ROUTLEDGE COMPANION WEBSITE

STEPHEN BAILEY

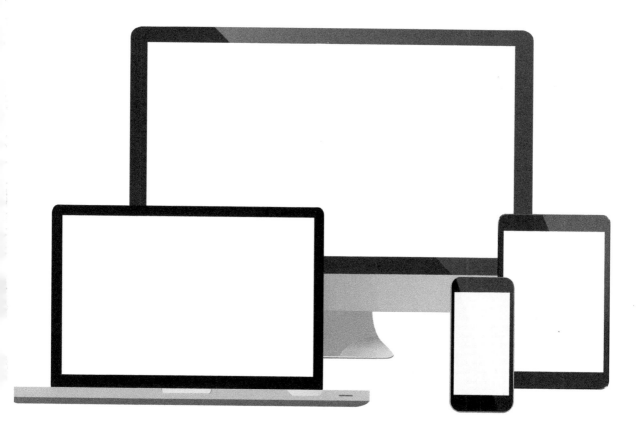

Enhancing online learning and teaching.

www.routledge.com/cw/bailey

Routledge
Taylor & Francis Group

Routledge... think about it
www.routledge.com

Academic Writing for International Students of Business and Economics

The third edition of *Academic Writing for International Students of Business and Economics* is written to help international students succeed in writing essays, reports and other papers for their English-language academic courses. Thoroughly revised and updated to reflect issues such as diversity and sustainability, this book is designed to let students and teachers easily find the help they need, both in the classroom and for self-study.

The book is divided into five parts, comprising a total of 42 units:

- The Writing Process
- Elements of Writing
- Language Issues
- Vocabulary for Writing
- Writing Models

New topics in this edition include Writing in Groups, Written British and American English and Reflective Writing. In addition, the new interactive website has a full set of teaching notes as well as more challenging exercises, revision material and links to other sources. Additional features of the book include:

- Models provided for writing tasks such as case studies and literature reviews
- Use of authentic academic texts from a range of sources
- Designed for self-study as well as classroom use
- Useful at both undergraduate and postgraduate level
- A complete set of answers to the practice exercises
- Cross-references across all units

Providing a glossary to explain technical terms and written to deal with the specific language issues faced by international students of Business and Economics, this practical, user-friendly book is an invaluable guide to academic writing in English.

Stephen Bailey has taught English for Academic Purposes at the University of Nottingham and Derby University in the UK. Previously he taught students in Barcelona, Tokyo, Johor Bahru and Prague. His other books include *Academic Writing, A Handbook for International Students* (Routledge), *The Essentials of Academic Writing for International Students* (Routledge) and *The Old Roads of Derbyshire* (Matador).

Academic Writing for International Students of Business and Economics

Third Edition

Stephen Bailey

Routledge
Taylor & Francis Group

LONDON AND NEW YORK

Third edition published 2020
by Routledge
2 Park Square, Milton Park, Abingdon, Oxon, OX14 4RN

and by Routledge
52 Vanderbilt Avenue, New York, NY 10017

Routledge is an imprint of the Taylor & Francis Group, an informa business

First edition published by Routledge 2011
Second edition published by Routledge 2015

British Library Cataloguing-in-Publication Data
A catalogue record for this book is available from the British Library

Library of Congress Cataloging-in-Publication Data
Names: Bailey, Stephen, 1947 – author.
Title: Academic writing for international students of business and
    economics/Stephen Bailey.
Description: 3rd edition. | Abingdon, Oxon; New York:
    Routledge, 2020. | Includes bibliographical references and index.
Identifiers: LCCN 2019041442 (print) | LCCN 2019041443 (ebook) |
    ISBN 9780367280307 (hardback) | ISBN 9780367280314
    (paperback) | ISBN 9780429299278 (ebook)
Subjects: LCSH: Authorship. | Academic writing. | Business writing.
    Classification: LCC PN151.B26 2020 (print) | LCC PN151 (ebook) |
    DDC 808.02–dc23
LC record available at https://lccn.loc.gov/2019041442
LC ebook record available at https://lccn.loc.gov/2019041443

ISBN: 978-0-367-28030-7 (hbk)
ISBN: 978-0-367-28031-4 (pbk)
ISBN: 978-0-429-29927-8 (ebk)

Typeset in Galliard
by Swales & Willis, Exeter, Devon, UK

Visit the companion website: www.routledge.com/cw/bailey

Contents

Acknowledgements

I would like to thank all the teaching colleagues that I have worked with over the years in different parts of the world. They have always been ready to share ideas, and their encouragement and suggestions have helped me develop these materials.

Closer to home, my wife Rene, who has a remarkable grasp of the finer points of good English in academic style, has been an invaluable critic and adviser, while my daughter Sophie has provided vital feedback to help me appreciate the other side of the academic whirl.

Introduction for Teachers

Aims

The third edition of *Academic Writing for International Students of Business and Economics* has been designed to help students successfully complete their written academic work. They may be studying in a range of different situations: on full-time pre-sessional courses, on part-time in-sessional classes, in subject-specific classes or in multi-discipline courses, or studying entirely by themselves: due to its flexible structure this book can be used in all these situations.

This course is aimed at both undergraduate and postgraduate students, since although they are studying at different levels the requirements of their teachers are similar: for written work that is precise, objective, accurate and correctly referenced.

The structure of this book recognises that all language courses are inevitably time-constrained, and that some students may prefer or need to work by themselves. Each unit aims to involve students in completing a variety of exercises, which can be analysed and discussed in the classroom. Most of the exercises can be done individually or in pairs and groups, and students can check their work using the answer key.

The book is designed for ease of access and simplicity of reference, which is achieved via the format shown below.

Structure

Part	Topic	Main application
1	**The Writing Process** from finding sources to proofreading	Classroom use
2	**Elements of Writing** from argument to visual information	Classroom and self-study
3	**Language Issues** from cohesion to time markers	Classroom, self-study and reference

Part	Topic	Main application
4	**Vocabulary for Writing** from abbreviations to synonyms	Classroom, self-study and reference
5	**Writing Models** from case studies to reflective writing	Self-study and reference

Part 1 guides students through the entire process of writing essays or similar papers, and is best taught as a progressive series of lessons, with feedback from the practice exercises.

Part 2 teaches related writing skills, and like Parts 3 and 4 is organised alphabetically.

Part 3 examines the language issues that pose particular problems for international students, and Part 4 deals with the vocabulary problems which are an understandable concern for such students.

Finally, Part 5 provides models of some of the most common types of assessed writing tasks. All the units in Parts 2–5 can be taught in conjunction with units from Part 1, or can be suggested to individual students on a remedial basis for self-study.

The first three units in Part 1 are designed as a basic introduction to the subject and assume a fairly low level of writing ability. With stronger students teachers may choose to progress rapidly through these to more difficult materials starting with Unit 4, Avoiding Plagiarism. At the end of Parts 1, 2, 3 and 4 there is a Progress check to allow students to revise their work.

Note that *Academic Writing for International Students of Business and Economics* uses authentic reading texts taken from a range of relevant sources, but selected to be of interest to all students of business or economics. At the end of the book there is a glossary of academic terms and an index.

Cross-referencing to relevant sections in other units is provided like this:

▶ **See Unit 3.4 Passive and Active and Unit 4.5 Conjunctions**

The companion website provides a full set of teaching notes, plus relevant web links for each unit in the Teachers' Area. Further practice exercises for certain units plus web links and quizzes are found in the Students' Area. See www.routledge.com/cw/bailey

Using the book

The materials in this course have been thoroughly tested in the classroom, but improvement is always possible, so that I would be grateful for any comments or suggestions from teachers for future editions.

Stephen Bailey
stephen.bailey@w3z.co.uk

Introduction for Students

The challenge of writing in English

Most international students who come to college or university to study on English-language courses can speak the language well enough for everyday activities such as shopping and travelling. But they may be surprised to find that writing notes, essays and reports in English is much more difficult. There are several reasons for this situation.

Firstly, while speaking is normally done face to face, so that you can see if the listener understands what you say, when writing we cannot see the reader, so we must write as clearly as possible, to make our work easy to understand. Additionally, with academic writing, writers and readers must learn special conventions, such as using capital letters in certain places. If you do not follow these rules, your meaning may be unclear and your teacher could find it hard to assess your work. There is also the issue of vocabulary, since in most academic subjects students are expected to use a semi-formal vocabulary which is different from the idiomatic language of normal speech.

The aim of the book

The main purpose of *Academic Writing for International Students of Business and Economics* is to help you succeed in the writing tasks which you may be asked to complete on your course. The kind of writing you are asked to do could be different from the work you have done before, and this may be the first time you have had to write long essays and reports in English.

Your teachers know that English is not your native language, and will be sympathetic to the problems you have in your writing. But at the same time you will want to learn to write as clearly and accurately as possible, not only to succeed on your present course, but also in preparation for your future career. Most large companies and organisations now expect their staff to be able to communicate effectively in written English, as well as orally. During your studies you have an ideal opportunity to learn to write English well, and this book can help you achieve that goal.

As well as achieving accuracy, students are generally expected to take a critical approach to their sources. This means that you are expected to question and evaluate everything you read, asking whether it is reliable and relevant. Your teachers also expect you to refer carefully to the sources of your ideas, using a standard system of referencing. *Academic Writing for International Students of Business and Economics* will help you develop these skills.

Using the book

The organisation of the course is explained by this chart:

Part	*Topic*	*Main application*
1	**The Writing Process** from finding sources to proofreading	Classroom use
2	**Elements of Writing** from argument to visual information	Classroom and self-study
3	**Language Issues** from cohesion to time markers	Classroom, self-study and reference
4	**Vocabulary for Writing** from abbreviations to synonyms	Classroom, self-study and reference
5	**Writing Models** from case studies to reflective writing	Self-study and reference

The book can be used either with a teacher or by yourself for self-study and reference. To help you get the most out of the course, note the following points:

Instructions are printed like this:

■ **Read the following text**

Cross-referencing to relevant sections in other units is provided like this:

▶ **See Unit 3.4 Passive and Active and Unit 4.5 Conjunctions**

Answers to most exercises are provided in the answer key at the end of the book. If there is no definite answer, a model answer is usually given.

The **glossary** on page 259 explains academic terms you may not be familiar with. The **index** on page 313 can be used to find specific information.

The Students' Area of the **companion website** provides further practice exercises for some units, plus web links and quizzes. See www.routledge.com/cw/bailey

I hope you find this new edition helpful in progressing your studies, and I would be glad to receive your comments and suggestions on any part of the book to help develop future editions.

Stephen Bailey
stephen.bailey@w3z.co.uk

The Importance of Writing for Students of Business and Economics

During your business school course you may be asked to write a variety of tasks, such as reports, case studies, proposals, essays or a dissertation. These vary in length, format and complexity, but all should be written in academic English, as explained in the five parts of this book.

At first writing may seem the most difficult part of your work, but studying in English gives you a great opportunity to improve your writing skills for future employment. This is essential for the following reasons:

- Writing about a topic helps you to understand the subject better
- Writing enables you to organise and examine your ideas clearly
- Writing allows you to show your knowledge in tests and exams
- Writing allows you to communicate with your teachers
- Most companies expect employees to be able to communicate effectively in written English

■ **Discuss the following questions with a partner.**

a) What experience do you have of writing in English?

b) What is the longest piece of writing you have done in English?

c) What do you find most challenging about writing in English?

d) How do you plan to improve your written English?

Written British and American English – A Short Guide

Speakers of British and American English can usually understand each other easily, with only minor confusions due to some variations in vocabulary or pronunciation. However, with written academic work more differences need to be understood. The main issues are explained below.

NB: Academic writers in Australia, New Zealand and many other English-speaking areas tend to use British English; in Canada American English is more common.

1. Vocabulary

There are many vocabulary items which differ between British (UK) and American (US) English e.g. *autumn* (UK) and *fall* (US). However, these are mainly well-known and widely understood. But the two main problematic areas in everyday vocabulary are:

a)   words which are not commonly understood in both countries e.g. *tap* (UK) and *faucet* (US).

b)   words with different meanings in each country e.g. *gas* is used for cooking in Britain but in the USA *gas* powers cars (or automobiles).

Further examples:

UK	US
flat	apartment
underground	subway
queue	line
timetable	schedule
high street	main street

UK	US
lorry	truck
lift	elevator
toilet	restroom or bathroom

In the business field, these are examples of further differences:[1]

UK	US
share capital	capital stock
company	corporation
current account	checking account
merchant bank	investment bank
property	real estate
trade union	labor union
unit trusts	mutual funds

For a full list of differences see:
https://en.oxforddictionaries.com/usage/british-and-american-terms

2. Spelling

There are many minor differences in spelling, but among those worth noting are:

a)   In American English the 'u' is commonly dropped from words ending in -our (e.g. *neighbour* becomes *neighbor*).

b)   Words ending in -ise or -yse in British English (e.g. *sanitise, analyse*) change to *sanitize* and *analyze* in American English.

c)   A group of technical nouns such as *haemophiliac* and *foetus* lose the 'ae' or 'oe' in American English and become *hemophiliac* and *fetus*.

d)   British English spells the noun *practice* but the verb *practise*. In American English both forms are spelt with an 's'. The same applies to *license*.

e)   Many words ending in -re in British English (e.g. *metre, theatre*) become *meter* and *theater* in American English.

NB: If you are writing in an environment using British English, you should retain American spelling when providing references i.e. do not change the original spelling.

3. Academic language

There are many minor variations between the language of the educational systems of Britain and the US. These are some of the more important:

a)   A *college* in the UK is usually any post-school institution which provides mainly vocational training, but doesn't award degrees (but a few universities such as Oxford are organised in *colleges*). In the US a *college* is usually part of a university and does give first degrees.

b)   Most teaching in UK universities is done by *lecturers*, while a *professor* is a senior position. In US colleges and universities teaching is mainly done by *professors* and *assistant professors*.

c)   In Britain students *read/do/study* a subject. In the US they *study* or *major* in a subject (the latter as the main part of a two-part degree).

d)   Someone studying for a Master's degree in the UK is a *postgraduate*, while in the US they are a *graduate student*.

e)   Students in Britain *sit* or *take* exams, in America exams are just *taken*. Before taking an exam, British students may *revise* the subject, but in the US they *review* the topic.

   UK students generally receive *marks* for their work, while American students get *grades*.

f)   In Britain a *thesis* is the paper submitted for a PhD. This is called a *dissertation* in the US. (In the UK a *dissertation* may be written for a Master's degree.)

4. Punctuation

a)   In Britain quotations are shown by single quotation marks, while nested quotations (those inside quotations) use double. In the US the convention is, confusingly, the opposite.

   UK: *As Kauffman remarked: 'His concept of "internal space" requires close analysis'.*

   US: *As Kauffman remarked: "His concept of 'internal space' requires close analysis."*

   Note that in British English the full stop comes after the quotation marks, while in the US it is inside them.

b)   In American English the 'Oxford comma' is standard, i.e. the comma before the final 'and' in a list:

   Vision, knowledge, courage, and luck are the attributes of a successful entrepreneur.

   In British English this is usually omitted:

   Vision, knowledge, courage and luck are the attributes of a successful entrepreneur.

c) Dates are generally written with the month first in American English:

11.30.2019 = 30 November 2019

In British English dates usually begin with the day:

30.11.2019 = 30 November 2019

5. Capitals

In Britain titles are generally written with only the first word and proper nouns capitalised:

A study of inflation in India since the millennium

In the US all relevant elements have capital letters:

A Study of Inflation in India since the Millennium

▶ **See Unit 1.8 References and Quotations and Unit 3.5 Punctuation**

Academic Writing Quiz

How much do you know about academic writing? Find out by doing this fun quiz.

1. The main difference between academic writing and other writing is that academic writing:
   a) uses longer words
   b) tries to be precise and unbiased
   c) is harder to understand

2. Italics are used for <u>two</u> of the following reasons:
   a) to emphasise a word
   b) words from other languages
   c) for idioms

3. Teachers frequently complain about students:
   a) not answering the question given
   b) not writing enough
   c) writing in pencil

4. The best time to write an introduction is often:
   a) first
   b) last
   c) after writing the main body

5. The purpose of an introduction is:
   a) to give your aims and methods
   b) to amuse the reader
   c) to summarise your ideas

6. Making careful notes is essential for:
   a) writing essays
   b) revising for exams
   c) all academic work

7. An in-text citation looks like:
   a) (Manton, 2008)
   b) (Richard Manton, 2008)
   c) (Manton, R. 2008)

8. Paraphrasing a text means:
   a) making it shorter
   b) changing a lot of the vocabulary
   c) adding more detail

9. Paragraphs always contain:
   a) six or more sentences
   b) an example
   c) a topic sentence

10. Proofreading means:
    a) getting a friend to check your work
    b) checking for minor errors
    c) rewriting

11. Teachers expect students to adopt a critical approach to their sources:
    a) sometimes
    b) only for Master's work
    c) always

12. This punctuation mark (') is called:
    a) comma
    b) colon
    c) apostrophe

13. A suitable synonym for 'business' is:
    a) firm
    b) organisation
    c) outfit

14. 'Progress' and 'research' are both nouns. What kind of noun?
    a) countable
    b) uncountable
    c) proper

15. An abstract is normally found:
    a) on the back cover of books
    b) before journal articles
    c) in exam questions

16. The word 'unreliable' contains:
    a) a prefix
    b) a suffix
    c) both

17. When making notes you should always include:
    a)   your own ideas
    b)   a full reference
    c)   the date

18. A pie chart is used to show:
    a)   changes in time
    b)   proportion
    c)   structure of an organisation

19. Acknowledgements are generally used:
    a)   to admit possible errors
    b)   to suggest more research
    c)   to thank people who helped

20. The conclusion to an article usually includes:
    a)   results of the study
    b)   additional data
    c)   references

Answers on p. 264

---

1 Kutateladze, M. (2014) 'Major Differences between American and British English in Business Communication'. *Journal in Humanities* 3(2), 23–25.

The Writing Process

This section explains and practises all the stages of producing a piece of academic writing, from analysing the title, reading the sources, note-making and referencing through to rewriting and then proofreading the final draft.

1. The writing process

■ Study the flowchart below, which illustrates the process of academic writing.

Each stage is fully explained in the relevant units.

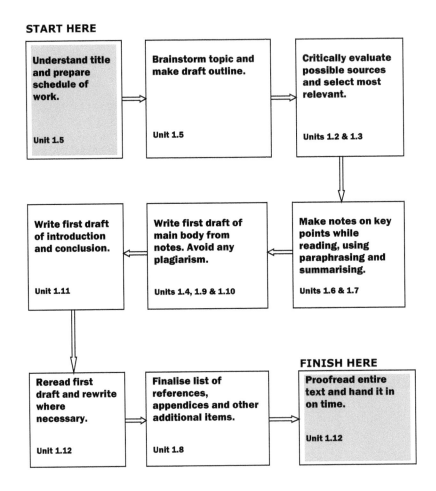

Basics of Writing

Most business schools assess students through written assignments of various kinds. These tasks include coursework, which may take weeks to write, and exam answers, which often have to be written in an hour. This unit deals with:

- the main features of academic writing
- the names of different writing tasks
- the format of short and long writing tasks
- the structure of sentences and paragraphs.

1. The purpose of academic writing

Students should be clear why they are writing. The most common reasons include:

- to report on a piece of research the writer has conducted
- to answer a question the writer has been given or chosen
- to discuss a subject of common interest and give the writer's view
- to synthesise research done by others on a topic

■ **Can you suggest any other reasons?**

- _____
- _____

2. Features of academic writing

Although there is no fixed standard of academic writing, and style may vary from subject to subject, academic writing is clearly different from the written style of newspapers or novels. For example, it is generally agreed that academic writing attempts to be accurate, so that instead of 'sales fell sharply' it is better to write 'sales fell by 35%'. What are some of the other features of academic writing?

■ Working alone or in a group, list your ideas below.

- *Impersonal style - generally avoids using 'I' or 'we'*

• _____

• _____

• _____

3. Common types of academic writing

Below are the most common types of written work produced by business students.

■ Match the terms on the left to the definitions on the right.

Report	*The longest piece of writing normally done by a student, often for a higher degree (20,000+ words).*
Essay	*A general term for any extended piece of academic writing.*
Dissertation/ Thesis	*A persuasive text written to convince a potential customer of the value of a new product or strategy.*
Paper	*A description of a situation or process, often with suggestions for dealing with a problem.*
Case study	*The presentation of the results of a piece of research you have conducted, using interviews or questionnaires.*
Survey report	*The answer to a question set by the teacher, often on a theoretical subject.*
Reflection	**A detailed report on a particular situation or organisation.**
Proposal	*A piece of writing in which you critically examine how you dealt with a situation or task and what you learned from it.*

4. The format of written assignments

Essays and reports (1,000–5,000 words) generally include the following items.

■ Discuss the meanings of these elements with a partner.

Introduction

Main body

   Literature review

   Case study

Discussion

Conclusion

References

Appendices

▶ See Unit 5.3 Writing Longer Papers

Dissertations and journal articles may have:

Abstract

List of contents

List of tables

Introduction

Main body

    Literature review

    Case study

    Findings

    Discussion

Conclusion

Acknowledgements

References

Appendices

Business reports and proposals often have a short section at the beginning called:

Executive summary

In addition, books may also include:

Foreword

Preface

Bibliography/Further reading

■ Match the following definitions to terms in the lists above:

a) A short summary which explains the paper's purpose and main findings.

_____

b) A list of all the sources the writer has mentioned in the text.

_____

c) A section, after the conclusion, where additional information is included.

_____

d) A short section where people who have helped the writer are thanked.

_____

e) Part of the main body in which the views of other writers on the topic are discussed.

_____

f) A section where one particular example is described in detail.

_____

g) A preliminary part of a book in which the author often explains her reasons for writing.

_____

ACADEMIC JOURNALS

There are thousands of academic journals published in English and other languages around the world. The purpose of these journals is to provide a forum for academics within a specific discipline (e.g. accounting or marketing) to share cutting-edge research. Most journals publish several issues a year and are often available either online or in a hard copy.

One important feature of journals is that the articles they publish are generally peer-reviewed. This means that when an article is submitted the editors ask other specialists in that field to read the article and decide if it is worth publishing. Reviewers may make comments that lead to the article being modified.

Students need to get to know the leading journals in their subject, which are generally available via the university library.

► **See Unit 1.2.5 Using library websites to search journals and electronic resources**

5. The components of academic writing

There is considerable variation in the format of academic writing required by different business schools and departments. Your teachers may give you guidelines, or you should ask them what they want. But some general features apply to most formats.

■ Read the text below and identify the features underlined, using the words in the box.

a) **The Effectiveness of Microcredit**

b) An evaluation of programmes in India and the Philippines

c) Introduction

d) In the last ten years considerable claims have been made about the value of micro-credit (also known as microfinance); the provision of unsecured small loans to the

e) poor in developing countries. But it has proved surprisingly difficult to accurately measure the effectiveness of these loans, without interference from other non-commercial factors.

f) Two recent studies have attempted to compare the effects on randomly-chosen groups of people with access to microcredit, compared to those without. The first (Bannerjee *et al.*, 2009), based at Massachusetts Institute of Technology (MIT), looked at slumdwellers in the city of Hyderabad in India, while the second (Karlan and Zinman, 2009) compared borrowers and non-borrowers in the Philippines. Overall, neither study found evidence that microcredit had any effect in reducing poverty, although it may have some other positive aspects such as reducing the consumption of alcohol or tobacco.

sentence	heading	subtitle	paragraph	title	phrase

a) _____

b) _____

c) _____

d) _____

e) _____

f) _____

6. Some other common text features

a) Reference to sources using **citation**:
   . . . *while the second (Karlan and Zinman, 2009) compared borrowers and non-borrowers*

b) The use of **abbreviations** for convenience:
   Massachusetts Institute of Technology (MIT)

c) **Italics:** used to show words from other languages, or add emphasis:
   Bannerjee *et al.* (= and others)

d) **Brackets:** used to give extra information or to clarify a point:
   (also known as microfinance)

e) **Numbering systems** (1.1, 1.2) are often used in reports, less so in essays.

f)   Writers may choose to use **bold**, or vary the font size for titles and headings.

g) Some departments may specify the typeface (e.g. Times New Roman) or line spacing which assignments should use.

▶ **See Unit 4.2 Abbreviations**

7. Simple and complex sentences

◾ Study the table below.

Analysis of writing assignments by student level in business school

Type	Undergraduate	Graduate	Total
Case study	22	57	79
Article/book report	13	43	56
Business report	11	19	30
Business proposal	7	6	13
Reflection paper	7	4	11
Research proposal	1	4	5

All sentences contain verbs:

> *Case studies **are** the most common type of assignment.*

> *More graduates than undergraduates **wrote** case studies.*

Simple sentences such as these are easier to read and write, but longer sentences are also necessary to explain more complex ideas:

> *Articles and book reports are more commonly required from graduates, who were given about three quarters of the total set.*

Students should make clarity a priority and avoid writing very lengthy sentences with several clauses until they feel confident in their ability.

Sentences containing two or more clauses use **conjunctions**, **relative pronouns** or **punctuation** to link the clauses:

> *Undergraduates were rarely asked to write research proposals, **but** business proposals were more common. (conjunction)*

> *Business reports were commonly required at both levels: 11 on the undergraduate programme and 19 for the postgraduates. (punctuation)*

■ Write two simple and two longer sentences using data from the table below.

a) _____

b) _____

c) _____

d) _____

Borchester Business School: gender balance by programme, 2019 (percentages)

	Accounting	Finance	Marketing	Economics	Human resources
Male	69	71	43	52	27
Female	32	29	57	48	73

▶ See Unit 3.7.5 Varying sentence length

▶ See Unit 4.5 Conjunctions

8. Writing in paragraphs

■ Discuss the following questions:

What is a paragraph?

Why are texts divided into paragraphs?

How long are paragraphs?

Do paragraphs have a standard structure?

▶ *For answers see Unit 1.10 Organising Paragraphs*

■ Read the text below and divide it into a suitable number of paragraphs.

The unpredictable effects of energy efficiency
It has often been argued that by raising standards of energy efficiency, for example making cars more fuel efficient, both consumers and the planet would benefit. In other words, drivers would spend less on petrol, and less fossil fuel would be burnt. In fact, the International Energy Agency recently claimed that if the world's GDP doubled by 2040, higher standards of fuel efficiency would only cause a small increase in demand for energy. However, some economists have disputed this claim. They point out that as countries get richer, their energy use rises. A new study (Rausch and Schwerin, 2018) explores the example of the USA since 1960. As efficiency gains made energy cheaper, demand for energy rose: people drove further, but also had spare money for other energy-demanding products. Described as 'rebound

effects', these unexpected results mean that energy savings are often reduced or eliminated. But this effect is likely to vary in relation to a country's level of economic development. In more developed countries there is less appetite for driving extra distances, while in developing economies there may be more latent demand, resulting in a larger potential increase in total energy use. The macro-economic model created by Rausch and Schwerin relates energy use to efficiency-increasing technological development, and aims to predict energy consumption by relating energy consumption to changes in the cost of capital and energy. Their conclusion was that gains in fuel efficiency in America between 1960 and 2011 resulted in higher energy use overall, resulting in no benefit for the environment.

9. Practice

■ **Write two simple and two longer sentences on energy efficiency.**

a) _____

b) _____

c) _____

d) _____

1.2 Reading

Finding Suitable Sources

Students often underestimate the importance of effective reading, but on any course it is vital to be able to find and understand the most suitable relevant sources quickly. This unit:

- examines the most appropriate types of text for academic work
- explores ways of locating relevant material in the library
- explains the use of electronic resources
- demonstrates different reading methods.

1. Academic texts

You will need to read a variety of sources such as books, websites or journal articles for your course. With some assignments your teacher will give you a reading list, but in other situations you will have to identify the most suitable texts and recognise their features, which will help you to assess their value.

■ You are studying water management. Read the following text extracts A–C and discuss with other students if they are suitable for academic use, and why.

Text	Suitability?
A	
B	
C	

A. WORLDWIDE PRESSURES

The global nature of the crisis is underlined in reports from many regions. In south Asia, there have been huge losses of groundwater, which has been pumped up with reckless lack of control over the past decade. About 600 million people live on the 2,000 sq. km. area that extends from eastern Pakistan, across the hot dry plains of northern India and into Bangladesh, and the land is the most intensely irrigated in the world. Up to 75% of farmers rely on pumped groundwater to water their crops and water use is intensifying – at the same time that satellite images show that supplies are shrinking alarmingly.

Changing precipitation and melting snow and ice are already altering hydrological systems in many areas. Glaciers continue to shrink worldwide, affecting villages and towns downstream. The result, says the Intergovernmental Panel for Climate Change, is that the proportion of the global population experiencing water scarcity is bound to increase throughout the twenty-first century. More and more, people and nations will have to compete for resources. An international dispute between Egypt and Ethiopia over the latter's plans to dam the Nile has only recently been resolved. In future, far more serious conflicts are likely to erupt as the planet dries up.

Even in high latitudes, the one region on Earth where rainfall is likely to intensify in coming years, climate change will still reduce water quality and pose risks due to a number of factors: rising temperatures; increased levels of sediments, nutrients, and pollutants triggered by heavy rainfall; and disruption of treatment facilities during floods. The world faces a water crisis that will touch every part of the globe, a point that has been stressed by Jean Chrétien, former Canadian prime minister and co-chair of the InterAction Council. 'The future political impact of water scarcity may be devastating', he claimed. 'Using water the way we have in the past simply will not sustain humanity in future'.

B. A DRYING WORLD?

It is easy to think that water will always be plentiful, as it covers 70% of our planet. However, freshwater – the stuff we drink, bathe in, irrigate our farm fields with – is extremely rare. Only 3% of the world's water is fresh water, and two-thirds of that is tucked away in frozen glaciers or otherwise unavailable for our use.

As a result, some 1.1 billion people worldwide lack access to water, and a total of 2.7 billion find water scarce for at least one month of the year. Inadequate sanitation is also a problem for 2.4 billion people – they are exposed to diseases such as cholera and typhoid fever and other water-borne illnesses. Two million people, mostly children, die each year from diarrheal diseases alone.

Many of the water systems that keep ecosystems thriving and feed a growing human population have become stressed. Rivers, lakes and aquifers are drying up or becoming too polluted to use. More than half the world's wetlands have disappeared. Agriculture consumes more water than any other source and wastes much of that through inefficiencies. Climate change is altering patterns of weather and water around the world, causing shortages and droughts in some areas and floods in others. This situation will only get worse at the current rate of consumption. By 2025, two-thirds of the world's population may face water shortages, and ecosystems around the world will suffer even more.

C. MEASURING SCARCITY

It is surprisingly difficult to determine whether water is truly scarce in the physical sense at a global scale (a supply problem) or whether it is available but should be used better (a demand problem). Rijsberman (2006) reviews water scarcity indicators and global assessments based on these indicators. The most widely used indicator, the Falkenmark indicator, is popular because it is easy to apply and understand but it does not help to explain the true nature of water scarcity. The more complex indicators are not widely applied because data are lacking to apply them and the definitions are not intuitive.

Water is definitely physically scarce in densely populated arid areas, such as Central and West Asia, and North Africa, with projected availabilities of less than 1,000 m^3/capita/year. This scarcity relates to water for food production, however, and not to water for domestic purposes that are minute at this scale. In most of the rest of the world water scarcity at a national scale has as much to do with the development of the demand as the availability of the supply. Accounting for water for environmental requirements shows that abstraction of water for domestic, food and industrial uses already has a major impact on ecosystems in many parts of the world, even those not considered 'water scarce'.

■ The main features of academic texts are listed in the table below. Find examples of each in the texts above.

Feature	Examples
Formal or semi-formal vocabulary	
Sources are given	
Objective, impersonal style	

2. Types of text

■ The table below lists the most common types of written sources used by students. Work with a partner to consider their likely advantages and disadvantages.

Text type	Advantages	Disadvantages
Textbook	*Written for students*	*May be too general or out-dated*
Website		
Journal article		
Official report (e.g. from a government body)		
Newspaper or magazine article		
E-book		
Edited book		

3. Using reading lists

Your teacher may give you a printed reading list, or it may be available online through the library website. The list will usually include books, journal articles and websites. If the list is electronic there will be links to the library catalogue to let you check on the availability of the material. If the list is printed, you will have to use the library catalogue to find the texts.

You do not have to read every word of a book because it is on the list. Your teacher will probably suggest which parts to read.

On reading lists you will find the following formats:

Books	Griffin, R.C. *Water Resource Economics: The Analysis of Scarcity, Policies, and Projects/*2nd ed. MIT Press, 2016
Journal articles	Falkenmark, M., Lundqvist, J. and Widstrand, C. (1989), Macro-scale water scarcity requires micro-scale approaches. *Natural Resources Forum*, 13: 258–267.
Websites	http://www.un.org/waterforlifedecade/scarcity.shtml

4. Using library catalogues

University and college libraries usually have online catalogues. These allow you to search for the materials you want in various ways. If the title and author's name are known it is easy to check if the book is available. But if you are searching for material on a specific topic you may have to vary the search terms. For instance, if you want information about exploration for oil, you might try:

- oil exploration
- exploring for oil
- hydrocarbon exploration
- exploring for hydrocarbons

You have been given an essay title: 'Outline the current state of global exploration for oil, and relate this to future levels of production'.

■ **You have entered the term 'oil exploration' in the library catalogue search engine, and these are the nine results. Which would you select to borrow? Give your reasons.**

Full details	Title	Edition/ year	Location	Holdings
1	History, Exploration & Exploitation of Oil and Gas/Silvia Fernanda Figueirôa (Ed.), Gregory A. Good (Ed.), Drielli Peyerl (Ed.).	2019	Science Library	Availability
2	Upstream: Oil and Gas Exploration and Production: An Overview/Levonne Louie.	2015	Main Library	Availability
3	Oil exploration and human rights violations in Nigeria's oil producing communities/Olubayo Oloduro.	2013	Main Library	Availability
4	Oil and gas exploration and production [electronic resource]: Reserves, costs contracts/Nadine Bret-Rouzaut and Jean-Piere Favennec.	3rd ed. 2011	Main Library	Availability
5	Deepwater petroleum exploration & production [electronic resource]: a nontechnical guide/William L. Leffler, Richard Pattarozzi, Gordon Sterling.	2011	Main Library	Availability
6	Hydrocarbon exploration and production/by Frank Jahn, Mark Cook and Mark Graham.	2nd ed. 2008	Science Library	Availability
7	China and the global energy crisis: development and prospects for China's oil and natural gas/Tatsu Kambara, Christopher Howe.	2007	Main Library	Availability

Full details	Title	Edition/ year	Location	Holdings
8	Operational aspects of oil and gas well testing [electronic resource]/Stuart McAleese.	2000	Main Library	Availability
9	Geophysical exploration: an outline of the principal methods used in the search for minerals, oil, gas and water supplies/ F.W. Dunning.	1970	Science Library	Availability

Full details
If you click on this you will get more information about the book, including the number of pages and a summary of the contents. If a book has more than one edition it suggests that it is a successful title. This may help you decide whether to borrow it.

Year
The most recent books are listed first; always try to use the most up-to-date sources.

Location
Many large universities have more than one library. This tells you which one the book is kept in.

Holdings
If you click on availability it will tell you how many copies the library holds and if they are available to borrow or out on loan.

5. Using library websites to search journals and electronic resources

Journals are specialised academic publications produced on a regular basis, containing recent research (see p. 6). You need to be familiar with the main journals in your subject area. They are usually available in paper or electronic formats (e-journals).

E-journals and other electronic resources such as subject databases are becoming increasingly important. Their advantage is that they can be accessed by computer, saving the need to visit the library to find a book. Most library websites have a separate portal or gateway for searching electronic resources. This allows you to enter the name of a specific journal, or look for possible journals in your subject area by entering a term such as 'international business law'. In this case, the database may offer the following titles:

European Business Law Review
European Business Organisation Law Review
International Trade and Business Law Review

In each case, you can access a list of issues available. In the case of *European Business Organisation Law Review*, the list would include:

Dec 2019 Vol. 20 Issue 4
Sep 2019 Vol. 20 Issue 3
Jun 2019 Vol. 20 Issue 2
Mar 2019 Vol. 20 Issue 1

By clicking on any of these issues you can read a full list of articles. It is usually sufficient to read the abstract to find out if the article will be relevant to your work. Note that most journal websites contain a search engine to allow you to search all back issues by subject. They may also offer links to articles in other journals on the same topic.

The best way to become familiar with these methods is to practise. Library websites usually contain tutorials for new students, and librarians are always willing to give help and advice when needed.

■ **Select a specific topic from your subject area.**

a) **Use the library catalogue to search for relevant books. Write down the most useful titles.**

b) **Look for a few relevant journal articles, using the library portal. Write a reference for each article.**

6. Titles, sub-titles and text features

Many books and articles have both a title and a sub-title, often divided by a colon:

International Publishing Patterns: An Investigation of Leading UK and US Accounting and Finance Journals

The title is usually shorter and may aim to be eye-catching; the sub-title often gives more information about the specific focus. After finding a text relevant to your studies, it is worth checking the following text features before starting to read:

Author
Is the writer well-known in his/her field? What else has she/he published?

Publication date and edition
How old is the book? Do not use a first edition if there is a (revised) second or later edition available.

Abstract
See Section 9 below.

Contents
A list of the main chapters or sections. This should tell you how much space is given to the topic you are researching.

Introduction or preface
This is where the author often explains his/her reasons for writing, and also describes how the text is organised.

References
This list shows all the sources used by the author and cited in the text. It should give you some suggestions for further reading.

Bibliography
These are the sources the author has used but not specifically referred to. A bibliography is not required for short writing tasks.

Index
This is an alphabetical list of all the topics and names mentioned in a book. If, for example, you are looking for information about a person, the index will tell you whether that person is mentioned, and how often.

7. Reading methods

Reading academic texts in the quantity required for most business courses is a demanding task, especially for international students. Yet students will not benefit from attending lectures and seminars unless the preparatory reading is done promptly, while most writing tasks require extensive reading.

Moreover, academic texts often contain new vocabulary and phrases, and may be written in a rather formal style. This means that special methods have to be learnt to cope with the volume of reading needed, which is especially important when you are reading in another language.

Clearly, you do not have time to read every word published on the topic you are studying, so you must adopt a two-stage process of selection:

- carefully choose which texts you read
- only read the sections of the texts which are relevant to your task

The chart below illustrates the best approach to assessing texts for suitability.

■ **Complete the empty boxes in the chart with the following techniques:**

- Read intensively to make notes on key points
- Survey text features (e.g. abstract, contents, index)
- Ask yourself how this relates to your own knowledge of the subject and reasons for reading.

Choosing suitable texts

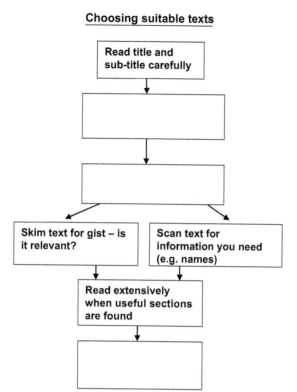

■ Can you suggest any other reading skills to add to the chart above?

● _____

● _____

8. Practice

■ You are writing a report on the impact of the internet on wage levels. Using the reading skills discussed above, decide if the following text is worth reading intensively by:

a) skimming quickly for relevance b) scanning for useful sources.

The internet gap: the effect of the world wide web on wage inequality
A recent study of the adoption of broadband by Brazilian companies (Poliquin: 2018) looked at the results of this process between 2000 and 2009. Employees of adopting companies enjoyed a 2.3% rise in real wages compared to those in companies which failed to adopt, while managers' pay increased by 8% and directors gained 18%. These results suggest that the internet boosted productivity throughout the companies. Poliquin's research duplicates the result of a

Norwegian study (Akerman, Gaarder and Mogstad: 2015) which stresses the benefits which were gained by skilled workers, while the work of unskilled employees was often automated.

Research which compares the situation of companies in different sectors (Song *et al.*: 2019) suggests the emergence of a high-wage sector such as technology, and a low-wage sector, for example in retail. A contributing factor may be the development of outsourcing, by which functions such as catering are moved to low-wage businesses. It seems that there may be a shortage of workers with digital skills, which may be surprising, given the prominence of social media platforms such as Facebook in everyday life. But a 2016 study by the OECD found that less than half of all adult were capable of doing more than writing a simple email.

9. Reading abstracts

Abstracts are normally found in journal articles, where they act as a kind of summary to allow researchers to decide if it is worth reading the full article. Students do not normally have to write abstracts, but it is important to be able to read them effectively.

■ **Study this example:**

Firming up inequality
Jae Song, David J Price, Fatih Guvenen, Nicholas Bloom, Till von Wachter
We use a massive, matched employer–employee database for the United States to analyse the contribution of firms to the rise in earnings inequality from 1978 to 2013. We find that one-third of the rise in the variance of (log) earnings occurred within firms, whereas two-thirds of the rise occurred due to a rise in the dispersion of average earnings between firms. However, this rising between-firm variance is not accounted for by the firms themselves but by a widening gap between firms in the composition of their workers. This compositional change can be split into two roughly equal parts: high-wage workers became increasingly likely to work in high-wage firms (i.e., sorting increased), and high-wage workers became increasingly likely to work with each other (i.e., segregation rose). In contrast, we do not find a rise in the variance of firm-specific pay once we control for the worker composition in firms. Finally, we find that two-thirds of the rise in the within-firm variance of earnings occurred within mega (10,000+ employee) firms, which saw a particularly large increase in the variance of earnings compared with smaller firms.

(Source: Song *et al.* (2018) *The Quarterly Journal of Economics*, 134 (1) 1–50)

■ **Underline the following standard features of an abstract in the example above.**

a) Purpose/aim of research
b) Method of research
c) Findings/results of research
d) Explanation of results.

Note that some abstracts may begin by giving background information, but all should state purpose, method and findings.

1.3 Reading

Developing Critical Approaches

> Students are expected to take a critical approach to sources, which means challenging what they read, rather than passively accepting it as reliable. Clearly this approach requires a thorough understanding of the text using the skills practised in the previous unit. This unit explores and practises critical analysis of texts.

1. Fact and opinion

When reading, it is important to distinguish between facts:

Kuala Lumpur is the capital of Malaysia.

and opinions:

Kuala Lumpur is a welcoming, bustling city.

In addition, the reader needs to decide if the facts given are true:

Singapore lies near the equator. (true)

Singapore was an ancient trading port. (false)

You need to be careful with texts that contain unsupported opinions or 'facts' that you think are wrong.

a) ■ Read the following and underline what is presented as a fact (_____) or opinion (_ _ _). Then decide if the 'facts' are true.

Example: <u>Sydney is the capital of Australia.</u> *Not true – the capital is Canberra*

a) Australia is a dynamic, prosperous and enterprising country.

b) The majority of Australians live on sheep farms.

c)   Most Australians are open-minded and friendly.

d)   Australia is the largest island in the world, and has extensive mineral deposits.

e)   Among the 22 million Australians are some of the world's best cricket players.

b)   ■   Read the paragraph on New Zealand and underline facts and opinions as above. Then rewrite the paragraph in an objective style, correcting the 'facts' where needed.

New Zealand is a proud island nation in the southern Pacific Ocean, consisting of three main islands. Nearly 1,000 miles west of Australia, it was one of the last places on Earth to be settled by man: the Polynesians who arrived in about 1250 CE, and who developed the fascinating Maori culture. In the eighteenth century European settlers started to land, and in 1841 New Zealand became part of the British Empire. Due to its long period of isolation many distinctive plants and animals evolved, such as the kiwi fruit, now the nation's symbol. Sadly, the country suffers from frequent earthquakes, such as the one that hit Christchurch in 2011, causing serious damage and loss of life.

2. Assessing internet sources critically

■   Compare these two texts about a pharmaceutical company, Evergreen. Discuss with a partner which is more reliable.

A. Our success is based on a commitment to discovery, finding new ideas that are inspired by life and which in turn help to inspire the lives of our stakeholders. We discover new medicines that are designed to improve the health and quality of life of patients around the world – medicines which are innovative, effective and which offer added benefits such as reduced side effects or better ways of taking the treatment. We also focus on getting the best from every medicine we make by exploring all the ways it can be used or improved. With a global business comes a global responsibility for consistently high standards of behaviour worldwide. We aim to effectively manage that responsibility and help to find new ways of bringing benefit to society to ensure that Evergreen continues to be welcomed as a valued member of the global community.

B. Recent trading results from Evergreen show an apparently healthy position, with pre-tax profit rising by 24% and total revenues up 5%. These figures, however, were inflated by some one-off gains, such as a $152 million sale of swine flu vaccine to the US government. Sales of the ZX high blood pressure drug also increased sharply due to its main rival being temporarily off the market due to safety concerns. Costs were very significantly lower in the last quarter, falling 14% due to productivity improvements. The anti-cholesterol drug Hixx also sold very well, becoming the market leader, but there are concerns that a pending US court case may soon challenge Evergreen's patent on this product. There are also worries that re-organisation of the American healthcare system may affect Evergreen's long-term profits, and the company's shares have recently fallen by 6%.

The first text contains little or no precise information about the company's performance and is full of statements that cannot be checked (medicines that are innovative, effective). It appears to be taken from the company website. By contrast the second seems to be based on a recent financial report and contains both facts (profits rising by 24%) and some comment (may affect Medmax's long-term profits). The first text is of little use to a student; the second could be used, with care, for analysis of the company's current state.

Internet sources are plentiful and convenient, but you cannot afford to waste time on texts which are unreliable or out of date. If you are using material that is not on the reading list you must assess it critically to ensure that the material is trustworthy, by asking several questions about each site:

- is this a reputable website, for example with ac. (= academic) in the URL?
- is the name of the author given, and is she well-known in the field?
- is the language of the text in a suitable academic style?
- are there any obvious errors in the text, e.g. factual mistakes, which suggest a careless approach?

3. Critical thinking

Even when you feel that a text is reliable and that you can safely use it as a source, it is still important to adopt a critical attitude towards it. This approach is perhaps easiest to learn when reading, but is important for all other academic work (i.e. listening, discussing and writing). Critical thinking means not just passively accepting what you hear or read, but instead actively questioning and assessing it. As you read you should ask yourself the following questions:

a)   What are the key ideas in this?
b)   Does the argument of the writer develop logically, step by step?
c)   Are the examples given helpful? Would other examples be better?
d)   Does the author have any bias (leaning to one side or the other)?
e)   Does the evidence presented seem reliable, in my experience and using common sense?
f)   Do I agree with the writer's views, based on my own knowledge?

■   Critically read the two articles below on universities, using the questions above.

A. COLLEGE CONCERNS

Despite their dominance of global league tables (e.g. Shanghai Rankings Consultancy) American universities currently face significant criticism. The American Enterprise Institute (AEI) and the Goldwater Institute have recently published negative reports on US universities, while a highly critical book *Higher Education?* (Hacker and Dreifus) was published in 2010. The critics focus on the rising costs of American higher education, which have increased at a much faster rate than inflation, resulting in a situation where even middle-class families are finding the expense unsupportable.

In the past, many American students paid for their education by working part-time while studying, but now the higher fees mean that students finish their education with significant levels of debt. This debt can be a serious burden at the start of their working lives, when they may be hoping to get married or buy a property.

Another target of criticism is the focus on research at the expense of teaching. Students rarely meet the 'star' professors, being taught instead by badly-paid graduate students, who work on short-term contracts. It is claimed that in one year nearly half of Harvard's history professors were on sabbatical leave. As a consequence, students work less; according to the AEI they currently study for 14 hours per week, whereas 50 years ago the figure was 24 hours per week. Despite this the proportion of students gaining a first or 2.1 degree has increased significantly: a situation described by the critics as 'grade inflation'. It seems incredible that working less should really be rewarded by better grades.

(Source: *Atlantic Digest*, July 2014, p. 119)

B. A BRIGHTER TOMORROW?

There is little doubt that a university degree is the key to a better future for any student. Despite the costs involved in terms of fees, it has been calculated that the average UK university graduate will earn £400,000 ($600,000) more over their lifetime compared to a non-graduate. Possession of a degree will also assist a graduate to find a satisfying job more quickly and give greater prospects for promotion inside the chosen career. A degree from a British university is recognised all over the world as proof of a high quality education.

A university course will not only provide students with up-to-date knowledge in their subject area, but also provide practice with the essential skills required by many employers today, such as the ability to communicate effectively using ICT, or the skills of team working and problem solving. In addition, living away from home in an international atmosphere gives the opportunity to make new friends from all over the world, and build networks of contacts that may be invaluable in a future career.

Studying at university is a unique opportunity for many young people to develop individually by acquiring independence, free from parental control. They will learn to look after themselves in a secure environment, and gain useful life skills such as cooking and budgeting. Most graduates look back at their degree courses as a valuable experience at a critical period of their lives.

(Source: *Borchester University Prospectus*, 2018, p. 5)

■ List any statements from the articles that you find unreliable and add comments to explain your doubts in the table below. Then decide which article you find more reliable overall.

Statements	Comments
A. College concerns	
B. A brighter tomorrow?	

▶   See Unit 2.1 Argument and Discussion

4. Practice

■ You are researching for a report on the economic and social impact of electric cars. Read the following texts critically and, working alone or with a partner, assess their value by completing the box below.

A. VOLKSWAGEN PLUGS IN

Herbert Diess, the tough-talking CEO of Volkswagen (VW) recently promised to develop 70 new models of electric vehicles (EVs) in the next ten years, significantly increasing the company's commitment to this exciting new technology. Diess moved to VW from BMW three years ago, promising to confront the powerful labour unions which many shareholders feel have held back VW's profitability for far too long. Despite producing nearly 11 billion vehicles per year the company's productivity and profitability are poor, so that the group depends on its upmarket brands, Audi and Porsche, for earnings.

The unions are strongly represented on the company's board and resist any attempt to move production away from Wolfsburg, VW's base, to cheaper locations outside Germany. Their sole priority is preserving the roughly 300,000 VW jobs inside the country, and they have even opposed plans to sell off subsidiary companies such as Ducati, a motorbike business.

Officially, VW claims that the new focus will help reduce global emissions of carbon dioxide, and also meet stringent new European regulations. But the emphasis on EVs can also be seen as a welcome move to weaken union power, since EVs, having fewer components, are simpler to make and thus require a smaller workforce. However, the unions point out that VW's involvement in the recent exhaust emissions scandal, which cost the company over £1 billion and damaged its reputation, was more harmful than their labour practices.

(Source: *European Business Weekly*, 8 February 2019)

B. HOW ELECTRIC CARS WILL CHANGE THE WORLD

There is a clear global shift away from petrol and diesel cars. China, the world's largest car market, is working on a timetable to stop the production and sale of vehicles powered by fossil fuels. India has declared its intention to make all new vehicles electric by 2030. Like Britain and France, these two markets are planning to phase out the sale of petrol and diesel vehicles over the next 20 years or so.

Vehicle manufacturers, the oil industry and governments are starting to wake up to the disruption that vehicle electrification could bring about. Automakers recognise that they cannot afford to be legislated out of these lucrative markets. Volvo, Jaguar and Land Rover, Volkswagen, Mercedes, Audi and BMW have all promised to roll out electric models over the next decade. Electro-mobility now seems inevitable, but the impact this shift will have on jobs, the oil economy and even national tax systems will be profound.

The global impact on jobs

Electric vehicles, including their batteries, generally require less manufacturing labour than ones that run on petrol. For this reason, among others, a phase-out of combustion engines by 2030 could cost an estimated 600,000 jobs in Germany alone, according to one report from the country's Ifo Economic Institute.

But there may be some positive outcomes. According to the Australian Federation of Automotive Parts Manufacturers (FAPM), the ban may be good news for suppliers to the Chinese market, including Australia. As electric vehicles become easier to build the manufacturing process may become simplified and robotised, creating new manufacturing and business opportunities for the right investor.

Going all-electric by 2030 will place considerable budgetary stress on major oil-producing countries, and change the geopolitical map. Stanford economist Tony Seba and his team push the vision of an electric vehicle revolution a step further, and predict that the disruption will come earlier, during the 2020s. They argue that oil demand will peak at 100 million barrels per day by 2020 and fall to 70 million barrels per day by 2030. According to their 2017 study, net exporting countries like Venezuela, Nigeria, Saudi Arabia and Russia will feel the greatest impact.

They also claim that the geopolitics of lithium, which along with nickel, cobalt and cadmium is key to electric vehicles, are entirely different from oil politics. Although there is potential for supply disruption, lithium is not as critical as oil in the life of a car.

The impact on government coffers

By 2030, revenues from petrol taxes could be reduced significantly, with the shift from individual ownership of petrol vehicles to shared (and ultimately autonomous) electric vehicle fleets. Governments whose budgets rely on this revenue stream could find themselves shifting to road pricing, such as charging per kilometre of travel or congestion charging. Modelling by Seba and his team shows that US$50 billion from petrol taxes could disappear from the American economy.

In Australia, according to the Bureau of Infrastructure, Transport and Regional Development, public sector road-related revenue totalled A$28.7 billion in 2014–2015. Fuel excise contributed about A$11.03 billion or 38%, down from about 44% in the early 2000s. This revenue will come under direct threat with increasing electric vehicle market adoption. My research also shows that under some future scenarios of shared autonomous mobility, the car fleet size could shrink to around 80%, meaning less income from vehicle registration fees and sale taxes, maintenance, insurance and parking.

(Source: Dia, H. (2017) 'Jobs, tax and politics: three ways electric vehicles will change our world'.)

	A. Volkswagen plugs in	B. How electric cars will change the world
Negative points		
Positive points		

1.4 Avoiding Plagiarism

Plagiarism is a concern for both teachers and students, but it can be avoided by clearly understanding the issues involved. In the English-speaking academic world it is essential to use a wide range of sources for writing, and to acknowledge these sources correctly – otherwise there is a risk of plagiarism. This unit introduces the techniques students need to do this. Further practice is provided in Units 1.7 Summarising and Paraphrasing and 1.8 References and Quotations.

1. What is plagiarism?

Essentially plagiarism means taking ideas or words from a source (e.g. a book or journal article) without giving credit (acknowledgement) to the author. It is seen as a kind of theft, and is considered to be an academic crime. In academic work, ideas and words are seen as private property belonging to the person who first thought or wrote them. Therefore it is important for all students, including international ones, to understand the meaning of plagiarism and learn how to prevent it in their work.

This situation may appear confusing, since students are expected:

a) **to show that they have read the relevant sources on a subject (by giving citations)**

   BUT

b) **to explain these ideas in their own words and come to their own conclusions.**

However, mastering this requirement is vital to achieving success in the academic community. Reasons why students must avoid plagiarism include:

- copying the work of others will not help them develop their own understanding
- plagiarism is easily detected by teachers and computer software, such as Turnitin
- plagiarism may lead to failing a course or even having to leave college.

2. Acknowledging sources

If you borrow from or refer to the work of another person, you must show that you have done this by providing the correct acknowledgement.

■ **Read this paragraph from an article called 'The morale effects of pay inequality' by Emily Breza, Supreet Kaur and Yogita Shamdasani (2018).**

We find evidence that relative pay enters workers' utility function, with the potential for sizable negative impacts on labor supply and group cohesion. However, our findings indicate that pay inequality in itself is not necessarily problematic – at least not if it is clearly justified in the workers' eyes.

There are two ways to use this idea in your work and acknowledge the source:

1. Summary and citation
   Breza et al. (2018) found that pay inequality could have a negative effect on employees, unless it could be justified in their terms.

2. Quotation and citation
   According to Breza et al.: 'relative pay enters workers' utility function, with the potential for sizable negative impacts on labor supply and group cohesion. However, our findings indicate that pay inequality in itself is not necessarily problematic . . .' (Breza et al., 2018:623).

These in-text **citations** are linked to a list of **references** at the end of the main text which includes the following details:

Authors	Date	Title	Journal title	Details
Breza, E., Kaur, S., Shamdasani, Y.	2018	The morale effects of pay inequality	*The Quarterly Journal of Economics*	Volume 133, Issue 2, May 2018, pp. 611–663.

The citation makes it clear to readers that you have read Breza, Kaur and Shamdasani and borrowed this idea from them. This reference also gives readers the necessary information to find the source if they want to study the original article.

► **See Unit 1.8 References and Quotations**

3. Degrees of plagiarism

Although plagiarism essentially means copying somebody else's work, in some situations it can be difficult to decide if plagiarism is involved.

■   Working with a partner, consider the following academic situations and decide if they are plagiarism or not.

	Situation	Plagiarism?
1.	Copying a paragraph, but changing a few words, and not giving a citation.	Yes
2.	Cutting and pasting a short article from a website, with no citation.	
3.	Taking two paragraphs from a classmate's essay, without citation.	
4.	Taking a graph from a textbook, giving the source.	
5.	Taking a quotation from an article, giving a citation but not using quotation marks.	
6.	Using something that you think of as general knowledge, e.g. the earth's climate is getting warmer.	
7.	Using a paragraph from an essay you wrote and had marked the previous semester, without citation.	
8.	Using the results of your own unpublished research, e.g. from a survey you did, without citation.	
9.	Discussing an essay topic with a group of classmates and using some of their ideas in your own work.	
10.	Giving a citation for some information but misspelling the author's name.	

This exercise shows that plagiarism can be accidental. For example, Situation (10) above, when the author's name is misspelt, is technically plagiarism but really carelessness. In Situation (9) your teacher may have told you to discuss the topic in groups, and then write an essay on your own, in which case it would not be plagiarism. Self-plagiarism is also possible, as in Situation (7). It can be difficult to decide what is general or common knowledge (Situation 6), but you can always try asking colleagues.

However, it is not a good excuse to say that you didn't know the rules of plagiarism, or that you didn't have time to write in your own words. Nor is it adequate to say that the rules are different in your own country. In general, anything that is not common knowledge or your own ideas and research (published or not) must be cited and referenced.

4. Avoiding plagiarism by summarising and paraphrasing

Quotations should not be over-used, so you must learn to paraphrase and summarise in order to include other writers' ideas in your work. This will demonstrate your understanding of a text to your teacher.

- Paraphrasing involves re-writing a text so that the language is significantly different while the content stays the same.
- Summarising means reducing the length of a text but retaining the main points.

▶ **See Unit 1.7 Summarising and Paraphrasing**

Normally both skills are used at the same time, as can be seen in the examples (a–e) below.

■ **Read the following text and then compare the five paragraphs below which use ideas and information from it. Decide which are plagiarised and which are acceptable, and give your reasons in the table below.**

The Z generation

Researchers have recently been studying the behaviour of 'Generation Z', who are defined as young people born since 1997. This group appear to have different concerns compared with their predecessors, the so-called 'Millenials' or 'Generation Y'. The youngest group (i.e. Z), who now comprise about 25% of the population of the USA, cannot imagine living without smartphones or social media.

Pew Research Centre's 2018 report, which surveyed nearly 1,000 young Americans aged between 13 and 17, finds that they are lonelier but better behaved than previous groups, and their prime concern is with mental health issues such as depression. These youngsters feel little pressure to use drugs or get drunk, but more than half mention bullying on social media as a worry. Doing well at school is the leading issue for nearly 90% of those questioned, far more important than finding a sexual partner.

However, it appears that anxiety and depression increasingly affect people of all ages, and the WHO reckons that the cost to the global economy is roughly $1 trn. annually. At the moment the US only spends 0.05% of its total health budget on psychiatric care, and increasing this total would have positive results in terms of greater happiness and productivity.

(Source: Carroll, J. (2019) *The New Consumers*, p. 15)

a) A recent study by Pew Research Centre of the concerns of teenage Americans shows that this generation is surprisingly different from older groups. Instead of using drugs and alcohol, these youngsters are mainly worried about academic success and bullying on social media. Mental health is an important issue for them, but this appears to be something that increasingly affects young and old, globally.

b) Academics have recently been studying the behaviour of 'Generation Z': young people born since 1997, who now comprise about 25% of the population of the USA. A 2018 report, which surveyed nearly 1,000 young Americans, finds that they are lonelier but better behaved than previous groups, and their main concern is with mental health issues like depression. These youngsters feel little pressure to use drugs or get drunk, but more than half mention bullying on social media as a worry. Doing well in college is the leading issue for most of those questioned, far more important than finding a sexual partner. (Carroll, 2019:15)

c) Generation Z is the name given to people born since 1997, who have grown up with smartphones and social media. A report by Pew Research Centre in 2018 identifies this cohort as mainly concerned with success at school and abuse on social media sites. They seem less interested in sex, drink or drugs, but more concerned with mental health, although apparently this is a growing concern for people all over the world. (Carroll, 2019:15)

d) Recent research on American youngsters (age 13–17) reveals that their dominant concerns are with school grades and mental health issues, such as depression. According to Carroll: 'These youngsters feel little pressure to use drugs or get drunk, but more than half mention bullying on social media as a worry'. (Carroll, 2019:15)

e) The main issues for young Americans appear to be doing well academically, bullying on social media sites and dealing with mental health problems. This has been revealed by research carried out by Pew Research Centre, published in 2018. This contrasts markedly with the behaviour of older groups, who were more likely to be concerned with alcohol or drug taking, or finding a partner. (Carol, 2019:15)

	Plagiarised or acceptable?	Reason
a		
b		
c		
d		
e		

5. Avoiding plagiarism by developing good study habits

Few students deliberately try to cheat by plagiarising, but some develop poor study habits which result in the risk of plagiarism.

■ **Working with a partner, add to the list of positive habits.**

- Plan your work carefully so you don't have to write essays at the last minute.
- Take care to make notes in your own words, not copying from the source.
- Keep a full record of all the sources you use (e.g. author, date, title, page numbers, place of publication, publisher).

▶   **See Unit 1.6 Finding Key Points and Note-Making**

6. Practice

■   **Read this text on the link between Olympic success and national prosperity.**

Wealth is an important advantage in pursuing Olympic medals. Clearly, a large population also has benefits, since this is more likely to include people with sporting abilities. But countries must be able mobilise their human resources: in the London Olympics in 2012 India, with its huge population, only won six medals, while New Zealand (with just 4 million) won 13. When many people are affected by poverty and illness it is not easy to be ordinarily healthy, let alone be an Olympic athlete. In fact richer countries have both healthier populations and can also spend more on encouraging sport. China won only 58 medals in 2000, when its GDP per person was under $4,000. But at the 2012 London Olympics, when its GDP figure had risen to $16,000, China won a total of 88. Governments are also finding that there are benefits in focusing efforts on a limited number of sports in which there is less competition: this was the tactic that led to British success in the cycling events in 2016.

(Source: Kaufman, S. (2017) *Gold, Silver, Bronze*, p. 3)

■   **Add a citation to the summary and quotation below.**

(Summary)
Kaufman argues that wealth (expressed as GDP per head) rather than size of population is the key to national success in the Olympics.

(Quotation)
Large populations alone do not guarantee good national results at the Olympics. Countries must also be wealthy enough to have healthy citizens and be able to provide resources for training. As Kaufman points out: 'When many people are affected by poverty and illness it is not easy to be ordinarily healthy, let alone be an Olympic athlete'.

7. Further practice

■   Revise this unit by matching the words on the left with the definitions on the right.

a **Source**	To gain advantage dishonestly
b Citation	**The origin of ideas or information**
c To summarise	To reduce the length of a text while keeping the main points
d Quotation	Short in-text note giving the author's name and publication date
e Reference	Using different words or word order to restate a text
f To cheat	Using the exact words of the original text in your work
g Paraphrase	Full publication details of a text or other source

8. Research

Look on your college or university website to find out the policy on plagiarism. It may raise some issues that you want to discuss with colleagues or your teachers.

If you can't find anything for your particular institution try one of these sites:

http://owl.english.purdue.edu/owl/resource/589/01/

http://www.uefap.com/writing/plagiar/plagfram.htm

1.5 From Understanding Titles to Planning

In both exams and coursework it is essential for students to understand what an essay title is asking them to do. A plan can then be drawn up, which should prevent time being wasted, while ensuring the question is answered fully. This unit looks at:

- key words in titles
- essay length and organisation
- methods of essay planning.

1. The planning process

Teachers frequently complain that students do not answer the question set, but this can be avoided by care at the planning stage. Planning is necessary in all academic writing, but clearly there are important differences between planning in exams, when time is short, and for coursework, when preparatory reading is required. However, in both cases the process of planning should include these four steps:

a) analyse the title wording

b) study the evaluation criteria

c) decide how long each section should be

d) prepare an outline using your favourite method.

Note that when writing coursework, your outline will probably be revised as you develop your ideas.

▶ **See Unit 5.3 Writing Longer Papers**

2. Analysing essay titles

Titles contain key words which tell the student what to do. Note that titles often have two (or more) parts:

*What is meant by a demand curve and **why** would we expect it to slope downwards?*

In this case, 'what' is asking for a description and 'why' for a reason or explanation.

■ **Underline the key words in the following titles and consider what they are asking you to do.**

a) Summarise the main reasons for the growth of e-commerce, and discuss the likely results of this.

b) 'The internet has rendered obsolete the traditional theories of the internationalisation of firms'. Critically evaluate this statement.

c) Describe the barriers and challenges to managing diversity and critically examine organisational practices.

d) Discuss the relationship between knowledge and power in organisations. Consider the implications for managers.

3. Practice: key words

■ **Match the key words on the left to the definitions on the right.**

Analyse	Explain a topic briefly and clearly
Assess /Evaluate	**Divide into sections and discuss each critically**
Describe	Break down into the various parts and their relationships
Discuss	Make a proposal and support it
Examine /Explore	Look at various aspects of a topic, compare benefits and drawbacks
Illustrate	Give a detailed account of something
Outline /Trace	Give examples
Suggest/Indicate	Decide the value or worth of a subject
Summarise	**Deal with a complex subject by reducing it to the main elements**

Many essay titles also include a context, such as a time period or a geographical area:

Instruction	Subject	Context
Compare	*the effects of privatisation on the economies*	*of Poland and Hungary 1990–2010.*

Clearly, it is important to limit your answer to the given context; you will lose marks if you ignore this limitation.

4. Evaluation criteria

It is always worth spending time finding out exactly what your teacher is looking for. When setting an assignment, your teacher will often give you a very clear picture of how the work will be assessed. This example from an MBA course explains how the mark scheme is organised. It is worth noting, for instance, that 30% of the mark is given for the conclusion – which should give you a guide to how much time to spend on this part.

SECTION	CRITERIA TO BE ASSESSED
OVERALL STRUCTURE (5%)	The written work is structured clearly and coherently without any spelling errors; the language and grammar are appropriate.
PART 1: INTRODUCTION (20%)	The objectives are clearly stated as are the main sources of information and the focus of the work.
PART 2: THEORETICAL FRAMEWORK/ MODELS (40%)	Theoretical framework(s) and/or model(s) are adequately stated, described and applied with a clear discussion and interpretation of the analysis of a chosen company. A critical analysis of the topic should be carried out.
PART 3: CONCLUSIONS (30%)	Key findings are clearly presented and discussed with evidence of critical thinking.
REFERENCING (5%)	The work contains academic references and/or citations. Please consult the specific reference style in the module handbook or follow the Harvard reference system.

You may also be given grade descriptors, as in the following example. These tell you what is expected at different marking levels:

INDICATOR %	PRESENTATION WILL OFTEN DEMONSTRATE SOME OF THE FOLLOWING FEATURES
90–100	An exceptional level of analysis, showing deep critical engagement with a comprehensive range of contextual material. Demonstration of independent thought resulting in creative and original responses to the assignment brief. Clear evidence of understanding of current scholarship and research based on an extensive range of relevant sources. Clarity of structure demonstrating complete focus of argument. Virtually no errors in referencing/grammar and/or syntax.
80–89	Excellent links between relevant ideas, theories and practice. Clear evidence of independent scholarship and the ability to engage critically and analytically with a range of contextually relevant resource material. Demonstration of insights supported by extremely well structured overall argument. Very few errors in referencing/grammar and/or syntax.
70–79	Very good links between a range of different ideas and theories. Places issues in a wider context. Clear evidence of a critical understanding of a range of relevant theories and application of these appropriately. Independent ideas, well-argued and supported. Few errors in referencing/grammar and/or syntax.
60–69	Clear links between theory and practice. Good coverage of assignment issues. Full understanding of core issues. Evidenced level of understanding of appropriate theory and concepts. Some small repeated errors in referencing/grammar and/or syntax.
50–59	Identifies main issues and relevant theory. Coverage of most assignment issues. Competent application of relevant theory and states obvious links to practice. Some repeated errors in grammar or syntax. Failure to apply Harvard referencing standard correctly in places.

5. Brainstorming

In an exam, it is often helpful to start thinking about a topic by writing down the ideas you have, in any order. Taking the example from 2a) above:

'Summarise the main reasons for the growth of e-commerce, and discuss the likely results of this'.

You might collect the following points:
Growth of e-commerce and likely results
Main reasons

- Businesses can offer a wider range of products via the internet
- Delivery service more convenient for customers than travelling to shops
- Businesses can reduce overheads by centralising distribution centres
- Prices can often be lower reflecting lower costs

Likely results

- Decline in conventional shops
- Growth in delivery businesses
- Shopping centres become entertainment areas

■ **Working with a partner, brainstorm ideas for the title below:**

'How and why has the market for international tourism segmented since the end of the twentieth century? What are the economic forces that have driven this process?'

6. Essay length

Coursework essays and reports usually have a required length, normally between 1,000 and 5,000 words. You must keep to this limit, although differences of 5% more or less are generally acceptable. However, at the planning stage you need to consider what proportion of the essay to allocate to each part of the question. As a basic guide, 20% is usually sufficient for the introduction and conclusion together (references are not included in the word count). Therefore, in a 2,000 word essay the main body would have 1,600 words.

If this was the length given for title 2a) above, you might decide on the following division for the main body:

Reasons that benefit businesses: reduced overheads/wider range	600 words
Reasons that benefit customers: convenience and lower prices	450 words
Likely results: fewer shops/change in use/more deliveries	550 words
Total	**1,600 words**

This calculation is useful since it can guide the amount of reading you need to do, as well as providing the basis for an outline. Moreover, it prevents you from writing an unbalanced answer, in which part of the question is not fully developed.

Essays in exams do not have a word limit, but it is equally important to plan them in similar terms e.g. part 1, 40%, part 2, 60%.

■ **Identify the key words in the following titles and decide what percentage of the main body to give to each part.**

a) 'Monopolies are inefficient in using resources'. Explain and discuss.

b) What problems do East Asian businesses face in integrating with the global economy? Discuss with reference to a country example.

c) Choose a company which you work for, or you are familiar with, examine the environmental challenges which face your chosen company from political, economic and cultural perspectives when entering or expanding into a foreign country.

7. Outlines

An outline should help the writer to answer the question as effectively as possible. Care at this stage will save wasted effort later. The more detail you include in your outline, the easier the writing process will be.

Note that for coursework it is usually better to write the main body first, then the introduction and finally the conclusion. Therefore you may prefer to outline just the main body at this stage.

There is no fixed pattern for an outline; different methods appeal to different students. For example, with the first part of title 2a) above:

'Summarise the main reasons for the growth of e-commerce'.

a) The outline might be a list:
1. Benefits for buyers
    – greater convenience in shopping by computer at any time
    – lower prices
    – better choice
2. Benefits for sellers

    – cost saving by centralising distribution
    – global customer base
    – 24/7 trading

b) An alternative is a mind map:

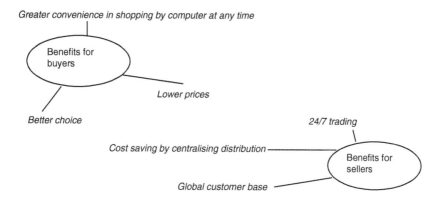

- What are the advantages and drawbacks of each method?

8. Practice

- You have to answer the second part of the title 'Summarise the main reasons for the growth of e-commerce, and discuss the likely results of this'. In preparation read the following text, and then prepare an outline using either method.

BRITISH SHOPPERS GO ONLINE

People in Britain do more of their shopping (currently 20%) through the internet than in most other countries. This figure, which is increasing rapidly, is having significant effects on many industries. Britain's geography makes it ideal for the spread of e-commerce, due to it being a small and densely populated country, so that most households can be easily reached from giant warehouses in the Midlands. The popularity and convenience of smartphones is also encouraging internet shopping.

The result is that retailers have had to focus on logistics to compete for trade. The efficient management of parcels is the key to success: over a billion packages were sent out in 2018. One effect has been a revival in the fortunes of the Royal Mail, which had been suffering from a decline in its letter business. Most internet orders are sent from huge 'fulfilment centres' in central England; these structures now cover 40 million square metres. However, intense competition on delivery times has recently led to a trend to build warehouses on the edge of cities, especially London, to be near customers. As a result, the cost of rents for these has risen sharply, since this land is also in demand for housing.

Another concern for internet retailers is the legal obligation to accept returned goods within two weeks of sale. This amounts to about 6% of sales overall, but as much as 40% with items of clothing. This increases costs for the seller, but has also created a new niche business in dealing with these goods. The volume of parcel deliveries, coupled with the food delivery services run by the major supermarkets, has led to more traffic on the roads. In addition, there is a shortage of drivers for the trucks and vans involved, since this work is demanding and low-paid. One solution may be to use driverless vehicles, and trials of these have begun.

At the moment about 3 million people work in UK shops, but the increase in e-commerce and the inevitable closure of many shops may lead to the loss of about a third of these jobs within the next ten years. Some of the closed stores may re-open as cafes, bars or restaurants, other may develop into 'shopping experiences' which give customers a taste of the product instead of just selling it. In any case it is likely that Britain's high streets will drastically change their character in the years to come.

(Source: Kuyper, J. (2017) *Tomorrow's Cities*, p. 232)

1.6 Finding Key Points and Note-making

> After finding a suitable source and identifying relevant sections of text, the next step is to select the key points that relate to your topic and make notes on them. This unit explains and practises this process, which also involves skills further developed in Unit 1.7 Summarising and Paraphrasing.

1. Finding key points

Before making notes you need to find the main ideas in a text.

■ **Read the following article about financial fraud, underline the key points and then choose a title for the article.**

Title:_____

It is difficult to make an accurate estimate of the cost of internet scams, but the fraud research centre at Stanford University gives a total of more than $50 bn. per year in the USA. The scammers are steadily becoming more sophisticated and may clone authentic websites, or make phone calls that seem to come from real banks or the tax authorities.

Many of the victims are wealthier retired people, who are deceived by fake websites offering tax refunds or fraudulent dating profiles. Such people may be well educated, but often over-estimate their financial ability, and they may be especially vulnerable if suffering from a recent emotional trauma such as divorce. Many people find it hard to admit, even to themselves, that they have been swindled out of their savings, and some never report their losses.

Normally banks refuse to compensate people who have lost money through these schemes, although many victims argue that the banks are partly responsible for the functioning of some of the scams. In turn, the banks maintain that some responsibility lies with the internet companies that give a platform to the fraudsters. In Britain a voluntary code has been prepared which would compensate some victims who made bank payments after getting fake messages from 'police' or other authorities. But the question remains: who will fund the compensation scheme?

2. Finding relevant points

When preparing to write an essay you have to search for information and ideas relevant to your subject. Therefore the key points that you select must relate to that topic.

You are given an essay title: 'Taxation as an instrument of social policy – Discuss'.

■   Read the following article and underline the key points that link to your essay topic.

CAN TAXATION REDUCE OBESITY?

Taxation has been imposed by governments for thousands of years, and initially the basis of taxation was something easily assessed, such as land, fire hearths or windows, all of which were difficult to hide from the tax collector. But in more recent times governments have sought to use taxes not just to raise revenue, but also to reward virtue and discourage vice.

The practice of imposing taxes on products which are thought to have a negative social impact, such as alcohol, has been accepted for several hundred years, and they are now called Pigouvian taxes (after the twentieth-century economist Arthur Pigou). Tobacco, gambling and carbon taxes are common examples. It has recently been suggested in the USA that so-called junk food should be taxed in order to compensate for the social costs of the obesity it is believed to cause. This proposal is based on the estimate of the medical costs of obesity, which is thought to be linked to cancer, diabetes and heart disease. These costs are shared by all taxpayers, not just the obese, so it is claimed that taxing items such as hamburgers and sugary drinks would both reduce consumption and help pay for medical care.

A study of the long-term effects of changes in food prices (Goldman, Lakdawalla and Zheng, 2009) argues that significant changes in consumption, and hence obesity levels, can be achieved over time. They claim that raising the price of calories by 10% could eliminate nearly half the increase in obesity over a 20-year span. But the link between junk food and ill-health is not easily determined. A physically active person could eat hamburgers daily and still keep slim. In this respect it is quite different from drinking alcohol or causing air pollution.

It has even been suggested that such a 'fat tax' might have the opposite effect and reduce activity levels by forcing people to spend more time preparing food for themselves, instead of buying it from fast-food outlets (Yaniv, Rosin and Tobol, 2009). Additionally, other studies on the effects of alcohol and tobacco taxes indicate that the heaviest users of these products are the least influenced by price rises, so that raising the price of hamburgers may do little to curb consumption among the keenest consumers. As these are often also the poorest, the tax would not only fail to improve their health, but would be regressive, making them even poorer.

(Source: Rohan, J. (2010) *Public Health Review 8*, p. 36)

3. Why make notes?

■ What are the main reasons for note-making? Add to the list below.

a) *To prepare for writing academic assignments* _____

b) _____

c) _____

d) _____

e) _____

4. Practice A

■ You are looking for information on the everyday effects of technological change. Study the text below (key points underlined) and the notes in the box. What do you notice about the language of the notes?

- _____
- _____
- _____
- _____

A CASHLESS CONTINENT?

There are significant differences between payment methods among European countries. In Scandinavia many shops and cafes no longer accept cash: all payments are made with credit or debit cards. By contrast, in Italy and other southern states the majority of transactions are still made in cash. The reasons for the variations are both historical and cultural.

Sweden is the leader in the 'plastic revolution', with about 95% of all payments (by value) made by card. This method is seen as quicker and more convenient for both customers and businesses, and also cheaper for the latter, since bank notes need to be sorted, checked and protected. It is also thought that the use of cash encourages tax avoidance, while banks are forced to maintain a large branch network to provide ATM facilities and also accept cash deposits. A further argument against cash use is that cashless shops are less likely to be robbed, so that the staff feel more secure.

In contrast, people in both Italy and Germany are far less enthusiastic about a cashless society: here more than 75% of transactions are still made in cash. Their banks charge more to handle card payments, so that shop keepers are less keen to accept them. In Germany there also seem to be fears about security and privacy, perhaps as a legacy of state control in the past, while some Italians apparently prefer to keep their transactions hidden from the government.

Everywhere there are poorer people who have no bank account and consequently need to operate in cash, and ultimately cash provides security in case the system breaks down. But despite these considerations, cultural as well as economic, the benefits of a cashless economy seem likely to result in a steady shift towards the use of plastic cards across Europe.

(Source: *East-West Monthly*, December 2017, p. 112)

EUROPEAN PAYMENT TRENDS

1. Wide variation in payment methods in Europe – historical and cultural causes

2. In Scandinavia (esp. Sweden) most payments by card:

<u>Reasons</u>

    a)   fast and convenient + saves outlets money

    b)   prevents tax evasion

    c)   safer for shops

    d)   banks need fewer branches

3.   In Germany and Italy most payments in cash:

    a)   higher bank charges for cards

    b)   security concerns

    c)   worries re. govt. interference

4.   Cash needed by poor (no bank accounts) and for back-up but general trend >
cashless economy

(Source: *East-West Monthly*, December 2017, p. 112)

5. Effective note-making

Notes are for your personal use and you should create your own style.

a)   To avoid the risk of plagiarism you must use your own words and not copy phrases from the original.

b)   The quantity of notes you make depends on your task: you may only need a few points, or a lot of detail.

c)   Always record the source of your notes, which will save time when you have to write the list of references.

d)   Notes are written quickly, so keep them simple. Do not write sentences. Leave out articles (a/the) and prepositions (of/to).

e)   If you write lists, it is important to have clear headings (<u>underlined</u>) and numbering systems (a, b, c, or 1, 2, 3,) to organise the information. Do not crowd your notes.

f)   Use symbols (+, >, =) to save time.

g)   Use abbreviations (e.g. = for example). You need to make up your own abbreviations for your subject area. But do not abbreviate too much, or you may find your notes hard to understand in the future!

▶   **See Unit 4.2 Abbreviations**

6. Practice B

■   Complete the set of notes for 'Can taxation reduce obesity?' using the key points underlined in (2) above.

(Source: Rohan, J. (2010) *Public Health Review* 8, p. 36)
<u>Taxing junk food</u>

1.   Goods > social harm e.g. alcohol have been taxed since 18th C.

2.   US proposal to tax junk food > reduce obesity > cut medical costs (diabetes, heart disease).

3.   _____

4.   _____

5.   _____

6.   _____

7. Practice C

You have to write an essay titled: 'What is the value of anti-monopoly legislation?'

■   Read the following text, underline the relevant key points and make notes on them.

THE DIFFICULTY OF ASSESSING PREDATORY PRICING

Small companies often feel that larger rivals want to put them out of business by discounting, for example the corner shop which cannot match the supermarket's bargain offers. In 1890 the United States passed the Sherman Antitrust Act, which was an attempt to prevent large companies exploiting their semi-monopoly position, and many countries have adopted similar legislation. This is a response to concerns that big businesses will lower prices to drive competitors to bankruptcy, and then be able to raise prices at will.

But clearly low prices are an advantage to consumers, and proving predation in court is a difficult process. Firms may have legitimate reasons for selling below cost, such as promoting a new product or because they expect their costs to fall when volume increases. In these cases current losses can be offset against future profits.

Bundling goods, i.e. selling two or more products as a package, makes it even harder to establish malpractice. This is because the profit margin on each item in the bundle may vary. So a company that makes little profit on printers may sell them with higher profit margin ink cartridges. By doing this it can claim that other costs are being saved, for example on distribution.

In May 2009 the European Union found the chip-maker Intel guilty of predatory pricing against a rival, AMD, and fined the company 1.06 billion Euros, claiming that European consumers of computers had suffered as a result of Intel providing incentives to manufacturers to favour its chips. But Intel appealed against the verdict, and the complexity of the case (the court verdict ran to over 500 pages) is an example of the difficulty of policing companies in this area.

(Source: Caballero J. and Poledna Z. (2010) *European Business Prospects*, London: Capital University Press, p. 351)

1.7 Summarising and Paraphrasing

Summarising and paraphrasing are normally used together in academic writing.

- Summarising aims to reduce information to a suitable length, allowing the writer to condense lengthy sources into a concise form.
- Paraphrasing means changing the wording of a text so that it is significantly different from the original source, without changing the meaning.
- Both are needed to avoid the risk of plagiarism, and this unit practises them separately and jointly.

1. What makes a good summary?

Summarising is a common activity in everyday life. It is used to describe the main features of the subject in order to give a clear and simple impression. For example, if you have been to Tokyo, you might tell a friend:

Tokyo is a huge city with mainly modern buildings and a dense network of public transport. It has many busy shopping centres which are crowded day and night.

■ Write a short description of one of the topics below in no more than 30 words.

    a) A company you have worked for

    b) A product you have recently bought

    c) A film you have recently watched

■ Compare your summary with others in your class. Discuss what is needed for a good summary.

- _____
- _____
- _____

2. Stages of summarising

Summarising is a flexible tool. You can use it to give a one-sentence outline of an article, or to provide much more detail, depending on your needs. Generally a summary focuses on the main ideas and tends to exclude examples or supporting information. When writing a summary the same basic steps need to be followed in order to meet the criteria discussed in 1) above.

■ Study the stages of summary writing below, which have been mixed up. Put them in the correct order (1–5).

a)   Write the summary from your notes, re-organising the structure if needed.

b)   Make notes of the key points, paraphrasing where possible.

c)   Read the original text carefully and check any new or difficult vocabulary.

d)   Mark the key points by underlining or highlighting.

e)   Check the summary to ensure it is accurate and nothing important has been changed or lost.

3. Practice A

■ Read the following text and the summaries which follow. Which is best? Put them in order 1–3 and give reasons.

DISRUPTIVE TECHNOLOGY

This phrase was first used by Joseph Bower and Clayton Christensen of the Harvard Business School in 1995. They employed it to describe a new technology that appeals to a minority section of the market, but a large enough minority to allow the technology to take root and develop. Companies that continue to use the older technology run the risk of being left behind if they do not adopt the innovation at the right moment. A clear example in the mid-1990s was the digital camera. The first models had lower picture quality than film cameras and were expensive. But their important advantages were that they allowed the photographer to see the results immediately, and had the ability to download the images to a computer for storage, printing or emailing. Since then, digital cameras have completely transformed the industry, and are now standard in many devices such as mobile phones. The business of making film has almost vanished, and the vast majority of cameras sold are now digital.

a) Disruptive technology is a new invention which attracts enough buyers to become established in the market, and then to improve and grow. For example, the first digital cameras, launched years ago, took poor quality pictures and were costly, but had some important benefits. Today they dominate the market, and the older type of camera, which uses expensive film, is now less popular.

b) Bower and Christensen from Harvard introduced the term 'disruptive technology' in 1995, to characterise a new technology which sold well enough to enter the market, and could then be developed further. The digital camera, for instance, was originally expensive and had low picture quality. However, it had some advantages which quickly allowed it to virtually replace the traditional film camera.

c) Digital cameras are a good example of a disruptive technology, a term used by Bower and Christensen of Harvard Business School in 1995 to describe a new technology that initially wins enough market share to survive and develop. These cameras at first produced inferior pictures, but had the critical advantages of showing the picture instantly, and allowing the user to download the image. In a few years they dominated the camera market, while traditional film cameras almost became redundant.

1. _____

2. _____

3. _____

4. Practice B

a) ■ Read the following text and underline the key points.

AFRICA CALLING

In many African countries mobile phone ownership is aiding new businesses to get started. Farmers can easily find current market prices for their crops, and traders can use mobile money services to make payments. It seems clear that as more people use these phones national GDP rises, but it is difficult to quantify this precisely. Ten years ago there were only 130 million mobile users in the entire continent: now the number is over one billion. However, this figure is deceptive: many Africans have two or more SIM cards, and in reality only about half of Africa's 1.2 billion people have access to a mobile phone.

Inevitably, the Africans who have phones tend to be better-educated urban dwellers, but even these are often unable to access the internet, according to an estimate by the International Telecommunications Union (ITU). They claim that 75% of

Africans are unable to use the net, with figures as high as 95% in places like Chad. This is because much of the continent is rural and sparsely populated, so that providing mobile phone masts in these districts is uneconomic. Even fewer people can receive a fast 4G signal, and when available, costs are high.

But the situation may be improving due to advances in technology. New cables are facilitating the connection with other continents, and fibre optic networks are being installed in major cities. Modern satellites are also lowering transmission costs, and solar powered phone masts are cheaper to run in remote villages. But one significant obstacle to these developments is the heavy taxation many governments impose on the telecom companies, which can be as high as 50% in places such as Tanzania.

(Source: Weiss, J. and Evans, P. (2019) *African Perspectives*, pp. 213–214)

▶ **See Unit 1.6 Finding Key Points and Note-making**

b) ■ Complete the notes of the key points below.

    i)   Mobile phones have helped _____

    ii)   Link between higher phone ownership _____

    iii) Only half of Africans _____

    iv) New developments _____

    v)   But _____

c) ■ Join the notes together and expand them to make the final summary in about 70 words. Check that the meaning is clear and no important points have been left out. Find a suitable title.

Title:_____

d) This summary is about 25% of the length of the original, but it could be summarised further.

■ Summarise the summary in no more than 30 words.

5. Practice C

■ Summarise the following text in about 50 words.

THE ECONOMICS OF HAPPINESS

Since 2005 Gallup has been surveying adults in over 100 countries to find their life satisfaction, measured on a ten-point scale. When this score is correlated with the national GDP per person, we might expect to find that people in countries with strong increases in GDP would report greater happiness. This is true overall, but there are many exceptions, creating a phenomenon known as the 'Easterlin Paradox', after Richard Easterlin, the economist who demonstrated that, despite a 65% increase in average wealth in the USA between 1946 and 1970, there had been no improvement in life satisfaction scores.

The same paradox is evident today. The latest Gallup figures (2019) show a significant improvement in Chinese happiness, alongside a doubling of GDP during the past 10 years. But over the same period the data from India tells a different story: while GDP has risen by 80% happiness has dropped from 5 to 4 on the ten-point scale. Other countries experiencing a similar decline include Tanzania, Japan and Spain, while among those reporting increased satisfaction are Pakistan, Greece and Germany. Economists continue to debate the reasons for the paradoxical results, but it seems likely that there are special, complex factors at work in every case.

---

6. Paraphrasing

Paraphrasing and summarising are normally used together in essay writing, but while summarising aims to **reduce** information to a suitable length, paraphrasing attempts to **restate** the relevant information. For example, the following sentence:

> *There has been much debate about the reasons for the Industrial Revolution happening in eighteenth-century Britain, rather than in France or Germany.*

could be paraphrased:

> *Why the Industrial Revolution occurred in Britain in the eighteenth century, instead of on the continent, has been the subject of considerable discussion.*

Note that an effective paraphrase usually:

- has a different structure to the original
- has different vocabulary
- retains the same meaning
- keeps some phrases from the original which are in common use e.g. 'Industrial Revolution'.

7. Practice D

■ **Read the text below and then rank the three paraphrases (a–c) in order of accuracy, clarity and use of original language.**

THE CAUSES OF THE INDUSTRIAL REVOLUTION

Allen (2009) argues that the best explanation for the British location of the Industrial Revolution is found by studying demand factors. By the early eighteenth century high wages and cheap energy were both features of the British economy. Consequently, the mechanisation of industry through such inventions as the steam engine and mechanical spinning was profitable, because employers were able to economise on labour by spending on coal. At that time, no other European country had this particular combination of expensive labour and abundant fuel.

---

a) A focus on demand may help to explain the UK origin of the Industrial Revolution. At that time British workers' pay was high, but energy was cheap. This encouraged the development of mechanical inventions based on steam power, which enabled bosses to save money by mechanising production (Allen, 2009).

b) The reason why Britain was the birthplace of the Industrial Revolution can be understood by analysing demand in the early 1700s, according to Allen (2009). He maintains that, uniquely in Europe, Britain had the critical combination of cheap energy from coal and high labour costs. This encouraged the adoption of steam power to mechanise production, thus saving on wages and increasing profitability.

c) Allen (2009) claims that the clearest explanation for the UK location of the Industrial Revolution is seen by examining demand factors. By the eighteenth century cheap energy and high wages were both aspects of the British economy. As a result, the mechanisation of industry through inventions such as the steam engine and mechanical spinning was profitable because employers were able to save money on wages by spending on coal. At that time, Britain was the only country with significant deposits of coal.

1) _____

2) _____

3) _____

8. Techniques for paraphrasing

a)   Changing vocabulary by using synonyms:

argues > claims/eighteenth century > 1700s/wages > labour costs/economise > saving

b)   Changing word class:

explanation (n.) > explain (v.)/mechanical (adj.) > mechanise (v.)/profitable (adj.) > profitability (n.)

c)   Changing word order:

. . . the best explanation for the British location of the Industrial Revolution is found by studying demand factors.

> A focus on demand may help explain the UK origin of the Industrial Revolution.

Note that in practice all these three techniques are used at the same time. Do not attempt to paraphrase every word, since some have no true synonym e.g. demand, or economy.

▶   **See Units 4.3 and 4.4 Academic Vocabulary and 4.8 Synonyms**

9. Practice E

◼   **Read the following text.**

GREEN DREAMS?

It is often argued that governments can create employment and reduce carbon emissions by investing in renewable energy projects. These so-called 'green jobs' also have the appeal of helping to combat global warming while reducing a country's dependence on imported fuels. An American think-tank has calculated that the spending of $100bn. by the US government would result in the creation of two million jobs. A number of countries such as Germany, Spain and Indonesia have spent heavily on subsidising low-carbon technology.

However, critics of these schemes claim that the results are not as beneficial as they seem. Firstly, if the money was spent on other projects such as road building, jobs would also be created. Secondly, higher government borrowing to pay for the investment has to be financed by the taxpayer, and it may eventually affect the cost of borrowing for all businesses. In addition, subsidising relatively inefficient energy sources such as solar and wind power may raise the price of electricity for consumers.

A study in Spain looked at the cost of subsidising renewable energy over 25 years. The estimated expenditure of €29bn. will provide 50,000 jobs, but they will have cost €570,000 each to create. If, however, the government had allowed private industry to spend the same amount, it would have created 113,000 posts; more than twice as many. So it can be argued that the Spanish scheme will have actually destroyed over 50,000 jobs. Although these figures ignore both the environmental benefits and the advantages for Spain of reducing demand for imported fossil fuels, it is clear that such green schemes do not automatically bring benefits to all.

a) ■ **Find synonyms for the words underlined. Re-write the sentences using these.**

It is <u>often argued</u> that governments can create<u> employment</u> and <u>reduce</u> carbon emissions by investing in renewable energy <u>projects</u>. These so-called 'green jobs' also have the <u>appeal</u> of helping to <u>combat</u> global warming while <u>reducing</u> a <u>country's </u>dependence on imported fuels.

b) ■ **Change the word class of the underlined words. Re-write the sentences using the changes.**

However, critics of these schemes <u>claim</u> that the results are not as <u>beneficial</u> as they seem. First, if the money was <u>spent</u> on other projects such as road building, jobs would also be <u>created</u>.

c) ■ **Change the word order of these sentences, re-writing the paragraph so the meaning stays the same.**

Second, higher government borrowing to pay for the investment has to be financed by the taxpayer, and it may eventually affect the cost of borrowing for all businesses. In addition, subsidising relatively inefficient energy sources such as solar and wind power may raise the price of electricity for consumers.

d) ■ Combine all three techniques to paraphrase the next paragraph.

> A study in Spain looked at the cost of subsidising renewable energy over 25 years. The estimated expenditure of €29bn. will provide 50,000 jobs, but they will have cost €570,000 each to create. If, however, the government had allowed private industry to spend the same amount, it would have created 113,000 posts; more than twice as many. So it can be argued that the Spanish scheme will have actually destroyed over 50,000 jobs.

10. Practice F

a) ■ Use the same techniques to paraphrase the following text.

THE POWER OF THE BID

Two American researchers, Philip Cook of Duke University and John MacDonald from the University of Pennsylvania, have studied the effectiveness of Business Improvement Districts (BIDs) in Los Angeles. These not-for-profit bodies were set up to combat crime in commercial areas of the city, mainly by providing private security guards. Their research shows that BIDs, which are financed by levies on firms in the district, do reduce crime in a cost-effective way.

It appears that because the guards are only responsible for a limited area they can work more efficiently than police; moreover they are paid less. The companies that finance the scheme benefit by enjoying a safer environment and higher property values. In addition, the police can concentrate their efforts on other parts of the city, though there is no evidence that crime is displaced from the BIDs to neighbouring areas. Overall, Cook and MacDonald conclude that BIDs are a valuable crime-reduction tool.

b) ■ Summarise the same text in 50 words.

1.8 References and Quotations

Academic work is based on the research and ideas of others, so it is vital to show which sources you have used in your work, in an acceptable manner. This unit explains:

- the format of in-text citation
- the main reference system for students of Business
- the use of quotations
- the layout of lists of references.

1. Why use references?

There are three principal reasons for providing references and citations:

a) to show that you have read some of the authorities on the subject, which will give added weight to your writing

b) to allow readers to find the source, if they wish to examine the topic in more detail

c) to avoid plagiarism and demonstrate that you understand the rules of the academic community.

▶ **See Unit 1.4 Avoiding Plagiarism**

■ Decide if you need to give a reference in the following cases.

	Yes/No
a) Data you found from your own primary research	_____
b) A graph from an internet article	_____
c) A quotation from a book	_____

d) An item of common knowledge e.g. exercise is good for you   _____

e) A theory from a journal article   _____

f) An idea of your own based on reading several sources   _____

g) A comment made by a person you interviewed for your project   _____

2. Citations and references

It is important to refer correctly to the work of other writers which you have used. You may present these sources as a summary or paraphrase, as a quotation, or use both. In each case a citation is included to provide a link to the list of references at the end of your paper:

Smith (2009) argues that the popularity of the Sports Utility Vehicle (SUV) is irrational, as despite their high cost most are never driven off-road. In his view 'they are bad for road safety, the environment and road congestion' (Smith 2009:37).

> **Reference**
> Smith, M. (2009) *Power and the State*. Basingstoke: Palgrave Macmillan.

■ Underline the citations in the example above. Which is for a summary and which a quotation? What are the advantages of each?

Giving citations

A quotation	Author's family name, date of publication, page no.	(Smith 2009:37)
A summary	Author's family name, date of publication	Smith (2009)

3. Reference verbs

Summaries and quotations are usually introduced by a reference verb:

*Smith (2009) **argues** that . . .*

*Janovic (1972) **claimed** that . . .*

These verbs can be either in the present or the past tense. Normally the use of the present tense suggests that the source is recent and still valid, while the past indicates that the source is older and may be out-of-date, but there are no hard-and-fast rules. In some cases an older source may still be relevant.

The meaning and use of the different verbs of reference is explained in Part 4.

▶   **See Unit 4.4.3 Using verbs of reference**

4. Reference systems

There are various systems of referencing employed in the academic world, each used by different subjects. Many Business schools use the Harvard system, which is explained here. If you are not sure which system to use you should ask your teacher. With any system, the most important point is to be consistent e.g. to use the same pattern of punctuation and capitalisation throughout.

Each system specifies how to reference a wide variety of sources: not only books and journals but also sources such as films, music, blogs and oral testimony. Referencing is a complex subject and students should use an online reference guide for detailed information, such as Anglia Ruskin's guide to Harvard at:

https://libweb.anglia.ac.uk/referencing/harvard.htm?active=11

5. Using quotations

■   **Discuss with a partner reasons for using quotations in your written work.**

Using a quotation means bringing the original words of a writer into your work. Quotations are effective in some situations, but must not be over-used (e.g. to pad out your work). They can be valuable:

•   when the original words express an idea in a distinctive way

•   when the original is more concise than your summary could be

•   when the original version is well-known.

All quotations should be introduced by a phrase which shows the source, and also explains how this quotation fits into your argument:

Introductory phrase	Author	Reference verb	Quotation	Citation
This view is widely shared;	as Friedman	stated:	'Inflation is the one form of taxation that can be imposed without legislation'	(Friedman, 1974:93).

a)   Short quotations (1–2 lines) are shown by single quotation marks. Quotations inside quotations (nested quotations) use double quotation marks:

As Kauffman remarked: 'his concept of "internal space" requires close analysis'.

b) Longer quotations (3 or more lines) are either indented (given a wider margin) and/or are printed in smaller type. In this case quotations marks are not needed:

As Sarah Nuttall and Achille Mbembe suggest in relation to their work on Johannesburg:

> *The two processes of formalisation and informalisation work together. How they work together and how this working together ends up producing city forms and urban economies seems to be the question that we need to pursue (Nuttall and Mbembe, 2004:9).*

c) Page numbers should be given after the date.

1974:93

d) Care must be taken to ensure that quotations are the exact words of the original. If it is necessary to delete some words which are irrelevant, use dots (…) to show where the missing section was:

'Few inventions . . . have been as significant as the mobile phone'.

e) It may be necessary to insert a word or phrase into the quotation to clarify a point. This can be done by using square brackets [ ]:

'[this category of] products is distinguished by its high brand recognition . . .'.

f) If you want to show that you are aware of a mistake in the original use [*sic*]:

He claimed that 'the company was to [sic] big to fail'.

g) If a writer has published more than one book or article in a year it is necessary to add a/b/c to the date:

(Nussbaum, 2011b:28)

6. Practice

■ **Read the following text, from an article called 'Dealing with transition' in the journal *Education Review* (Autumn 2016, pp. 45–47) by A. Kelman.**

Students entering Higher Education (HE, i.e. degree-level study) often find the transition from school to university difficult to manage. This can be especially true of the demands of essay writing, a skill required in the majority of subjects. A study by McEwan (2015) explored the reasons for difficulties at this stage by comparing the expectations of staff and students towards writing essays. He found significant differences between the two, and suggested ways in which the differences could be reduced.

It often takes time for new students to adjust to the learning culture of HE, and much depends on their previous academic experience. Teaching staff at degree level expect students to study independently and not to need regular supervision, although recently universities have begun to provide more support for first-year students to help them adjust to these expectations.

■ **Compare the following:**

a) **Summary**
Kelman (2016) maintains that the transition from school to university study is particularly hard in terms of writing essays. She refers to McEwan's research on the mis-match between student and teacher expectations, and highlights the need to give students time to adapt to a new academic culture.

b) **Quotation**
Kelman discusses McEwan's research on the gap between the expectations of staff and students with regard to essay writing at first-year university level:

> It often takes time for new students to adjust to the learning culture of HE, and much depends on their previous academic experience. Teaching staff at degree level expect students to study independently and not to need regular supervision.
> (Kelman, 2016:45)

c) **Summary and quotation**
Kelman (2016) points out that one area of serious concern for first-year university students is writing essays. She looks at the study done by McEwan on the differences between teachers' and students' perceptions of essay writing, which highlighted one distinct difficulty: 'Teaching staff at degree level expect students to study independently and not to need regular supervision' (Kelman, 2016:45).

■ **Read the next part of the same text, also on p. 45.**

McEwan argues that student success at university level is partly dependent on narrowing the difference between student and staff expectations. This is particularly important now that the student body includes an increasing proportion of international students, who may take longer to adapt to the university culture. The same is also true of the increasingly diverse university staff, who often come from very different academic cultures.

> The two most significant findings of the study concerned plagiarism and essay focus. In both cases there was a substantial difference between staff and student opinion. While all the students claimed to understand the meaning of plagiarism, a majority of teachers (over 60%) felt that they didn't. Similarly, nearly all the students claimed to focus on answering the question in the essay title, but only one fifth of the teachers thought that they did.

a) ▓ **Write a summary of the main point, including a citation.**

b) ▓ **Introduce a quotation to show the key point, referring to the source.**

c) ▓ **Combine the summary and the quotation, again acknowledging the source.**

7. Abbreviations in citations

In-text citations use the following abbreviations, derived from Latin and printed in italics:

et al.: used when three or more authors are given. The full list of names is given in the reference list:

Many Americans fail to vote (Hobolt *et al.*, 2006:137)

ibid.: taken from the same source (i.e. the same page) as the previous citation:

Older Americans are more likely to vote than the young (ibid.)

op cit.: taken from the same source as previously, but a different page

Note that journal articles increasingly tend to use full citations at each occurrence, but students should still use the above in their work.

▶   **See Unit 4.2 Abbreviations**

8. Secondary references

It is quite common to find a reference to an original source in the text you are reading. For instance, in the text by Kelman in 6) above she says:

A study by McEwan (2015) explored the reasons for difficulties at this stage by comparing the expectations of staff and students towards writing essays.

You may wish to use this information from the original (i.e. McEwan) in your writing, even if you have not read the whole work. This is known as a secondary reference. If it is not possible to locate the original, you can refer to it thus:

*McEwan (2015), **cited in Kelman (2016:45)** compared the expectations of . . .*

You must ensure that you include the work you have read, i.e. Kelman, in the list of references.

9. Internet references

Note that references to websites should include the hyperlink to the website and the date at which it was accessed in square brackets. If no author is given use the title of the publication. For example:

Higher Education Funding Council for England (HEFCE) (2010) Research Impact. Available from www.hefce.ac.uk/rsrch/REFimpact/ [accessed 21 July 2016]

10. Organising the list of references

> There are many software systems available, e.g. RefWorks or Endnote, which automate the making of a list of references. Using one of them not only saves time, but may also help to produce a more accurate result. Some are free and others require payment, but if you search your library website you may find one which you can access without charge.

At the end of an essay or report there must be a list of all the sources cited in the piece of writing. In the Harvard system, illustrated here, the list is organised alphabetically by the family name of the author. You should be clear about the difference between first names and family names. On title pages the normal format is first name, then family name:

Sheila Burford, Juan Gonzalez

But in citations only the family name is usually used:

Burford (2001), Gonzalez (1997)

In reference lists use the family name and the initial(s):

Burford, S., Gonzalez, J.

If you are not sure which name is the family name, ask a classmate from that cultural background.
    Remember that consistency is most important when preparing a list of references e.g. if you use a full stop at the end of a reference, make sure that every reference has the same.

■ **Study the reference list below, from an article about attempts to reduce youth crime in Chicago, and answer the questions which follow.**

REFERENCES

Aizer, A. and J. Doyle (2015) 'Juvenile incarceration and adult outcomes: Evidence from randomly assigned judgest'. *Quarterly Journal of Economics* 130, 759–803.

Allensworth, E. and J. Easton (2005) 'The on-track indicator as a predictor of high school graduation'. Chicago: Consortium on Chicago School Research, University of Chicago.

Anderson, E. (1999) *Code of the Street*. New York: Norton.

Anderson, M. (2008) 'Multiple inference and gender differences in the effects of early intervention: A re-evaluation of the Abecedarian, Perry Preschool, and Early Training projects'. *Journal of the American Statistical Association* 103, 1481–1495.

Anon. (1990) *Coping Better, Anytime, Anywhere: The Handbook of Rational Self-Counselling*. Alexandria, VA: RBT Center.

Beck, J. (2011) *Cognitive Therapy: Basics and Beyond*. New York: Guilford.

Benjamini, Y. and Y. Hochberg (1995) 'Controlling the false discovery rate: A practical and powerful approach to multiple testing'. *Journal of the Royal Statistical Society* 57, 289–300.

Blattman, C., J. Jamison and M. Sheridan (forthcoming) 'Reducing crime and violence: Experimental evidence on adult noncognitive investments in Liberia'. *American Economic Review*.

Cunningham, T. (2015) 'Hierarchical aggregation of information and decision-making'. Unpublished Manuscript, New York: Columbia University.

Deming, D. (2015) 'The Growing Importance of Social Skills in the Labor Market'. NBER Working Paper No. 21473.

Doe v. Cook County (2007) No. 99 C 3945 (N.D. Ill.).

Ellis, A. (1957) 'Outcome of employing three techniques of psychotherapy'. *Journal of Clinical Psychology* 13, 344–350.

Ellis, A. and R. Harper (1975) *A New Guide to Rational Living*. Upper Saddle River, NJ: Prentice Hall.

Jensen, R. (2010) 'The (perceived) returns to education and the demand for schooling'. *Quarterly Journal of Economics* 125, 515–548.

Kahneman, D. (2011) *Thinking, Fast and Slow*. London: Macmillan.

Manski, C. (1993) 'Dynamic choice in social settings: Learning from the experiences of others'. *Journal of Econometrics* 58, 121–136.

Nisbett, R. and R. Lee (1991) *The Person and the Situation*. New York: McGraw-Hill.

a) Find an example of:

   i)   a book by one author

   _____

   ii) a journal article by three authors

   _____

   iii) a court case

   _____

   iv) an unpublished article

   _____

   v)   a journal article by one author

   _____

   vi) a book by two authors

   _____

   vii) a book by an unknown author

   _____

   viii) an article to be published shortly

   _____

b) What are the differences between the format of references for books and journal articles?

   Books:_____

   Journal articles:_____

c) When are italics used?

d) How are capital letters used in titles?

e) How is a source with no given author listed?

f) Write citations for summaries of the first three sources in the list of references above.

   i)   _____

   ii) _____

   iii) _____

1.9 Contrasting Sources

For most assignments students are expected to read a range of sources, often containing conflicting views on a topic. In some cases the contrast between the various views may be the focus of the task. This unit explains how writers can present and organise a range of contrasting sources.

1. Referring to sources

In the early stages of an essay it is common to refer to the views of other writers on the subject, to show that you are familiar with their work, and that your work will take their research into account. In a longer essay or thesis this may form a section headed 'Literature review'.

■ **Read the following example, from a study of social skills in the workplace, and answer the questions below.**

> A vast literature in economics explains increasing returns to skill as a product of the complementarity between technology and high-skilled labor, or skill-biased technological change (SBTC) (e.g., Bound and Johnson 1992; Katz and Murphy 1992; Juhn, Murphy, and Pierce 1993; Acemoglu and Autor 2011). Beginning in the 1990s, the labor market 'hollowed out' as computers substituted for labor in middle-skill routine tasks and complemented high-skilled labor, a phenomenon referred to as job polarization (Autor, Levy, and Murnane 2003; Autor, Katz, and Kearney 2006; Goos, Manning, and Salomons 2014; Michaels, Natraj, and Van Reenen 2014).
>
> (Source: Deming, D. (2017) 'The growing importance of social skills in the labor market', *The Quarterly Journal of Economics*, 132 (4), pp. 1593–1640.)

a) How many sources are mentioned here?

b) How many sources deal with job polarization?

c) Name two sources which discuss higher rewards for highly skilled workers.

■ Read another paragraph from the same study, and answer the following questions.

However, while job polarization implies rising demand for skilled labor, there has been little or no employment growth in high-paying jobs since 2000, and this slow growth predates the Great Recession (Acemoglu and Autor 2011; Beaudry, Green, and Sand 2014, 2016). Beaudry, Green, and Sand (2016) show evidence of slow growth in cognitive skill–intensive occupations in the U.S. labor market during the 2000s, and Castex and Dechter (2014) find smaller returns to cognitive test scores in the 2000s compared to the 1980s. These findings are especially puzzling in light of the rising heterogeneity in worker-specific pay premiums found in studies that use matched employer-employee data (Card, Heining, and Kline 2013; Card, Cardoso, and Kline 2016). If technological change is skill-biased, why have the returns to cognitive skill not increased over the past decade?

---

d) What is the main subject of the paragraph?

e) What is the author's reason for citing all these sources?

▶ See Unit 5.2 Literature Reviews and Book Reviews

2. Contrasting sources

Most subjects worth studying are the subject of debate. Therefore it is important to compare a range of views on a topic to show that you are familiar with all sides of a discussion.

■ The following texts are on the subject of gender pay equality. Read both texts and discuss their differences with a partner.

MIND THE GAP

The gender pay gap is the difference between what women and men earn in different companies or sectors of the economy. According to the latest figures the gap in Britain is nearly 12%, a percentage which has hardly changed since businesses were first required to report their gap in 2017. There were no sectors of the economy in which women earned more than men, while fewer than 500 organisations, out of a total of 10,500 claimed to have a pay gap of 0%.

Some of the companies which reported a reduced gap, such as Monzo bank, explained it as a result of more women being promoted to senior positions. The same occurred in some schools and academies, which tend to be dominated by female staff. But the complexity of the situation is highlighted by companies with the opposite outcome, a widening gap, such as the law firm Ashfords, which pointed out they had recruited a large number of women in junior positions. It is also notable that the pay gap in the public sector, at 16% is wider than in the private sector (11%).

The data is collected by the Equalities and Human Rights Commission, but this body has no power to check the accuracy of the figures, or force companies to reduce their gap. The government insists that the best way to promote equality is by encouraging businesses to adopt female-friendly employment practices, but given the evidence of the past few years it seems that more needs to be done to achieve full equality.

(Source: Björkman, 2019)

CAN SEX-SEGREGATION BE ELIMINATED?

During the 1970s most Western countries passed laws which required companies to treat male and female employees equally. The majority of jobs were open to applicants of either sex, so that the idea of a female firefighter or a male nurse was no longer considered abnormal. This process has brought significant economic gains: Chang-Tai Hsieh and colleagues at Chicago University calculate that a 25% increase in output per worker was achieved between 1960 and 2010, mainly due to this change.

However, it appears that most of the change has been seen in office work, and in other areas there has been little recent progress. In fact, across the economy men still work mainly with other men, and women with women. In the EU around 70% of working women are in sectors dominated by women, such as primary school teaching or catering. A similar situation exists in the USA, where occupations such as nursing are 80% female. This explains most of the gender pay gap, since female-dominated jobs tend to be worse paid than male ones, such as construction. In the US, 26 of the 30 highest paid occupations are male dominated.

Even well-qualified women, such as those who graduate in STEM subjects (science, technology, engineering and maths), are less likely than men to get work in that field, and are more likely to leave it, possibly due to discrimination. Motherhood poses a further barrier to integration.

But one effective method of improving female pay is a national minimum wage, as women tend to do the lowest-paid work. In America, those states with a minimum wage set above the federal level have smaller differences in their gender pay gap than those without. Additionally, if more men entered female dominated sectors, this would tend to push wage levels higher. However, it may be that the effective limits of de-segregation have been reached, and that there will always be a tendency for houses to be built by men and the sick to be nursed by women.

(Source: Ziadah, 2018)

■ Read this extract from a paper which compares the two previous sources.

WILL MEN AND WOMEN EVER EARN THE SAME?

Many countries now ask large organisations to report the difference in pay between their male and female employees. Björkman (2019) emphasises that the latest data from the UK shows little change from previous years, with a gap of about 12%. The recruitment situation in particular companies may explain year-on-year changes in the figures. She considers that just reporting the differences will have little effect on the behaviour of firms, and the government must do more to encourage female employment in higher-paid work. Ziadah (2018), however, points out that as there has been little recent progress in employment patterns, the process may have stalled. She argues that, although innovations such as minimum pay levels have aided women, beyond the white-collar sector traditional roles seem to be very resistant to change. Discrimination and the demands of their families, she maintains, are both significant contributory factors.

■ Note the way in which the paper summarises the sources:

2.1 Björkman	Summary
According to the latest figures the gap in Britain is nearly 12%, a percentage which has hardly changed since businesses were first required to report their gap in 2017.	According to Björkman (2019) the latest data from the UK shows little change from previous years, with a gap of about 12%.
. . . given the evidence of the past few years it seems that more needs to be done to achieve full equality.	. . . the government must do more to encourage female employment in higher-paid work.

■ Find more examples from the second text:

2.2 Ziadah	Summary

■ Read the summary again and answer the following questions:

a) Which verbs are used to introduce the summaries of the two sources?

b) Which word marks the switch from summarising Björkman to Ziadah?

c) Can you suggest any other words or phrases to use here?

3. Practice

The three texts below reflect different approaches to the topic of globalisation.

■ Read them all and then complete the paragraph from an essay entitled: 'Globalisation mainly benefits multi-national companies rather than ordinary people – Discuss', using all three sources, in approximately 100 words.

THE BENEFITS OF GLOBALISATION

It has been argued that globalisation is not a new phenomenon, but has its roots in the age of colonial expansion in the seventeenth and eighteenth centuries. However, its modern use can be dated to 1983, when Levitt's article 'The Globalisation of Markets' was published. Among the many definitions of the process that have been suggested, perhaps the simplest is that globalisation is the relatively free movement of services, goods, people and ideas world-wide. An indication of the positive effect of the process is that cross-border world trade, as a percentage of global GDP, was 15% in 1990 but is expected to reach 30% by 2024. Among the forces driving globalisation in the last two decades have been market liberalisation, cheap communication via the internet and telephony, and the growth of the economies of developing countries such as India.

(Source: Costa, 2016)

GLOBALISATION AND ITS DRAWBACKS

Considerable hostility to the forces of globalisation has emerged in both the developed and developing worlds. In the former, there is anxiety about the outsourcing of manufacturing and service jobs to countries which offer cheaper labour, while developing countries claim that only a minority have benefited from the increase in world trade. They point out that per-capita income in the 20 poorest countries has hardly changed in the past 40 years, while in the richest 20 it has tripled. The markets of Western nations are still closed to agricultural products from developing countries, and while there is free movement of goods and capital, migration of people from poor countries to rich ones is tightly controlled.

(Source: Lin, 2012)

MULTI-NATIONALS AND GLOBALISATION

Multi-national companies have undoubtedly benefited from the relaxation of the import tariff regimes which previously protected local firms, allowing them to operate more freely in markets such as India which have recently liberalised. These corporations have evolved two distinct approaches to the challenge of globalisation. Some, e.g. Gillette, have continued to manufacture their products in a few large plants with strict control to ensure uniform quality worldwide, while others, for instance Coca-Cola, vary the product to suit local tastes and tend to make their goods on the spot. They claim that an understanding of regional differences is essential for competing with national rivals. In either case, these giant companies are often able to minimise their tax liabilities by establishing headquarters in low-tax countries.

(Source: Brokaw, 2014)

Globalisation mainly benefits multi-national companies rather than ordinary people – Discuss.

There is good evidence that globalisation has resulted in a considerable increase in world trade over the past 20-30 years...

1.10 Organising Paragraphs

Paragraphs are the basic building blocks of academic writing. Well-structured paragraphs help the reader understand the topic more easily by dividing up the argument into convenient sections. This unit looks at:

- the components of paragraphs
- the way the components are linked together
- the linkage between paragraphs in the overall text.

1. Paragraph structure

■ Read the paragraph below and answer the following questions.

> Many countries around the world are currently moving government departments out of the capital city. Previously there were attempts to create entirely new capitals, such as Brasilia in Brazil or Islamabad in Pakistan. Now however these schemes are seen as too expensive and disruptive. Instead the trend is to disperse different ministries around various districts away from the capital. Mexico, for example, has moved its Ministry of Culture to Tlaxcala and Norway has shifted the competition authority to Bergen.

a) What is the topic of this paragraph?

b) How are the sentences in the paragraph linked together?

The paragraph can be analysed thus:

1. Topic sentence	Many countries around the world are currently moving government departments out of the capital city.
2. Supporting information	**Previously** there were attempts to create entirely new capitals, such as Brasilia in Brazil or Islamabad in Pakistan.
3. Reason	**Now, however** these schemes are seen as too expensive and disruptive.
4. Further detail	**Instead** the trend is to disperse different ministries around various districts away from the capital.
5. Examples	Mexico, **for example**, has moved its Culture Ministry to Tlaxcala and Norway has shifted the competition authority to Bergen.

This example shows that:

i)   A paragraph is a group of sentences which deal with a single topic. Dividing up the text into paragraphs helps both writer and reader to follow the argument more clearly.

ii)   The length of paragraphs varies significantly according to text type, but should normally be no less than four or five sentences.

iii) Usually (but not always) the first sentence introduces the topic. Other sentences may give definitions, examples, extra information, reasons, restatements and summaries.

iv)   The parts of the paragraph are linked together by the reference words, conjunctions and adverbs shown in bold in the table. They guide the reader through the arguments presented.

▶   **See Unit 3.1 Cohesion and Unit 4.5 Conjunctions**

2. Practice A

■   **The sentences in the following paragraph, from the same article on government re-location, have been mixed up. Use the table to put them in the right order.**

i)   Another benefit of dispersal is to improve the quality of life of the civil servants, detached from over-crowded and expensive capitals.

ii)   Today's civil servants no longer need to all work in the same district and be able to meet face-to-face.

iii) Finally there should be economic benefits for remote and possibly run-down regions in receiving an injection of well-paid employment.

iv) Recent developments such as emails and video-conferencing make this pattern of dispersal, which has many apparent benefits, more feasible.

v) Moreover, away from the pressures of the capital with its lobbyists and politicians, workers may have a more objective and detached viewpoint.

Topic sentence	
Restatement	
Result 1	
Result 2	
Result 3	

3. Practice B

a) *Analyse the next paragraph from the same text by completing the left-hand column of the table with suitable descriptors.*

b) *Underline the words and phrases used to link the sentences together.*

c) *Which phrase is used to link this paragraph to the one before?*

Topic sentence	Despite these advantages there are serious drawbacks to relocating government departments.
	One of the gravest is that many employees, especially younger ones, are reluctant to leave lively capital cities to live in remote provincial towns.
	In some cases more than half the staff has resigned rather than move, fearing the loss of social life.
	In addition, new locations may be chosen for political rather than economic reasons.
	Politicians may attempt to bring jobs to their own constituencies, as when Pinochet moved Chile's congress to his home town, Valparaiso.
	So although there are many apparent gains from relocation, putting such a move into practice can be full of problems.

4. Practice C

Read the full text on relocating government departments.

a)   *Choose a subtitle for each paragraph.*

b)   *Choose a title for the whole text.*

Title: _____

Subtitle: _____

Many countries around the world are currently moving government departments out of the capital city. Previously there were attempts to create entirely new capitals, such as Brasilia in Brazil or Islamabad in Pakistan. Now however these schemes are seen as too expensive and disruptive. Instead the trend is to spread different ministries around various districts away from the capital. Mexico, for example, has moved its Ministry of Culture to Tlaxcala and Norway has shifted the competition authority to Bergen.

Subtitle: _____

Today's civil servants no longer need to all work in the same district and be able to meet face-to-face. Recent developments such as emails and video-conferencing make this pattern of dispersal, which has many apparent benefits, more feasible. Moreover, away from the pressures of the capital with its lobbyists and politicians, workers may have a more objective and detached viewpoint. Another benefit of dispersal is to improve the quality of life of the civil servants, detached from over-crowded and expensive capitals. Finally there should be economic benefits for remote and possibly run-down regions in receiving an injection of well-paid employment.

Subtitle: _____

Despite these advantages there are serious drawbacks to relocating government departments. One of the gravest is that many employees, especially younger ones, are reluctant to leave lively capital cities to live in remote provincial towns. In some cases more than half the staff have resigned rather than move, fearing the loss of social life. In addition, new locations may be chosen for political rather than economic reasons. Politicians may attempt to bring jobs to their own constituencies, as when Pinochet moved Chile's congress to his home town, Valparaiso. So although there are many apparent gains from relocation, putting such a move into practice can be full of problems.

5. Introducing paragraphs and linking them together

The paragraph in Practice B begins with a phrase which links it to the previous paragraph, in order to maintain continuity of argument:

> *Despite these advantages . . .*

To begin a new topic you may use phrases such as:

> *Turning to the issue of child labour . . .*
>
> *Rates of bankruptcy must also be examined . . .*
>
> *Inflation is another area for consideration . . .*

Paragraphs can also be introduced with adverbs:

> *Traditionally, few examples were . . .*
>
> *Finally, the performance of . . .*
>
> *Currently, there is little evidence of . . .*
>
> *Originally, most families were . . .*

▶   **See Unit 4.4 Academic Vocabulary: Verbs and Adverbs and Unit 4.5 Conjunctions**

6. Practice D

■   Use the notes below to write two paragraphs on the subject of 'Trams'. Use conjunctions and other suitable phrases to introduce and link the paragraphs together.

- Trams (streetcars in the USA) first developed in late nineteenth century
- Provided cheap and convenient mass transport in many cities
- Rail-based systems expensive to maintain
- Fixed tracks meant system was inflexible
- During 1950s and 1960s many European and Asian cities closed tram systems
- Today trams becoming popular again
- Some cities e.g. Paris and Manchester building new systems
- Trams less polluting than cars and cheaper to operate
- Problems remain with construction costs and traffic congestion blocking tracks
- Expense of building modern tramways means that they remain controversial

1.11 Introductions and Conclusions

An effective introduction explains the purpose, scope and methodology of the paper to the reader. The conclusion should provide a clear answer to any questions asked in the title, as well as summarising the main points under discussion. With course-work, it may be better to write the introduction after writing the main body.

1. Introduction components

Introductions are usually no more than about 10% of the total length of an assignment. Therefore in a 2,000 word essay the introduction would be approximately 200 words.

▶ **See Unit 1.5 From Understanding Titles to Planning**

a) ■ **What components are normally found in an essay introduction? Choose from the list below.**

Components	Y/N
i) A definition of any unfamiliar terms in the title	
ii) Your personal opinion on the subject of the essay	
iii) Mention of some sources you have read on the topic	
iv) A provocative idea or question to interest the reader	
v) A suitable quotation from a famous authority	
vi) Your aim or purpose in writing	
vii) The method you adopt to answer the question	
viii) Some background or context of the topic	

ix)	Any limitations you set yourself	
x)	An outline of the main body	

b) ■ **Read the extracts below from introductions to articles and decide which of the components listed above (i–x) they are examples of.**

i)   The goal of the present study is to complement the existing body of knowledge on HR practices with a large scale empirical study, and at the same time contribute to the discussion on why some firms are more innovative than others.

ii) We consider three dimensions of customer satisfaction: service, quality and price. We argue that employees most directly influence customer satisfaction with service. We test this proposition empirically, and then examine the links between customer satisfaction and sales.

iii) Corporate governance is a set of mechanisms, both institutional and market-based, designed to mitigate agency problems that arise from the separation of ownership and control in a company, protect the interests of all stakeholders, improve from performance and ensure that investors get an adequate return on their investment.

iv) This study will focus on mergers in the media business between 2000 and 2014, since with more recent examples an accurate assessment of the consequences cannot yet be made.

v)   The rest of the paper is organised as follows. The second section explains why corporate governance is important for economic prosperity. The third section presents the model specification and describes the data and variables used in our empirical analysis. The fourth section reports and discusses the empirical results. The fifth section concludes.

vi) The use of incentive compensation, such as bonus and stock options, is an important means of motivating and compensating executives of private companies, especially executives of technology-orientated companies.

vii) There is no clear empirical evidence sustaining a 'managerial myopia' argument. Pugh *et al.* (1992) find evidence that supports such theory, but Meulbrook *et al.* (1990), Mahoney *et al.* (1997), Garvey and Hanka (1999) and a study by the Office of the Chief Economist of the Securities and Exchange Commission (1985) find no evidence.

2. Introduction structure

There is no standard pattern for an introduction, since much depends on the type of research you are conducting and the length of your work, but this is a common format:

a) Definition of key terms, if needed

b) Relevant background information

c)   Review of work by other writers on the topic

d)   Purpose or aim of the paper

e)   Your research methods

f)   Any limitations you imposed

g)   An outline of your paper

■   **Study the introduction to an essay entitled: 'Evaluate the experience of e-learning for students in higher education'.**

There are a range of definitions for this term, but in this paper 'e-learning' refers to any type of learning situation where content is delivered via the internet. Learning is one of the most vital components of the contemporary knowledge-based economy. With the development of computing power and technology the internet has become an essential medium for knowledge transfer. Various researchers (Webb and Kirstin, 2003; Honig *et al.*, 2006) have evaluated e-learning in a healthcare and business context, but little attention so far has been paid to the reactions of students in higher education (HE) to this method of teaching. The purpose of this study was to examine students' experience of e-learning in an HE context.

A range of studies was first reviewed, and then a survey of 200 students was conducted to assess their experience of e-learning. Clearly a study of this type is inevitably restricted by various constraints, notably the size of the student sample, which was limited to students of Pharmacy and Agriculture. The paper is structured as follows. The first section presents an analysis of the relevant research, focusing on the current limited knowledge regarding the student experience. The second part presents the methodology of the survey and an analysis of the findings, and the final section considers the implications of the results for the delivery of e-learning programmes.

■   **Underline the following sections (a–g) of the introduction above:**

a) Definition
Certain words or phrases in the title may need clarifying because they are not widely understood, or are used in a special sense.

b) Context
It is useful to remind the reader of the wider context of your work. This may also show the value of the study you have carried out.

c) Reference to other researchers

While a longer article may have a separate literature review, in a shorter essay it is still important to show familiarity with researchers who have studied this topic previously. This may also reveal a gap in research which justifies your work.

d) Aim

The aim of your research must be clearly stated so the reader knows what you are trying to do.

e) Method

The method demonstrates the process that you undertook to achieve the given aim.

f) Limitations

You cannot deal with every aspect of this topic in an essay, so you must make clear the boundaries of your study.

g) Outline

Understanding the structure of your work will help the reader to follow your argument.

▶   **See Unit 2.4 Definitions**

3. Opening sentences

It can be difficult to start writing an essay, but especially in exams, hesitation will waste valuable time. The first few sentences should be general but not vague, to help the reader focus on the topic. They often have the following pattern:

Time phrase	Topic	Development
Currently,	the control of water resources	has emerged as a potential cause of international friction.
Since 2016	electric vehicles	have become a serious commercial proposition.

It is important to avoid opening sentences which are over-general and vague.
  Compare:

  Nowadays there is a lot of competition among different news providers.   ✗

  In the last 20 years newspapers have faced strong competition from the internet for   ✓
  news and entertainment.

■   **Working quickly, write introductory sentences for three of the following titles.**

a)   How important is it for companies to have women as senior managers?

b)   What are the 'pull' factors in international tourism?

c)   Is there a relationship between inflation and unemployment?

d)   Monopolies are inefficient in using resources – Discuss.

▶   **See Unit 2.6 Generalisations**

4. Practice A

You have to write an essay titled 'State control of industry: does it have any benefits?'

■ **Using the notes below and your own ideas, write a short introduction for the essay (it is not necessary to refer to sources in this exercise).**

Definition – State control = public ownership, especially of 'natural monopoly' industries e.g. electricity, water supply

Background – Worldwide trend to privatise industries but subject to controversy in some areas e.g. postal service, railways

Aim – to establish what advantages may come from public ownership of these industries

Method – Compare advantages (security of supply, benefits of large-scale operation) and disadvantages (lack of competition, corruption, political control) in Germany and France, in two industries: railways and electricity

Limitation – From 2000–2010

5. Conclusions

Conclusions tend to be shorter and more varied in format than introductions. Some articles may have a 'summary' or 'concluding remarks'. But student papers should generally have a final section which summarises the arguments and makes it clear to the reader that the original question has been answered.

■ **Which of the following are generally acceptable in conclusions?**

a)   A statement of your methodology.

b)   A discussion of the implications of your research.

c)   Some new information on the topic not mentioned before.

d)   A summary of your main conclusions or findings.

e)   Some suggestions for further research.

f)   The limitations of your study.

g)   Comparison with the results of similar studies.

h)   A quotation which appears to sum up your work.

■ Match the extracts from conclusions below with the acceptable components above.

i)   Time constraints meant that we were only able to study three Dutch firms.

ii) Obviously, business expatriates could benefit from being informed that problem-focused coping strategies are more effective than symptom-focused ones.

iii) Another line of research worth pursuing further is to study the importance of language for expatriate assignments.

iv) Our survey of 25 e-commerce startups was followed by a series of in-depth interviews.

v)   These results of the Colombia study reported here are consistent with other similar studies conducted in other countries (e.g. Ganghof and Bell, 2008).

vi) This study has clearly illustrated that family ownership of retail businesses can severely limit their potential for growth.

6. Conclusion structure

Although there is no fixed pattern, a common structure for an essay conclusion is:

a) Summary of main findings or results
b) Link back to the original question to show it has been answered
c) Reference of the limitations of your work e.g. geographical
d) Suggestions for future possible related research
e) Comments on the implications of your research

7. Practice B

■ The following sentences form the conclusion to the essay titled 'Evaluate the experience of e-learning for students in higher education', whose introduction was given above. The sentences have been mixed up. Put them into a logical order (1–5).

a) This finding was clear, despite the agreed convenience of e-learning.

b) Given the constraints of the small and limited sample there is clearly room for further research in this field, in particular to explore whether certain disciplines are more suited to this mode of learning than others.

c) However, our survey of nearly 200 students found a strong preference for traditional classroom teaching.

d) But in general it would appear that e-learning is unlikely to be acceptable as a primary teaching method in higher education.

e) This study found that little relevant research on the HE student experience of e-learning has been conducted, and the research that has been reported indicates a mixed reaction to it.

1.12 Editing and Proofreading

> In exams you have little time for editing, but with coursework it is important to take time to revise your work to improve its clarity and logical development. In both situations proofreading is essential to avoid the small errors which may make parts of your work inaccurate or difficult to understand.

1. Editing

Good editing can make a huge difference to the quality of your writing. Although it is tempting to think that the first draft of an essay or report is good enough, it can almost certainly be improved. After completing the draft you should leave it for a day and then reread it, asking yourself the following questions:

a) Does this fully answer the question(s) in the title?

b) Do the different sections of the paper have the right weight, i.e. is it well balanced?

c) Does the argument or discussion develop clearly and logically?

d) Have I forgotten any important points which would support the development?

e) Is the paper the required length; not too short or too long?

f) Have I mentioned the main authorities on this subject?

g) Is the style suitably academic?

h) Are all the citations and references included correctly?

2. Practice A

As part of a module on Qualitative Research Methods, you have written the first draft of a 1,000 word paper titled: 'What would be an acceptable number of interviews to carry out for a Master's dissertation?'

■ Study the introduction to this paper below, and decide how it could be improved, listing your suggestions in the table.

> An interview can be defined as a conversation with a definite structure and objective. It goes beyond an everyday conversation with no particular purpose. There are many possible interview situations, but all involve an interviewer and an interviewee. It is normal for the former to ask the latter direct questions, and record the answers. The questions may be prepared in advance or they may occur as the interview develops. The recording is often done on paper, but may also be done by audio or video recording. Interviews can take place anywhere, in a street, café, office, bar, restaurant etc. It is hard to say how many interviews can be carried out in one day. I personally think that two is the maximum because it can get very tiring. A lot depends on the subject being researched.

	Suggestions for improvement
a)	No sources are mentioned.
b)	
c)	
d)	
e)	

■ See Answers on p. 281 for suggestions.

With these points in mind, the introduction could be rewritten as follows:

> Organising an interview involves a series of steps (Davies, 2007) including recruiting interviewees, finding a suitable venue and writing appropriate guidelines. However, depending on the research subject a more flexible approach can be adopted, resulting in a less structured interview (Cooper and Schindler, 2008). For a Master's dissertation, interviews must contain data relevant to the research topic which the interviewer can later process. As King states: 'gathering a large

volume of cases does not guarantee the credibility of a study' (King, 2004:16). Most writers agree that two one-hour interviews per day are effectively the maximum for one interviewer, given the time needed for preparation and subsequent processing. Moreover, if audio or video recording is used there is more content to be analysed, for instance in terms of facial expression. The analysis of one interview can take up to three days' work. In order to answer the question, clearly much depends on the research topic and the time the researcher has available.

3. Practice B

■ Read the following paragraph on 'Possible ethical issues raised by interview-based research'. Decide how it could be improved, and rewrite it.

> Any organisation that allows researchers to interview its employees runs a big risk. The interviewees may complain about the boss or about other workers. Another danger for the researcher is that employees may feel obliged to give positive answers to questions instead of their honest opinions. This is because they are afraid of their bosses finding out what they really think. Also the reputation of the organisation may suffer. I believe that researchers should make sure that this does not happen. They must make it clear why they are doing the research, and keep identities secret by using false names. If this is not done there's a good chance that the validity of the whole research project will be in danger.

4. Proofreading

After you have edited your work, the final stage is to proofread it. This means checking your work for small errors which may make it more difficult for the reader to understand exactly what you want to say. If a sentence has only one error:

> *The italian economy is burdened with massive debt.*

it is not difficult to understand, but if there are multiple errors, even though they are all quite minor, the effect is very confusing:

> *As keynes, a british economic, said: 'in the long run . . . we are all ded'.*

Clearly, you should aim to make your meaning as clear as possible. Note that computer spell-checks will not always help you, since they may ignore a word which is spelt correctly but which is not the word you meant to use:

> *Tow factors need to be considered.*

5. Practice C

■ Examples of the ten most common types of error in student writing are shown below. In each sentence underline the error and correct it.

i)   **Factual**
     Corruption is a problem in many countries such as Africa.

ii) **Word ending**
     The new airport added to the country's prosperousness.

iii) **Punctuation**
     What is the optimum size for a research team

iv) **Tense**
     Since 2017 there were new models produced every 18 months.

v)   **Vocabulary**
     The Bulgarian money is the lev.

vi) **Spelling**
     Pervious experience can sometimes be a disadvantage.

vii) **Singular/plural**
     It is one of the largest company in Asia.

viii) **Style**
     A multinational business that operates in many countries.

ix) **Missing word**
     This is an idea established by David Ricardo in nineteenth century.

x)   **Word order**
     Three skills are for needed success in the academic world.

6. Practice D

■ The following sentences each contain one type of error. Match each to one of the error types (i–x) above, and correct the error.

a) Research shows that some bosses are discriminating against older workers.

b) Both companies focus on mass marketing to promote its line of products.

c) Failure to find the right coffee may lead to torment for consumers.

d) They found that different researchers had differently effects on the research.

e) This was after the single European market was established in 1873.

f) Experienced researchers can most likely come over these problems.

g) The Arts Faculty has it's own library.

h) She selected Budapest in Hungry for setting up the research centre.

i) Companies from the rest of world are eager to do business in India.

j) From 2012 to 2018 there are few cases of cholera.

7. Practice E

▉ Underline the ten errors in the text below and then correct them.

THE PANAMA CANAL

Ship canals are important element in the development of world trade, as most manufactured things travel by ship. Unlike the Suez Canal in egypt, crossing the Panamanian isthmus involves lifting ship 26 metres and then lowering them on the other side. Construction was so difficult and danger that the original French engineers were defeated by disease, after over 20,000 men had died working on the project. On the early twentieth century the American government became involved and after ten years' work the canal opened to shipping 1914, thereby avoiding the difficult route around the tip of south America. But since the 1970s container ships have steadily grown to large to fit the canals locks, and so in 2007 the canal authority began a major development to expand canal's capacity with locks 60% wider. When this was completed in 2016, at a cost of over $5 billion, the canal was able to handle almost all ships, including the giant cruise vessels now being operated.

Progress Check 1

These exercises will help you assess your understanding of Part 1 – The writing process.

1. ■ *Complete the description of the process of essay writing by adding **one** suitable word to each gap in the text below.*

The first stage of essay writing is to read and understand the a) _____ _____, and then to prepare a b) _____ of work for the time available. Then the topic should be brainstormed and a draft c) _____ prepared. Next, possible d) _____ have to be carefully evaluated and the most relevant selected, after which you can start e) _____ notes, using paraphrasing and summarising f) _____. When you have collected enough material to answer the question the first g) _____ of the main body can written from the notes, taking care to avoid any h) _____. Subsequently you can write the first draft of the introduction and i) _____, ensuring that a logical approach to the title is developed. After this the whole draft must be j) _____ reread and revised for both clarity and accuracy. The penultimate stage is to prepare final lists of k) _____, appendices and other items such as graphs and maps. Finally the whole text should be thoroughly l) _____ before handing in the assignment on time.

2. ■ *Decide if the following statements are true or false.*

a) Academic writing aims to be accurate and impersonal.

b) A case study looks at the views of other writers on the same topic.

c) Academic journals are usually peer-reviewed.

d) Students should read every page of the books on their reading lists.

e) When searching library catalogues it is better to use very specific terms.

f) Abstracts generally have a four-part structure.

g) Plagiarism often means copying another writer's words without acknowledgement.

h) An essay introduction should explain the purpose of the paper.

i) Introductions are normally about 25% of the essay's length.

j) Note-making should always include the source of the notes.

k) Paraphrasing means changing both vocabulary and structure but keeping the meaning.

l) Reference verbs always use the past tense.

m) Paragraphs always begin with a topic sentence.

n) A good summary often includes several examples.

o) Conclusions often mention the constraints on the paper e.g. length.

p) Most essays can be improved by editing.

q) Proofreading means just checking for spelling mistakes.

r) An essay conclusion should make it clear that the question has been answered.

s) Websites are often less reliable sources than books.

t) The best kind of outline is a mind map.

3. ■ *Read the following extract and write a summary of about 80 words. Then write a full reference for the text.*

In the early twentieth century in Europe wild bison were nearly hunted to extinction. At one stage there were less than 60 of these fearsome beasts alive, all in zoos. Yet today there are flourishing herds of bison in Poland, Belarus and Romania. This is because parts of eastern Europe provide an ideal habitat for such large wild animals as deer, wolves and brown bears, as well as the birds and insects which have become scarce in western Europe due to more intensive agriculture. During the communist period marginal land was neglected agriculturally, causing forests to expand and encouraging ecological diversity. Since 1989 many rural areas in ex-communist countries have become depopulated, due to emigration to the cities of western Europe. The Caras-Severin region of Romania, for instance, has lost over a quarter of its population in the last 30 years. Although some of its older inhabitants have doubts about the arrival of these large animals, for others they create an opportunity to develop eco-tourism: the more entrepreneurial are establishing bed and breakfast businesses and organic farms, catering for visitors thrilled to see these creatures in the wild.

(Source: Christian Nitoiu, (2019) *Rewilding Europe*. Frankfurt: Freihaus p. 14)

Elements of Writing

This section explains and practises the essential skills needed for writing academic papers. Many essays, for instance, require definitions to be made, causes and effects to be studied, and examples to be given. Organised alphabetically, these skills range from presenting argument and discussion to displaying visual information.

2.1 Argument and Discussion

On most courses students are expected to study the conflicting views on a topic and engage with them, which means analysing and critiquing them if appropriate. This unit demonstrates ways of showing your familiarity with all sides of a debate and presenting your own conclusions in a suitably academic manner.

1. Discussion vocabulary

Essay titles commonly ask students to 'discuss' a topic:

Environmental concerns have no place in a company's strategy – Discuss.

This requires an evaluation of both the benefits and disadvantages of the topic, with a section of the essay, sometimes headed 'Discussion', in which a summary of these is made. The following vocabulary can be used:

+	–
benefit	drawback
advantage	disadvantage
a positive aspect	a negative feature
pro (informal)	con (informal)
a plus (informal)	a minus (informal)
one major advantage	a serious drawback
another significant benefit	a considerable disadvantage

*A **major benefit** of reducing carbon emissions is the saving on energy costs.*

*Gaining a reputation for poor environmental standards can be a **serious disadvantage**.*

■ Fill the gaps in the following paragraph using language from the lists above.

Study abroad
Every year millions of students choose to study in a foreign country. This can have considerable a) _____, such as the chance to experience another culture, and improve another language, but also involves certain b) _____ _____, which may include feelings of isolation or homesickness. Another c) _____ aspect may be the high cost, involving both fees and living expenses. However, most students appear to find that the d) _____ outweigh the e) _____ and that the chance to join an international group of students is a major f) _____ in developing a career.

2. Organisation

The discussion section can be organised in two ways; either by grouping all the benefits together and doing the same with the disadvantages (vertical), or by examining the subject from different viewpoints (horizontal). For example, the following essay title can be discussed in the two ways as shown:

'Environmental concerns have no place in a company's strategy – Discuss'.

a) (Vertical)
    Grouping all the drawbacks together in one or more paragraphs, then treating the benefits in the same way:

Drawbacks:
Environmental concerns may increase costs (e.g. using expensive 'green' electricity)/delay projects by needing more planning/create extra work for managers

Benefits:
In the long term these may save money (e.g. reduced packaging)/good PR leading to increased sales/employee job satisfaction may also be increased

Discussion:
Depends on nature of business/some costs will rise, others fall/important long-term benefits as consumers place more weight on 'green' considerations

b) (Horizontal)
Examining the subject from different viewpoints e.g. economic, ethical or social:

Economic:
Initial investment in energy-saving measures may increase costs but long-term benefits should follow

Ethical:
Responsible companies should play a part in combating climate change

Social:
Consumer-facing companies benefit from 'green' credentials = increased sales/employee job satisfaction may also be increased

Discussion:
Depends on nature of business/some costs will rise, others fall/important long-term benefits as consumers place more weight on 'green' considerations

■ **What are the advantages of each format (i.e. vertical and horizontal)?**

3. Practice A

You have to write an essay titled:

Working from home can be positive for many companies and their employees – Discuss.

■ **Brainstorm the positive and negative aspects with a partner, using the box below, and then write an outline using one of the structures (vertical or horizontal) above.**

+ Positive	– Negative
No time wasted commuting to work	*Homeworkers may feel isolated*

4. The language of discussion

In discussion avoid personal phrases such as *in my opinion* or *actually, I think.*
    Use impersonal phrases instead, such as:

It is generally accepted that	*working from home saves commuting time.*
It is widely agreed that	*email and the internet reduce reliance on an office.*
Most people	*appear to need face-to-face contact with colleagues.*
It is probable that	*more companies will encourage working from home.*
The evidence suggests that	*certain people are better at self-management than others.*

These phrases suggest a minority viewpoint:

It can be argued that	*homeworking encourages time-wasting.*
One view is that	*homeworkers become isolated.*

When you are supporting your opinions with reference to sources use phrases such as:

According to Ganghof (2013)	*few companies have developed clear policies on this.*
Poledna (2018) claims that	*most employees benefit from flexible arrangements.*

▶   **See Unit 1.9 Contrasting Sources**

5. Counter-arguments

Counter-arguments are ideas which are opposite to your own. In an academic discussion you must show that you are familiar with all the various opinions and positions on the topic, and provide reasons to support your own position. It is usual to deal with the counter-arguments first, before giving your view.

■   **What is the writer's position in the following example, on the topic of environmental concerns (Section 1 above)?**

It is frequently argued that the company's main responsibility is to its shareholders, who are the owners of the company, and need to get a return on their investment in terms of dividend payments. But simple pursuit of profit, without regard to the environmental damage that may be caused, is a very short-sighted policy. A long-term strategy to reduce waste is likely to bring greater benefits for all stakeholders.

■   **Study the example below, and write three more sentences using ideas on the topic of homeworking from the title in Section 3 above.**

Counter-argument	Your position
Some people believe that home-workers become isolated,	*but this can be avoided by holding weekly meetings for all departmental staff.*

6. Providing evidence

Normally your conclusions on a topic follow an assessment of the evidence. You must show that you have examined the relevant sources, since only then can you give a balanced judgement.

■ **Study the following text, which discusses the idea that young people today, who have grown up with computing and the internet, are different from previous generations. Then answer the following questions.**

DO 'DIGITAL NATIVES' EXIST?

Various writers have argued that people born around the end of the twentieth century (1990–2005) and who have been using computers all their lives have different abilities and needs to other people. Palfrey and Gasser (2008) refer to them as the 'net generation' and argue that activities such as putting videos on YouTube are more natural for them than writing essays. Similarly, Prensky (2001a) claims that the educational system needs to be revised to cater for the preferences of these so-called 'digital natives'.

But other researchers doubt that these claims can apply to a whole generation. Bennett, Maton and Kervin (2008) argue that these young people comprise a whole range of abilities, and that many of them only have a limited understanding of digital tools. They insist that the so-called 'digital native' theory is a myth, and that it would be a mistake to re-organise the educational system and abandon traditional means of assessment and enquiry such as essay writing to cater for their supposed requirements.

Clearly there are some young people who are very proficient in online technologies, and many more regularly use social media in their daily lives, but taking a global perspective, millions still grow up and are educated in a traditional manner. Teaching methods are constantly being revised, but there is no clear evidence of a need to radically change them.

a) How many sources are cited to support the 'digital native' theory?

b) What do these writers suggest changing?

c) Why do their critics disagree with them?

d) What is the opinion of the writer of this text?

e) What is your opinion of this subject?

7. Practice B

■ Write two paragraphs on the topic:

'Inflation can be a positive force in the economy – Discuss'.

Use the ideas below and give your viewpoint.

Pros:
- Encourages spending as people expect higher prices in future
- Reduces the value of debt
- The opposite, deflation, causes stagnation
- Moderate inflation signals a healthy economy

(Source: Costa *et al.*, 2012)

Cons:
- Workers demand large pay rises, leads to conflict
- Excessive inflation leads to loss of faith in money
- Cost of regularly revising price lists
- Creates uncertainty about future
- Can erode the value of savings – currency devalues

(Source: Patterson, 1998)

▶ See Unit 2.7 Problems and Solutions

2.2 Cause and Effect

Academic work frequently involves explaining a link between a cause, such as a price rise, and an effect or result, such as a fall in demand. Alternatively, research may begin with a result, such as the Industrial Revolution, and discuss possible causes. This unit demonstrates and practises two methods of describing the link, with the focus either on the cause or on the effect.

1. The language of cause and effect

A writer may choose to emphasise the cause or the effect. In both cases, either a verb or a conjunction can be used to show the link.

a) **Focus on causes (e.g. a poor harvest)**

With verbs

The poor harvest	*caused*	*higher prices*
	led to	
	resulted in	
	produced	

With conjunctions

Because of	*the poor harvest*	*prices rose*
Due to		
Owing to		
As a result of		

b) Focus on effects (e.g. higher prices)

With verbs (note use of passives)

The higher prices	*were caused by* *were produced by* *resulted from*	*the poor harvest*

With conjunctions

There were price rises	***due to*** ***because of*** ***as a result of***	*the poor harvest*

■ Compare the following:

Because *sales **were** poor, the workforce was cut.* (*because + verb*)

Because *of poor **sales**, the workforce was cut.* (*because of + noun*)

Since *sales **were** poor, the workforce was cut.* (*conjunction + verb*)

Due to *poor **sales**, the workforce was cut.* (*conjunction + noun*)

■ Note the position of the conjunction in this sentence:

*Online sales increased sharply, **therefore/so/consequently** they shut four shops.*

▶ See Units 3.4 Passive and Active and 4.5 Conjunctions

2. Practice A

■ Match the causes with their likely effects and write two sentences linking each together, one emphasising the cause and the other the effect.

Causes	Effects
The cold winter of 2015	stores closing on the high street
More people shopping on the internet	**increased demand for electricity**
Her aggressive management style	fewer journeys driven
A reduction in sales tax	lower cost of shipping to Europe
Retirement age raised to 70	higher levels of spending
The opening of the Panama Canal	more disputes with the union
A 15% rise in the price of oil	fewer jobs for young people

Example:

i. *Owing to the cold winter of 2015 there was increased demand for electricity.*

ii. *The increased demand for electricity was due to the cold winter of 2015.*

a) _____

_____

b) _____

_____

c) _____

_____

d) _____

_____

e) _____

_____

f) _____

_____

g) _____

_____

3. Practice B

■ Complete the following sentences with likely effects.

a)   Increasing use of email for messages _____

b)   Rising demand for MBA courses _____

c)   Storms in the Brazilian coffee-growing areas _____

d)   Building a high-speed railway line _____

e)   The invention of the jet engine _____

■ Complete these sentences with possible causes.

f)   The company's bankruptcy _____

g) The high price of bread _____

h) The fall in share prices _____

i) A significant rise in profits _____

j) The success of their café _____

4. Practice C

▧ Use conjunctions or verbs to complete the following text.

Unhappy workers

In recent years there appears to have been a growth in employee dissatisfaction with work. At its most extreme this is shown by high rates of suicide in some companies, apparently a) _____ the stress b) _____ re-structuring programmes. Surveys of both European and American employees have found that more than 50% were unhappy, often c) _____ a feeling of stagnation. Various theories have attempted to explain this situation. Employees in certain industries such as car production may feel stressed d) _____ industry-wide overcapacity, creating a sense of insecurity. More generally, recession can e) _____ fear of unemployment or short-time working. In addition, the constant drive to cut costs and increase productivity f) _____ a concern with meeting targets which takes its toll on the workforce. Furthermore, many younger employees are now hired on short-term contracts, which g) _____ an awareness that they could lose their jobs with little warning.

5. Practice D

▧ Study the flow chart below, which shows some of the possible effects of the introduction of driverless cars. Working with a partner, discuss further possible effects and add them to the chart by completing the empty boxes.

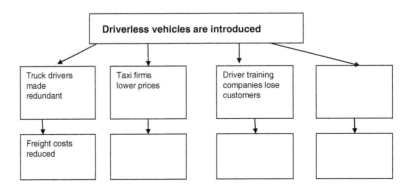

■ Complete the paragraph describing this sequence.

> The introduction of driverless cars and trucks would have various significant results. First, it would lead to ...

■ Choose a situation in your own subject. Draw a flow chart showing some probable effects, and write a paragraph to describe them.

2.3 Comparison

It is often necessary to make comparisons in academic writing. The comparison might be the subject of the essay, or might provide evidence for the argument. In all cases it is important to explain clearly what is being compared and to make the comparison as accurate as possible. This unit deals with different forms of comparison and practises their use.

1. Comparison structures

a) Some papers are based on a comparison:

The purpose of this study is to compare Chinese and American consumers on their propensity to use self-service technology in a retail setting.

In other cases a comparison provides useful context:

The first attempt to decode the human genome took ten years; now it can be done in less than a week.

b) The two basic comparative forms are:

i) *France is **larger** than Switzerland.*

*The students were **happier** after the exam.*

(-er is added to one-syllable adjectives and two-syllable adjectives ending in -y, which changes into an 'i')

ii) *Learning Chinese is **more difficult** than learning English.*

*Washington is **less crowded** than New York.*

(more/less … are used with other adjectives of two or more syllables)

c) These comparisons can be modified by the use of adverbs such as:

slightly, marginally (for small amounts)

considerably, significantly, substantially (for large amounts)

> *France is **substantially larger** than Switzerland.*
>
> *Switzerland is **slightly smaller** than Holland.*
>
> *Winters in Poland are **significantly colder** than in Portugal.*

d) Similarity or near-similarity can be noted by the use of *as . . . as* or *the same as:*

> *The population of France is **approximately the same as** the population of Britain.*
>
> *Summers in Tokyo are **as wet as** in Singapore.*

The 'as . . . as . . . ' form can be used for quantitative comparison:

> *Britain is **half as large as** France.*
>
> *The journey by plane is **five times as fast as** by train.*

▶   **See Unit 3.3 Numbers**

2. Using superlatives (e.g. the largest/smallest)

When using superlatives take care to define the group, e.g. 'the cheapest car' has no meaning:

> *The cheapest car **in the Ford range/in the USA.***

The most/the least are followed by an adjective:

> *The **most interesting** example is the position of Ireland.*

The most/the fewest are used in relation to numbers:

> ***The fewest** students studied insurance.* (i.e. the lowest number)

3. Practice A

■   Study the table, which shows the changes in house prices in ten countries between 2007 and 2017. Complete the following paragraph with one word in each gap.

Country	Real % change
Canada	+47
New Zealand	+36
Australia	+35
Germany	+31

Country	Real % change
China	+30
Japan	+5
United Kingdom	−4
USA	−15
Ireland	−35
Spain	−36

(Source: *The Economist*)

In the decade between 2007 and 2017, the a) _____ rise in house prices among these countries was in Canada, where prices rose by 47%. This increase was b) _____ greater c) _____ in New Zealand (36%) or Australia (35%). Rises in Germany were nearly the d) _____ as in China (31% and 30%). The e) _____ falls were in Spain and Ireland (−36% and −35%), f) _____ greater than declines in the USA (−15%) or the UK (−4%).

4. Forms of comparison

■ Compare these three possible structures:

House prices in China have risen more than in Japan.

Chinese house prices have risen more than Japanese.

The price of houses in China has risen more than in Japan.

Note that high/low are used for comparing abstract ideas (e.g. rates):

*The birth rate was **higher** 20 years ago.*

More/less must be used with *than + comparison*:

*This module is **more difficult than** the last one.*

*The current rate of inflation is **less than** last year's (rate).*

5. Practice B

■ Study the table, which shows the income of the top ten clubs in European football. Then read the comparisons. Each sentence contains one error. Find and correct it.

Income of top ten European football clubs (2017)

Club	Revenue $m.
Manchester United	703
Real Madrid	694
FC Barcelona	675
Bayern Munich	570
Manchester City	558
Arsenal	524
Chelsea	505
Liverpool	471
Juventus	415
Tottenham Hotspurs	310

(Source: Deloitte)

a) Manchester United had the highest income.
b) Bayern Munich's income was almost twice much as Tottenham's.
c) FC Barcelona earned marginally more than Juventus.
d) Juventus had less revenue Liverpool.
e) Arsenal's income was substantially less than Manchester City's.
f) Arsenal earned approximately same as Chelsea.

6. Practice C

■   The table shows the percentage of GDP spent on health in a range of countries. Complete the sentences below and write two more comparisons.

Country	Health spending as % of GDP
USA	14
Switzerland	11
Canada	9.5
South Africa	8.6
Denmark	8.4
Bangladesh	3.5

Country	Health spending as % of GDP
Oman	3.0
Indonesia	2.4
Madagascar	2.0
Azerbaijan	0.9

(Source: WHO)

a) There are wide _____ in the percentage of GDP spent on health globally.

b) The USA spends _____ times as much as Bangladesh.

c) South Africa spends _____ more than Denmark.

d) Madagascan spending on health is _____ the same as Indonesian.

e) _____

f) _____

7. Practice D

■ Study the table below, which shows the share of total energy consumption produced from renewable sources in various EU countries in 2016. Write a paragraph comparing them.

Country	% of total
Sweden	54
Finland	41
Denmark	35
Austria	32
Portugal	28
Romania	24
Italy	18
Germany	15
UK	10
Netherlands	6

(Source: Eurostat)

8. Practice E

■ Study the data below about Barcelona. Then complete the right-hand column about a city you know well and write a comparison of the two cities in 150–200 words.

	Barcelona	**Your city**
Location	Port city, on the northern Spanish Mediterranean coast	
History	A town has been on this site for over 2,000 years	
Status	Capital of the autonomous region of Catalonia	
Population	1.6 million	
Employment	Government offices, banking, tourism, car manufacturing	
Culture	Over 55 museums, plus many art galleries, theatres and cinemas	
Public transport	12 Metro lines, plus trams, buses and funicular railways	
Climate	Warm wet winters, hot dry summers. Summer average approximately 25°C	
Housing	Mainly flats, typically in blocks of six storeys	
Main visitor attractions	The buildings of Gaudi, especially the Sagrada Familia cathedral	

Definitions

Definitions are usually found in introductions (see Unit 1.11). They are not needed in every paper, but if the title includes an unfamiliar phrase, or if the writer wants to use a term in a special way, it is important to make clear to the reader exactly what is meant in this context. This unit presents ways of writing both simple and complex definitions.

1. Simple definitions

Basic definitions, as found in a dictionary, are formed by giving a category and the application:

Word	Category	Application
An agenda	is a set of issues	to be discussed in a meeting.
A Master's degree	is an academic award	for postgraduate students, given on successful completion of a dissertation.
A grant	is a sum of money	given for a specific purpose.
A seminar	is an academic class	meeting with a tutor for study.

2. Category words

These are useful for making definitions.

■ Complete the following definitions by inserting a suitable category word from the box.

organisation	period	financial instrument	loan	agreement	costs

a)   A mortgage is a type of _____ used for buying property in which the lender has the security of the property.

b)   A multinational company is a business _____ that operates in various countries.

c)   A recession is a _____ of negative economic growth.

d)   A cartel is an _____ between a group of companies for the purpose of price-fixing.

e)   Overheads are the fixed _____ of a business, not related to production.

f)   A bond is a _____ offering a fixed rate of return over a limited period.

■   Write definitions for the following:

g)   A trades union _____

h)   A monopoly _____

i)   Marketing _____

j)   A dividend _____

k)   A hostile takeover _____

3. Complex definitions

It can be difficult to explain terms that you may feel are widely used. For instance, what exactly is an 'urban area' or a 'non-governmental organisation'? This is the reason why it can be useful to make clear at the beginning of a paper what you understand by such a phrase.

The following examples illustrate the variety of methods that can be used in giving definitions.

■   Study the examples and underline the term being defined.

a)   The definition for a failed project ranges from abandoned projects to projects that do not meet their full potential or simply have schedule overrun problems.

b)   Development is a socio-economic-technological process having the main objective of raising the standard of living of the people.

c)   Electronic commerce is characterised by an absence of physical proximity between the buyer and seller in conducting the search, assessment and transaction stages of a transaction.

d) Corporate governance is a set of mechanisms, both institutional and market-based, designed to mitigate agency problems that arise from the separation of ownership and control in a company.

e) Globalisation, in an economic sense, describes the opening up of national economies to global markets and global capital, the freer movement and diffusion of goods, services, finance, people, knowledge and technology around the world.

f) Empathy as a concept has an interesting history. As Eisenberg and Strayer (1987) note: 'Some people take the term empathy to refer to a cognitive process analogous to cognitive role taking (e.g. Deutsch and Madle 1975); others take it to mean ...'

■ Working with a partner, decide which example(s)

i) gives a variety of relevant situations?

ii) defines the term in a negative way?

iii) quotes a definition from another writer?

iv) uses category words?

v) explains a process?

4. Practice

■ Study the following titles, underline the terms that are worth defining, and write definitions for three of them.

Example:

Title: Higher education should be free and open to all – Discuss.

Definition: *Higher education usually means university-level study for first or higher degrees, normally at the age of 18 or above.*

a) Do 'managing diversity' policies and practices in Human Resource Management add value?

b) How can the management of an entrepreneurial business retain its entrepreneurial culture as it matures?

c) Why is organisational culture of sustained interest not only for academics but also for practising managers?

d) Is it true that firms in perfect competition do not make a profit?

■ Think of a topic you are currently studying and write a definition for a term used in that topic that needs clarification.

2.5 **Examples**

> Examples are used in academic writing for support and illustration. Suitable examples can strengthen the argument, but they can also help the reader to understand a point. This unit demonstrates the different ways in which examples can be introduced, and practises their use.

1. Using examples

Generalisations are commonly used to introduce a topic:

> *It is often claimed that many mergers are unsuccessful . . .*

But if the reader is given an example for illustration the idea becomes more concrete:

> *It is often claimed that many mergers are unsuccessful,* **for instance the merger between Compaq and Hewlett-Packard in 2005.**

Without examples an argument may seem too theoretical:

> *E-commerce businesses are particularly vulnerable to security breaches.*

But an example makes the idea easier to understand:

> *E-commerce businesses are particularly vulnerable to security breaches.* **When Ebay was hacked into in 2014, for instance, 128 million members had to change their passwords.**

The example may also support the point the writer is making by providing more context:

> *. . . in recent years researchers have begun looking into corporate governance in transition economies . . .* **For example, Djankov and Murrell (2002) document that more than 150,000 large SOEs in transition economies have undergone enterprise restructuring . . .**

▶ **See Unit 2.6 Generalisations**

■ Read the following text and note the way that examples are used. Underline the examples.

Droning on

For some years there have been predictions that drones could be used to deliver goods to customers. Amazon was one company that expressed an interest. Yet issues with regulators have delayed the arrival of airborne parcels in most countries, owing to concerns with privacy and safety. However, in remote rural regions drone deliveries are already in operation. In Rwanda, for instance, an American startup called Zipline is flying medical supplies, especially blood, to isolated clinics and hospitals. There are various reasons for beginning to operate in these places: medicines are valuable yet lightweight, while most deliveries are between a small number of fixed points. By comparison, travel by road is likely to be slower and more expensive. The pioneer companies such as Zipline and Matternet claim to be operating profitably already, and there are plans to begin the service in less remote places: Zipline will bring its expertise from Africa to North Carolina.

2. Phrases to introduce examples

You will notice in the paragraph above that after the first sentence, a generalisation, the rest of the text consists of various examples which support the generalisation. Some of the examples (Rwanda) are introduced with a phrase (for instance) but others are not. More introductory phrases are shown in the box below.

---

a) **for instance, for example** (with commas)

Some car manufacturers, for instance Kia, now offer seven-year guarantees.

b) **such as, e.g.**

Many entrepreneurs such as Richard Branson have no formal business qualifications.

c) **particularly, especially** (to give a focus)

Certain MBA courses, especially American ones, take two years.

d) **a case in point** (for single examples)

A few countries have experienced deflation. A case in point is Japan.

■ Add a suitable example to each sentence and introduce it with a phrase from the box above.

Example: *Certain industries are experiencing labour shortages.*

*Certain industries, **for instance engineering**, are experiencing labour shortages.*

a)   Some twentieth-century inventions affected the lives of most people.

b)   A number of sports have become very profitable due to the sale of television rights.

c)   Various companies have built their reputation on the strength of one product.

d)   Some brands have remained successful for more than 50 years.

e)   In recent years the product life cycle has tended to get shorter.

f)   A variety of products are promoted by celebrity endorsement.

g)   Speculation in some commodities has created price bubbles.

h)   Investors are often advised to spread their risk by putting their money into a range of investments.

3. Practice A

■   Study the following text and add examples from the box where marked (^), using an introductory phrase from Section 2 above.

bookshops and record shops
clothing and footwear
cheaper prices
groceries
Amazon

THE CHANGING FACE OF SHOPPING

Widespread use of the internet has led to a major change in shopping habits, so that it is no longer necessary to visit shops to make routine purchases ^. With more specialised items internet retailers ^ can offer a wider range of products than brick-and-mortar shops. They can also provide extra incentives to customers ^, in addition to the convenience of not having to visit a real shop. As a result certain types of store ^ are disappearing from the high street. Other products however, ^ appear to require personal inspection and approval, and in addition many people enjoy the activity of shopping, so it seems unlikely that the internet will completely replace the shopping centre.

4. Practice B

■ Read the text below and insert suitable examples where needed to illustrate the points.

A NEW PERSPECTIVE?

Students who go abroad to study often experience a type of culture shock when they arrive in the new country. Customs which they took for granted in their own society may not be followed in the host country. Even everyday patterns of life may be different. When these are added to the inevitable differences which occur in every country students may at first feel confused. They may experience rapid changes of mood, or even want to return home. However, most soon make new friends and, in a relatively short period, are able to adjust to their new environment. They may even find that they prefer some aspects of their new surroundings, and forget that they are not at home for a while!

---

5. Restatement

Another small group of phrases is used when there is only one 'example'. This is a kind of restatement, or it can provide clarification:

> *The most profitable film of the twentieth century, namely 'Titanic', earned over $3 billion.*

in other words   namely   that is (to say)   i.e.   viz (very formal)

■ Add a suitable phrase from the box below to the following sentences to make them clearer.

   a)   The company's overheads doubled last year.

   b)   During a bear market few investors make money.

   c)   The Indian capital has a thriving commercial centre.

   d)   The best-selling car of all time has ceased production.

   e)   The world's lightest metal is used in car batteries.

---

namely lithium

i.e. the Toyota Corolla

in other words the fixed costs

that is, a period of falling share prices

namely New Delhi

2.6 **Generalisations**

Generalisations are often used to introduce a topic. They can be powerful statements because they are simple and easy to understand. But they must be used with care, to avoid being inaccurate or too simplistic. This unit explains how to generalise clearly and effectively.

1. Using generalisations

a) Generalisations are often used to give a simple introduction to a topic, before introducing more specific details:

Business has often been disrupted by natural forces. But now, however, global warming has added urgency to the problem. As there has been little real progress in cutting greenhouse gas emissions, businesses are threatened by worse floods, more powerful storms and deadlier wild fires, such as the blazes that devastated parts of California in 2018.

The writer must decide when accuracy is necessary, and when a generalisation will be acceptable. Compare:

- *54.9% of Spanish companies employ fewer than ten people.*

- *The majority of Spanish companies employ fewer than ten people.*

Although the first sentence is more accurate, the second is easier to understand and remember.

You must avoid using generalisations which cannot be supported by evidence or research, or are unclear:

- *Small businesses react faster to change than large ones.*

- *The best place to learn management skills is on the factory floor.*

Such statements are dangerous because there may well be exceptions. Instead, it is better to use cautious phrases such as:

- *Small businesses **can often** react faster to change than large ones.*

- *The best place to learn management skills **may be** on the factory floor.*

■ **Decide which of the following are valid generalisations:**

a) Recessions are often difficult to predict.

b) There appears to be a link between poverty and disease.

c) Women work harder than men.

d) Travel by air is faster than train travel.

▶ **See Unit 3.7.6 The use of caution**

2. Structure

Generalisations can be made in two ways:

a) Most commonly by using the plural:

Computers have transformed the way we live.

b) More formally using the singular + definite article:

The computer has transformed the way we live.

3. Practice A

■ **Write generalisations on the following topics:**

Example:
market research/new products
Market research can be vital for evaluating new products.

a) job satisfaction/rate of pay _____

b) weak currency/level of exports _____

c) spending on R&D/introduction of new models _____

d) unemployment/level of consumer spending _____

e) cold weather/demand for gas _____

f) industrial growth/pollution _____

4. Building on generalisations

Generalisations can be used in various ways when presenting the results of research or developing a thesis.

■   Read the following text and note the generalisations in italics. Answer the questions that follow.

WHAT WOMEN WANT

What we look for in choosing a mate seems to vary from place to place. A recent study (Jones and DeBruine, 2010) explores the idea that female preferences in a mate might vary according to the society in which she lives. In their research nearly 5,000 women in 30 countries were shown the same pictures of male faces and asked to state which they found more attractive. In countries where disease is common women chose men with more masculine features, while in countries such as America with more advanced health care and lower levels of disease, more effeminate-looking men were preferred. The researchers conclude that *in healthier societies women are more interested in men who may form long-term relationships and help with child-rearing, while in places where child mortality rates are high they choose strongly-featured men who seem more likely to produce healthy children.*

---

a)   What is the function of the first generalisation?

b)   What is the basis of the concluding generalisations?

c)   What is the purpose of the concluding generalisations?

5. Practice B

Most essays move from the general to the specific, as a generalisation has to be supported and developed. For example, an essay with the title 'The impact of globalisation on the Chinese economy' might develop in this way:

Generalisation >	Support >	Development > Specific
Since the mid-twentieth century there has been a remarkable increase in international trade.	*The reasons for this are a combination of international agreements such as GATT, better transport and improved communications.*	*China has played a significant part in this process, with its international trade growing by 16 times in just 20 years, while its GDP increased by nearly 10% per year.*

■ Choose a title from the list below, then write a generalisation and develop it in the same way.

a) To what extent has management theory made space for gender?

b) Should governments use taxation to promote public health?

c) Evaluate the contribution of Small and Medium Enterprises (SMEs) to the economy.

d) People are often positively disposed to their own country's products – Discuss.

Generalisation >	Support >	Development > Specific

▶ See Unit 1.11 Introductions and Conclusions

Problems and Solutions

Writing tasks frequently ask students to examine a problem and evaluate a range of solutions. This unit explains ways in which this kind of text can be organised. Note that some of the language is similar to that practised in Unit 2.1 Argument and discussion.

1. Vocabulary

*The main **problem** facing the company was a lack of skilled engineers. One **solution** to this was the expanded apprenticeship scheme. Another **proposal** was . . .*

The following words can be used as synonyms for *problem* and *solution*.

three main **difficulties** have arisen . . .	the best **remedy** for this may be . . .
the main **challenge** faced by managers . . .	two **answers** have been put forward . . .
one of the **concerns** during the recession . . .	another **suggestion** is . . .
the new process created two **questions** . . .	Matheson's **proposal** was finally accepted.
the team faced three main **issues** . . .	this was **rectified/solved** by . . .
our principal **worry/dilemma** was . . .	another **avenue/approach** worth exploring . . .

■ Complete the following text with a suitable word from the lists above.

How to motivate workers effectively is a(n) a) _____ which has been discussed and debated for many years. Higher pay is one obvious b) _____, but this alone may not be sufficient. A different c) _____ is to improve the job satisfaction of employees, although this d) _____ is not always easy to achieve. A third

e) _____ is to enhance working conditions, for instance by offering cheap meals in a workers' restaurant. But the best f) _____ will usually depend on the kind of work being done by the employees.

2. Paragraph structure

■ Study the organisation of the following paragraph:

Reducing road congestion

Currently roads are often congested, which is expensive in terms of delays to the movement of people and freight. It is commonly suggested that building more roads, or widening existing ones, would ease the traffic jams. But not only is the cost of such work high, but the construction process adds to the congestion, while the resulting extra road space may encourage more traffic, so it is only a short-term answer. Therefore constructing more roads is unlikely to solve the problem, and other remedies, such as road pricing or greater provision of public transport, should be examined.

Problem	Currently, roads are often congested, which is expensive in terms of delays to the movement of people and freight.
Solution A	It is commonly suggested that building more roads, or widening existing ones, would ease the traffic jams.
Arguments against Solution A	But not only is the cost of such work high, but the construction process adds to the congestion, while the resulting extra road space may encourage extra traffic, so it is only a short-term answer.
Conclusion in favour of Solutions B and C	. . . other remedies, such as road pricing or greater provision of public transport, should be examined.

3. Alternative structure

The same ideas could be re-ordered to arrive at a different conclusion:

How can road congestion be reduced?

Currently, roads are often congested, which is expensive in terms of delays to the movement of people and freight. It is commonly suggested that building more roads, or widening existing ones, would ease the traffic jams. This remedy is criticised for being expensive and liable to lead to more road use, which may be partly true, yet the alternatives are equally problematic. Road pricing has many practical difficulties, while people are often reluctant to use public transport. There is little alternative to a road building programme except increasing road chaos.

Problem	Currently, roads are often congested, which is expensive in terms of delays to the movement of people and freight.
Solution A	It is commonly suggested that building more roads, or widening existing ones, would ease the traffic jams.
Arguments against Solution A	This remedy is criticised for being expensive and liable to lead to more road use, which may be partly true . . .
Solutions B and C and arguments against	. . . yet the alternatives are equally problematic. Road pricing has many practical difficulties, while people are often reluctant to use public transport.
Conclusion in favour of Solution A	There is little alternative to a road building programme except increasing road chaos.

4. Practice A

■ Read the following text and then rewrite it to reach a different conclusion.

The housing dilemma

In many expanding urban areas there is a serious housing shortage, caused by people moving from the country to seek urban opportunities. There are various possible answers to this problem, but each has its drawbacks. The traditional response is to build family houses with gardens, which offer privacy and space but require a lot of land. Building these is slow and the growth of suburbs creates longer journeys to work. Another solution is to construct tall blocks of flats, which will accommodate more people at high density quite cheaply. However, families may find them noisy and cramped. A third option is to build prefabricated three-storey houses, which can be erected more quickly and cheaply than traditional houses, and can be designed to achieve a higher density of population. For many cities these may be the best solution, avoiding the growth of both extensive suburbs and high-rise blocks.

5. Practice B

■ Working with a partner, study the diagram, which shows a current environmental problem and offers four possible solutions. Discuss the value of the solutions, and then write a paragraph analysing the situation.

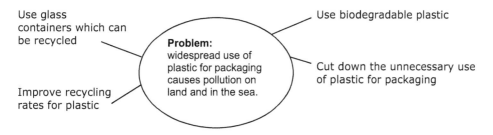

6. Practice C

■ Use the following points to write a paragraph on university expansion.

Topic	University expansion
Problem	Demand for university places is growing, leading to overcrowding in lectures and seminars
Solution A	Increase fees to reduce demand
Argument against Solution A	Unfair to poorer students
Solution B	Government pays to expand universities
Argument against Solution B	Unfair to average taxpayer who would be subsidising the education of a minority who will earn high salaries
Conclusion	Government should subsidise poorer students

7. Practice D

■ Think of a similar problem in your subject area. Complete the table and write a paragraph which leads to a conclusion.

Topic	
Problem	
Solution A	
Argument against Solution A	
Solution B	
Argument for/against Solution B	
(Solution C)	
Conclusion	

2.8 Visual Information

In many Business and Economics assignments it is essential to support your writing with statistical data. Visual devices such as graphs and tables are a convenient way of displaying large quantities of numerical information in a form that is easy to understand. This unit explains and practises the language connected with these devices.

1. Types of visuals

Below are examples of some of the main types of visual devices used in academic texts. Note that they are often combined e.g. a bar chart with a line graph.

■ Complete the box below to show the main use (a–i) and the example (A–I) of each type.

Types	Uses	Example
1. Diagram	g	F
2. Table		
3. Map		
4. Pie chart		
5. Flow chart		
6. Line graph		
7. Bar chart		
8. Plan		
9. Scatter graph/plot		

Use:

a) location – small scale

b) location – large scale

c) changes in time

d) sequence of process

e) comparison

f) proportion

g) structure

h) statistical display

i) relation between two sets of variables

A Cinema ticket sales

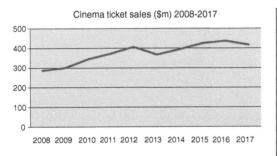

Cinema ticket sales ($m) 2008-2017

B Average life expectancy – both sexes (2015, in years)

Japan	83.7
France	82.4
United States	79.3
United Arab Emirates	77.1
India	68.3
South Africa	62.9
Afghanistan	60.5
Nigeria	54.5
Angola	52.4

C Electricity output from coal (2015)

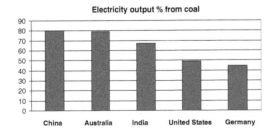

Electricity output % from coal

D Origins of international students

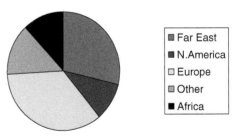

■ Far East
■ N.America
□ Europe
▣ Other
■ Africa

E Planning an essay

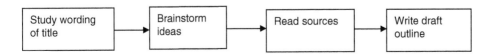

Study wording of title → Brainstorm ideas → Read sources → Write draft outline

F The human ear

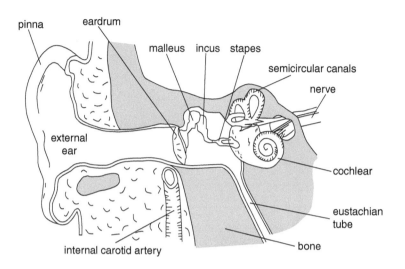

G Layout of the language centre

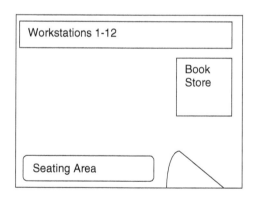

H The regions of Italy

I Height versus armspan

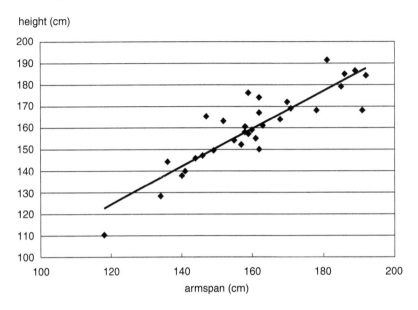

2. The language of change

(past tenses in brackets)

Verb ↗	Adverb	Verb ↘	Adjective + noun
grow (grew)	slightly	drop (dropped)	a slight drop
rise (rose)	gradually	fall (fell)	a gradual fall
increase (increased)	steadily	decrease (decreased)	a sharp decrease
climb (climbed)	sharply	decline (declined)	a steady decline
also: a peak, to peak, a plateau, to level off, a trough			

Average temperatures **rose steadily** until 2012 and then **dropped slightly**.

There was a **sharp decrease** in sales during the summer and then a **gradual rise**.

■ Study the graph and the description below.

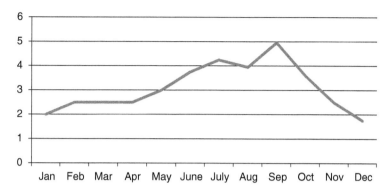

Figure 1 **Inflation (%) January–December 2019**

*The graph (Figure 1) shows that the rate of inflation was 2% in January, and then **rose** to 2.5% in February. After that it **levelled off** until April, and then **increased steadily** to over 4% in July. Inflation **fell slightly** in August, but then **climbed** to a **peak** of 5% in September. From there it **dropped sharply** to below 2% in December.*

3. Describing visuals

A. Although visuals do largely speak for themselves, it is common to help the reader interpret them by briefly commenting on their main features.

The graph	*shows*	*the changes in the price of oil since 1990.*
The map	*illustrates*	*the main sources of copper in Africa.*
The diagram	*displays*	*the organisation of both companies.*

■ Read the following descriptions of the chart below. Which is better, and why?

1. The chart (Figure 2) shows the quantity of tea consumed by the world's leading tea consuming nations. India and China together consume more than half the world's tea production, with India alone consuming about one-third. Other significant tea consumers are Turkey, Russia and Britain. 'Others' includes the United States, Iran and Egypt.

2. The chart (Figure 2) shows that 31% of the world's tea is consumed by India, 23% by China, and 8% by Turkey. The fourth largest consumers are Russia, Japan and Britain, with 7% each, while Pakistan consumes 5%. Other countries account for the remaining 12%.

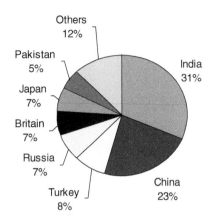

Figure 2 World tea consumption
(Source: The Tea Council)

B. ■ Complete the description of the bar chart below.

The bar chart (Figure 3) shows population a) _____ in a variety
of countries around the world. It b) _____ the extreme contrast c)
_____ crowded nations such as South Korea (475 people per sq. km.)
and much d) _____ countries such as Canada (3 people per sq. km.).
Apparently, climate plays a major e) _____ in determining population
density, f) _____ the least crowded nations g) _____ to have
extreme climates (e.g. cold in Russia and Canada or dry in Algeria).

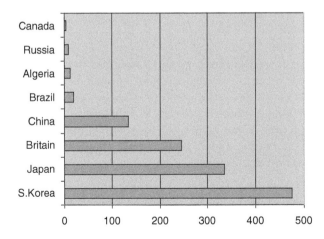

Figure 3 Population density (people per square kilometre)
(Source: OECD)

4. Practice A

■ Study the line graph below and write a paragraph commenting on its main features.

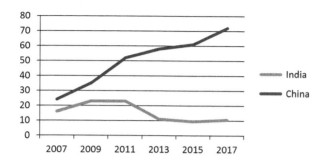

Figure 4 First-year university students in UK from India and China, 2007–2017 (000s)
(Source: HESA)

5. Labelling

- When referring to visual information in the text, the word 'figure' is used for almost everything (such as maps, charts and graphs) except tables (see examples above).
- Figures and tables should be numbered and given a title. Titles of tables are written above, while titles of figures are written below the data.
- As with other data, sources must be given for all visual information.
- If you are writing a lengthy work such as a dissertation you will need to provide lists of tables and figures, showing numbers, titles and page numbers, after the contents page.

6. Practice B

■ Complete the following description of the table below (one word per gap).

Table 1 Projected population changes in various European countries 2015–2050 (millions).

Country	Population 2015 (millions)	Projected population 2050	Change (%)
France	62	67	+5
Germany	82	71	−11
Italy	60	57	−3
Poland	38	32	−6

Country	Population 2015 (millions)	Projected population 2050	Change (%)
Portugal	10.7	10	−0.7
Russia	140	116	−24
Spain	45	51	+6
UK	62	72	+11

(Source: UN)

The table a) _____ the projected population changes in various

European countries b) _____ 2015 and 2050. It can be seen that in a

c) _____ the population is expected to fall, in some cases (e.g. Germany

and Russia) quite d) _____. However, the populations of France,

e) _____ and the UK are predicted to f) _____, in the case of

the latter by more g) _____ 10%.

7. Practice C

■ Write a paragraph commenting on the main features of the chart below.

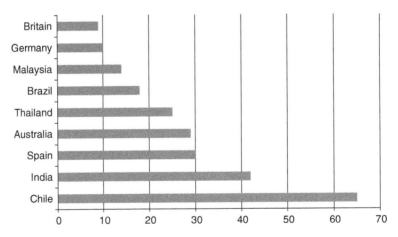

Figure 5 Private school enrolments % of total 2017

(Source: Govt. data)

8. Practice D

■ Write a paragraph commenting on the data in the table below.

Table 1 The world's largest companies by revenue, 2018

Rank	Company	Industry	Revenues $bn.
1.	Wal-Mart Stores	Retail	$500
2.	State Grid Corp of China	Electricity supply	$348
3.	Sinopec	Oil	$326
4.	China National Petroleum	Oil	$326
5.	Royal Dutch Shell Oil	Oil	$311
6.	Toyota	Vehicles	$265
7.	Volkswagen	Vehicles	$260
8.	BP	Oil	$244
9.	Exxon Mobile	Oil	$244
10.	Berkshire Hathaway	Financials	$242
11.	Apple	Electronics	$229
12.	Samsung	Electronics	$211

(Source: *Fortune magazine*)

Progress Check 2

These exercises will help you assess your understanding of Part 2 – Elements of writing

1. ■ *Give two synonyms for 'benefit' and two for 'disadvantage'.*

2. ■ *What is a counterargument?*

   ■ *Underline the counterargument in this sentence:*

State-owned companies are often seen as inefficient, but certain industries do involve a 'natural monopoly'.

3. ■ *Write sentences giving possible causes for the following effects:*

   a) A rise in unemployment

   b) A railway accident

   c) A power cut

4. ■ *Write three sentences comparing Australia with New Zealand, using the data below:*

	Australia	**New Zealand**
Area (square kilometres)	7.6 million	270,000
Population	21.5 million	4.3 million
GDP per head	$50,750	$32,370

5. ■ *Write definitions for:*

   a) A semester

   b) A limited company

   c) An invoice

   d) Bankruptcy

6. ■ *Insert suitable examples into each sentence.*

   a) Certain capital cities are smaller than the commercial centres of their country.

   b) Some recent inventions have changed the way we live.

   c) A number of successful entrepreneurs have had no formal business education.

   d) A few areas are famous for being hubs of technological innovation.

7. ■ *What are the two ways of making a generalisation?*

8. ■ *In the following, underline any generalisations you find unreliable.*

In the past century, photography has gone from being an exclusive hobby to something accessible to everyone. This is largely due to the invention of the digital camera. In the last 20 years this has made it simple to take colour photographs cheaply, and also to modify pictures easily by using editing programmes. So now that everyone has a smartphone, with its built-in camera, photography has become democratic and high quality photographs can be produced by anybody.

9. ■ *Complete each sentence with synonyms for 'problem' or 'solution'.*

   a) The main _____ facing the engineers was the extreme cold.

   b) The only _____ was to repeat the experiment.

   c) One _____ faced by the company was public mistrust of internet security.

   d) The safe disposal of nuclear waste is a _____ without an easy _____

10. ■ *What are the following visuals usually used to show?*

   a) Line graph b) Diagram c) Pie chart d) Table

   ■ *Write a paragraph commenting on the data in the table below.*

Table 2 Student survey of library facilities: % students rating facilities as good.

Library facilities	Undergraduates (%)	Postgraduates (%)
Opening hours	72	63
Staff helpfulness	94	81
Ease of using the electronic catalogue	65	87
Availability of working space	80	76
Café area	91	95
Availability of short loan stock	43	35
Quality of main book stock	69	54

(Source: Author)

Language Issues

This section deals with the language issues that international students find most challenging when writing in English. For example, accurate use of definite articles, punctuation and a suitable academic style can be problematic for any student. These units, again arranged alphabetically, can be studied on a remedial basis when a problem arises.

Cohesion

3.1

Cohesion means joining a text together with reference words (e.g. he, she, theirs) and conjunctions so that the whole text is clear and readable. This unit practises the use of reference words, while conjunctions are examined in Unit 4.5.

1. Reference words

These are used to avoid repetition:

John Maynard Keynes (1883–1946) was an influential British economist whose theories had a profound effect on economic thought during the 1930s and later. **He** argued that governments should spend money to stimulate the economy, even if **they** had to borrow to do so. **This** 'deficit spending' was the basis of the New Deal in the USA, which allowed **it** to overcome the Great Depression of 1929–1933. Keynes' theories became unfashionable in the 1970s, but **they** were revived following the recession of 2007–2009.

Here the reference words function as follows:

Keynes	governments	spend money	USA	theories
He	they	This	it	they

■ **Study these examples of reference words and phrases.**

Pronouns	he/she/it/they
Possessive pronouns	his/her/hers/its/their/theirs
Objective pronouns	her/him/them
Demonstrative pronouns	this/that/these/those
Other phrases	the former/the latter/the first/the second/the last

2. Practice A

■ Read the following paragraph and complete the table.

BUSINESS SHORT LIFE

La Ferrera (2007) has researched the life cycle of new businesses. She found that they have an average life of only 4.7 years, and considers this is due to two main reasons; one economic and one social. The former appears to be a lack of capital, the latter a failure to carry out sufficient market research. La Ferrera considers that together these account for approximately 70% of business failures.

Reference	Reference word/phrase
La Ferrera	*She*
new businesses	
average life of only 4.7 years	
one economic	
one social	
the former . . ., the latter . . .	

3. Preventing confusion

To avoid confusing the reader it is important to use reference words only when the reference is clear. For example:

The company was founded in 1953 and bought the mine in 1957. It was successful at first . . .

In this case it is not clear which noun (the company or the mine) 'It' refers to. So to avoid this write:

The company was founded in 1953 and bought the mine in 1957. The mine/the latter was successful at first . . .

4. Practice B

■ In the following paragraph, insert suitable reference words in the gaps.

Famous for?

When Andy Warhol died at the age of 58 in 1987 few people guessed that

a) _____ would soon become one of the most valuable artists in

the world. In 2007 total sales of b) _____ work at auction reached

$428 million dollars. When, a year later, c) _____ painting 'Eight

Elvises' sold for over $100 million, d) _____ was one of the

highest prices ever paid for a work of art. In e) _____ working life

f) _____ made about 10,000 artworks, and dealers believe that

g) _____ will continue to be popular with collectors in future.

h) _____ is because of Warhol's huge reputation as a super-cool

trendsetter and innovator. i) _____ is also remembered for

j) _____ remark: 'In the future everyone will be famous for

15 minutes', which seems to forecast today's celebrity culture.

5. Implied language

In various written forms certain words may be omitted for convenience. For instance, in emails the pronoun is frequently missed out:

(I) Hope to see you on Friday.

(We are) Looking forward to reading your article.

In other cases nouns may be implied, to avoid repetition:

Various metals are used to make alloys with nickel. One such (metal) is chromium.

Oil (production) and gas production have fallen since 2015.

It is hoped to select suitable candidates from the 10,000 (candidates) who apply each year.

In places a whole phrase might be implied:

They are hoping to reach that goal soon. By 2025 they probably will. (reach that goal)

Implied language is frequently found in comparisons:

The price of land in rural areas is much less than (the price of land) in cities.

Until you are a very confident writer it is better not to omit such words or phrases, but it is useful to understand why it is done.

6. Practice C

■ Read the paragraph below and replace the words in **bold** with reference words.

Velcro

Velcro is a fabric fastener used with clothes and shoes. **Velcro** was invented by a Swiss engineer called George de Mestral. **Mestral's** idea was derived from studying the tiny hooks found on some plant seeds. **The tiny hooks** cling to animals and help disperse the seeds. Velcro has two sides, one of which is covered in small hooks and the other in loops. When **the hooks and loops** are pressed together they form a strong bond.

Mestral spent eight years perfecting **Mestral's** invention, which **Mestral** called 'Velcro' from the French words 'velour' and 'crochet'. **The invention** was patented in 1955 and today over 60 million metres of Velcro are sold annually.

7. Practice D

■ In the following paragraph, insert suitable reference words in the gaps.

Gillette's blades

Thin, disposable razor blades were marketed in America by King Gillette

at the beginning of the twentieth century. a) _____ had realised that

as all men had to shave daily, there was a huge market for a product that would

make b) _____ easier. c) _____ was a simple idea, but at

first d) _____ found it very hard to sell e) _____.

f) _____ was because nobody had marketed a throw-away product

before. However, g) _____ use of advertising to stimulate demand

rapidly increased sales and h) _____ became very popular. Within a

few years i) _____ was a millionaire.

8. Practice E

■ Use the following information to write a paragraph about nylon, paying careful attention to the use of reference words.

Nylon

Inventor:	Wallace Carothers
Company:	DuPont Corporation (USA)
Carothers' position:	Director of the research centre

Carothers' background:	Chemistry student, specialising in polymers (molecules composed of long chains of atoms)
Properties:	Strong but fine synthetic fibre
Patented:	1935
Mass produced:	1939
Applications:	Stockings, toothbrushes, parachutes, fishing lines, surgical thread

3.2 **Definite Articles**

Students often find the rules for using articles ('a', 'an' and 'the') in English confusing. This unit focuses on the definite article, 'the', and provides guidelines, examples and practice.

1. Use of articles

Unless they are uncountable, all nouns need an article when used in the singular. The article can be either **a/an** or **the**. Compare:

a) *Research is an important activity in universities.*

b) ***The*** *research begun by Dr Mathews was continued by Professor Brankovic.*

c) ***An*** *interesting **piece** of research was conducted among 80 new business start-ups.*

In a) research, which is usually uncountable, is being used in a general sense.

In b) a specific piece of research is identified, started by Dr Mathews.

In c) the research is mentioned for the first time, and the word 'piece' is used to 'count' the research.

▶   **See Unit 3.6.3 – Uncountable nouns**

2. Using definite articles

The rules for using **the** (the definite article) are quite complex.

■   **Discuss with a partner why it is used, or not used, in the following examples.**

a)   One of the world's rarest minerals is rhodium.

b)   The USA was founded in the eighteenth century.

c)   The government increased taxation in the 1990s.

d)   The French Revolution was partly caused by bad harvests.

e)   The *Economist* is published every week.

f)   The south is characterised by poverty and emigration.

g)   John Maynard Keynes, the British economist, died in 1946.

h)   The River Seine runs through the middle of Paris.

i)   The World Bank was founded in 1946.

j)   The euro was introduced in 2002.

In general, **the** is used with:

i.   superlatives (*rarest*)

ii.   time periods (*eighteenth century/1990s*)

iii. unique things (*government, world*)

iv.   specified things (*French Revolution*)

v.   regular publications (*Economist*)

vi.   regions, seas and rivers (*south/River Seine*)

vii. very well-known people and things (*British economist*)

viii. institutions and bodies (*World Bank*)

ix.   positions (*middle*)

x.   currencies (*euro*)

It is **not** used with:

xi.   things in general (*bad harvests*)

xii. names of countries (except for the UK, the USA and a few others)

xiii. abstract nouns e.g. poverty, love

xiv. companies/things named after people/places e.g. Sainsbury's, Heathrow Airport

Note the alternate forms:

The deserts of Australia are expanding.

Australian deserts/Australia's deserts are expanding.

3. Practice A

It can be difficult to decide if a noun phrase is specific (with 'the') or general. Compare:

Climate change is a serious threat for millions.	(general)
The Russian climate is characterised by long cold winters.	(specific)
Mobile phones are vital tools for many businesses.	(general)
The mobile phone she bought was a Samsung.	(specific)

■ In the following sentences, decide if the words and phrases in bold are specific or not, and whether 'the' should be added.

Example:

_____ **inflation** was a serious problem for _____ **Brazilian government**.

Inflation was a serious problem for **the** Brazilian government.

a) _____ **engineering** is the main industry in _____ **northern region**.

b) _____ **insurance firms** have made record profits in _____ **last decade**.

c) _____ **global warming** is partly caused by _____ **fossil fuels**.

d) _____ **CEO** has been arrested on suspicion of _____ **corruption**.

e) _____ **moons of Jupiter** were discovered in _____ **eighteenth century**.

f) _____ **tourism** is _____ **world's** biggest industry.

g) _____ **forests of Scandinavia** produce most of _____ **Germany's** paper.

h) _____ **Thai currency** is _____ **baht**.

i) _____ **computer crime** has grown by 200% in _____ **last five years**.

j) _____ **main causes** of _____ **Industrial Revolution** are still debated.

k) 3% of _____ **working population** are employed in _____
    call centres.

l) _____ **latest forecast** predicts _____ **warmer winters** in
    the next decade.

m) Research on _____ **recruitment methods** is being conducted in
    _____ **business school**.

n) _____ **best definition** is often _____ **simplest**.

o) During _____ **last recession** there was a sharp increase in
    _____ **child poverty**.

4. Practice B

Note the difference in meaning between:

A government minister	(one of several/many)
The Minister of Health	(the only one)
Solar power is a principal source of renewable energy	(one of a few)
Solar power is the principal source of renewable energy	(the main one)

■ **Complete the following text by inserting a/the (or nothing) in each gap. (Note that in
some cases more than one answer is possible).**

A Northern model?

Norway is a) _____ global leader in b) _____ use of electric cars: in 2016
nearly 30% of vehicle sales were battery-powered or hybrid models. In
c) _____ past five years sales have increased sharply due to d) _____
development of better batteries, so now e) _____ country's 5 million people
are f) _____ world's largest electric car market. g) _____ Transport
Minister talks of ending sales of cars powered by h) _____ fossil fuels by
2025. i) _____ government is subsidising j) _____ installation of charging
points on main roads and shopping centres. In addition, drivers of
k) _____ zero-emission vehicles pay no sales tax or parking fees, and
may use bus lanes in cities. But this pattern may not be l) _____ model
for other countries: Norway has m) _____ surplus of cheap electricity
thanks to n) _____ hydropower, and it taxes petrol and diesel fuel heavily.

3.3 **Numbers**

Students of Business often have to write clearly and accurately about statistical data. This unit explains and practises the language of numbers and percentages. Presenting data in charts and tables is dealt with in Unit 2.8 Visual Information.

1. The language of numbers

a) In introductions numbers are often used to give an accurate summary of a situation:

Women account for fewer than 2% of Fortune 500 CEOs, 14% of Fortune 500 directors, and 8% and 5% of board directors and top managers, respectively, of the biggest west European companies.

The words **figures** and **numbers** are both used to talk about statistical data in a general sense:

*The **figures/numbers** in the report need to be read critically.*

But **number** is used more widely:

*She forgot her mobile phone **number.***

*13 is an unlucky **number** in some cultures.*

Digits are individual numbers.

*4,539 is a four-**digit** number.*

Both **fractions** (½) and **decimals** (0.975) may be used.

b) There is no final 's' with hundred/thousand/million used with whole numbers:

*Six **million** people live there.*

but:

> **Thousands** *of companies were formed in the dotcom boom.*

When discussing money put the currency symbol first: *$440 m.* (440 million US dollars).

Rates are normally expressed as percentages (e.g. *the rate of unemployment fell to 3.8%*) but may also be per thousand (e.g. *the Austrian birth rate is 8.7*).

It is normal to write whole numbers as words from one to ten and as digits above ten:

> *There were **16** students in the class, but only **eight** came to the lecture.*

Large numbers can be confusing. The USA and Britain now call 1,000,000,000 a **billion** (a thousand million). However, some European countries use 'billion' for 1,000,000,000,000 (a million million). In the USA and UK this number is a **trillion**.

2. Percentages

These are commonly used for expressing rates of change:

> *In the last three years internet sales have increased by 55%.*

■ **Complete the following sentences using the data in the table below.**

  a) Between 2016 and 2017, the number of students increased by _____ %.
  b) The number increased by _____ % the following year.
  c) Between 2016 and 2019 there was a _____ % increase.

Students studying Marketing 2016–2019

2016	2017	2018	2019
203	305	604	1,011

3. Simplification

Although the accurate use of numbers is vital, too many statistics can make texts difficult to read. If the exact number is not important, words such as *various, dozens* or *scores* may be used instead:

> *53 employees opted for voluntary redundancy.*

> ***Dozens** of employees opted for voluntary redundancy.*

■ Study these words and phrases.

a couple	2
few	a small number, less than expected
a few	approximately 3–6 depending on context
several	approximately 3–4
various	approximately 4–6
dozens of	approximately 30–60
scores of	approximately 60–100

■ Rewrite the following sentences using one of the words or phrases in the table above.

Example:

> **Only three** people attended the meeting.
> **Few** people attended the meeting.

a) 77 students applied for the scholarship.

b) In the past decade the bank has closed 55 branches.

c) The students thought of four good topics for their project.

d) Five names were suggested, but rejected, for the new chocolate bar.

e) Last year 49 books were published on insurance.

4. Further numerical phrases

The expressions listed below can also be used to present and simplify statistical information. For example:

> *The course fees rose from $1,200 to $2,500 in two years.*

could be written:

> *The course fees **doubled** in two years.*

If appropriate, *roughly/ approximately* can be added:

> *The course fees **roughly doubled** in two years.*

one in three	*One in three* accountancy students is from China.
twice/ three times as many	*Twice as many* women as men study business law.
a five/ tenfold increase	There was *a fivefold increase* in the price of oil.
to double/ halve	The rate of inflation *halved* after 2015.
the highest/ lowest	*The lowest* rate of home ownership was in Germany.
a quarter/ fifth	*A fifth* of all employees leave every year.
the majority/ minority	*The majority* of shareholders supported the proposal.
on average, the average	*On average*, each salesperson sells two cars per week.
a small/ large proportion	The website generates *a large proportion* of their sales.

Majority and minority

below 20%	=	a small minority
21–39%	=	a minority
40–49%	=	a substantial/ significant minority
51–55%	=	a small majority
56–79%	=	a majority
80% +	=	a large majority

▨ **Rewrite each sentence in a simpler way, using a suitable expression from the list above.**

a)   In 1973 a litre of petrol cost 12p, while the price is now £1.20.

_____

b)   Out of 18 students in the group 12 were women.

_____

c)   The new high-speed train reduced the journey time to Madrid from seven hours to three hours 20 minutes.

_____

d)   The number of students applying for the Statistics course has risen from 350 last year to 525 this year.

_____

e)   More than 80% of students in Britain complete their first degree course; in Italy the figure is just 35%.

_____

f) Tap water costs 0.07p per litre while bottled water costs, on average, 50p per litre.

g) The rate of unemployment in the EU ranges from 18.5% in Greece to 1.9% in the Czech Republic.

h) 57% of the members supported the suggestion, but of these 83% had some doubts.

i) Visitor numbers to the theme park show a steady increase. In 2015 there were 40,000 admissions, in 2016 82,000 and 171,000 in 2017.

5. Practice

■ The following data was collected about a group of 15 international students. Write sentences about the group using the data.

Mother tongue		Future course		Age		Favourite sport	
Arabic	2	Accounting	1	21	1	climbing	2
Chinese	8	Economics	3	22	3	cycling	1
French	1	Finance	2	23	9	dancing	3
Japanese	1	Management	6	24	–	football	3
Korean	2	MBA	2	25	–	swimming	5
Spanish	1	Tourism	1	26	1	tennis	1

a) *Roughly half the group speak Chinese.*

b) _____

c) _____

d) _____

e) _____

f) _____

■ Write a few sentences about the students in your class.

3.4 Passive and Active

The passive voice is more common in academic writing than in other genres, making it more impersonal and formal, but the passive should not be overused. This unit explains where it is appropriate to use the passive and provides practice in developing a balanced style.

1. Active and passive

The passive is used when the writer wants to focus on the result, not on the cause or agent:

> *The company was founded in 1858 by Parvez Alam.* (passive)

> *Parvez Alam founded the company in 1858.* (active)

In the first sentence, the emphasis is on the company, in the second on Alam. So the passive is often used in written English when the cause or agent (a person or thing) is less important or unknown.

> *Aluminium was first produced in the nineteenth century. (by someone)*

> *The currency was devalued in 1957. (for some reason)*

The cause of the action can be shown by adding 'by . . .':

> *The city was flooded by a severe hurricane.*

The passive is also used in written work to provide a more impersonal style:

> *The findings were evaluated. (not 'I evaluated the findings')*

▶ **See Unit 3.7 Style**

2. Structure

All passive structures have two parts:

Form of the verb to be	Past participle
is	constructed
was	developed
will be	reorganised

■ **Change the following sentences into the passive to make them more impersonal.**

   a) We collected the data and compared the two groups.

   b) I interviewed 120 people in three social classes.

   c) They checked the results and found several errors.

   d) We will make an analysis of the findings.

   e) He asked four managers to give their opinion.

   f) She wrote the report and distributed ten copies.

3. Use of the passive

The passive tends to be commonly employed in certain situations:

a) Describing a process

   *Urea can **be made** cheaply by mixing ammonia and carbon dioxide.*

   *Aluminium can **be used** to reduce weight.*

   *Nine so-called tech 'unicorns' **will be studied**.*

b) Describing a piece of research

   *The results **were adjusted** to allow for the variation.*

   *It **was found** that the smallest were the most effective.*

   *The process **was discovered** in the 2000s.*

   *One study **was conducted** in America and **published** in 2018.*

In both of these situations the use of the passive puts the emphasis on the action and not on the people involved.

■   Change the following sentences from active to passive.

a)   He argued that entrepreneurial skills should be taught in school.
b)   Some economists believe that the government should reduce its borrowing.
c)   Dr Weber suggests that foreign competition can damage that industry.
d)   Ryanair is offering eight new destinations this year.
e)   She claimed that productivity could be raised by more automation.

4. Adverbs with passives

An adverb can be inserted into a passive form to add information:

This process is **commonly** *called 'networking'.*

Students are **usually** *required to write a dissertation.*

■   Change the following sentences from active to passive and insert a suitable adverb from the box below. Decide if it is necessary to show a cause.

---

optimistically   helpfully   effectively   accurately   eventually   carefully profitably   vigorously

---

Example:

The recession forced the company to make redundancies.

The company was **eventually** *forced to make redundancies by the recession.*

a)   The Connors family ran the company until 2001.

b)   Economists debated the reasons for the Asian currency crisis.

c)   They provided pencils for all students in the exam.

d)   The staff of the advertising agency gave a presentation.

e)   The researchers calculated the percentages to three decimal places.

f)   They called their business the Grand Universal Trading Company.

g)   She researched the life cycle of over 240 companies.

▶   **See Unit 4.4 Academic Vocabulary: Adverbs and Verbs**

5. Practice

Overuse of the passive can make a text seem very formal. A balanced style mixes both active and passive.

■ **Read the following and change some of the passive forms into active.**

MAKING BREAD

Bread is traditionally made from wheat flour, salt, water and yeast. The wholemeal or white flour is mixed with a little salt and yeast, and then lukewarm water is gradually added. Other ingredients such as chopped nuts or seeds may be included. Then the dough is mixed until a soft ball is formed, which can be kneaded by hand. In the kneading process the dough is vigorously pounded and reshaped so that all the ingredients are fully combined. After being thoroughly kneaded the dough is left for a few hours to rise. When this is finished the dough is again worked by hand to shape it into loaves or rolls. After two more hours the loaves will have risen again, due to the action of the yeast. They are baked in a hot oven for about half an hour and then allowed to cool.

Bread is traditionally made from wheat flour, salt, water and yeast. You mix the wholemeal or white flour with a little salt and yeast . . .

3.5 **Punctuation**

Accurate punctuation and the correct use of capital letters help the reader to understand exactly what the writer means. While some aspects of punctuation, such as the use of commas, can be a matter of individual style, correct punctuation in such areas as quotation is vital.

1. Capital letters

It is difficult to give precise rules about the use of capital letters in modern English, where nowadays there is a tendency to use them less than before. However, they should always be used in the following cases:

a)	The first word in a sentence	*In the beginning . . .*
b)	Days and months	*Friday 21 July*
c)	Nationality words	*Indonesia and the Indonesians*
d)	Languages	*Most Swiss speak French and German*
e)	Names of people/ places	*Dr Martin Lee from Sydney, Australia*
f)	Book titles (main words only)	*Power and the State*
g)	Historical periods	*The Industrial Revolution, the Great Depression*
h)	Names of organisations	*Sheffield Hallam University*
i)	The first person pronoun	*By Monday I had finished the book*

NB seasons are not capitalised (*The course began in autumn*)

When discussing general concepts such as 'empire' no capital is needed:

Rome developed one of the world's earliest empires.

But should be used when specific:

The Roman Empire stretched from Britain to Syria.

2. Full stops (.) [*US: period*]

These are used to show the end of a sentence:

The first chapter provides a clear introduction to the topic.

They are also used with certain abbreviations formed from the first part of a word:

govt./Jan./p.397

But do not use full stops with acronyms such as:

BBC/UN/VIP

It is also now less common to use full stops with initials:

DH Lawrence

▶ **See Unit 4.2 Abbreviations**

3. Commas (,)

These are one of the commonest punctuation marks, but also one of the hardest to provide guidance for, because comma use is partly a matter of individual style. It may be useful to think of commas as providing a brief pause for readers, to give them a chance to make sense of a chunk of text. Overuse can slow down the reader, but equally the lack of commas can be confusing. Some instances of necessary comma usage are:

a) after introductory words or phrases:

However, more cases should be considered before reaching a conclusion.

b) around examples or comments (these are phrases that can be left out without loss of meaning):

Certain investments, for instance shares, are highly volatile.

Privatisation, it is widely recognised, has a positive and a negative side.

c) before some conjunctions:

Three hundred people were interviewed, and most of these expressed approval.

d) in lists of three or more items:

Apostrophes, colons, semi-colons and commas must all be used with care.

e) finishing direct speech:

'Don't forget the deadline', the teacher told them.

f) to show contrasting elements:

It was well-written, but badly spelt.

g) with a group of adjectives:

It was a long, rambling, humorous and controversial book.

4. Apostrophes (')

These can be one of the most confusing features of English punctuation, but their correct use is grammatically vital. They are mainly used in two situations:

a) to show contractions   *He's the leading authority on Marx.*

NB: contractions are not common in academic English. It is usually better to write the full form:

He is the leading authority on Marx.

b) with possessives   *The professor's secretary* (singular)

Students' marks (plural words ending in 's')

Dickens's novels (names ending in 's')

Women's rights (for irregular plurals)

NB: **it's** is the contraction of **it is**   *It's possible the course will be cancelled.*

The third person singular possessive form is **its**   *'Civilization and its Discontents' (Freud)*

There is no need to use the apostrophe with generic plurals: *1980s, HGVs*

5. Semi-colons (;)

Semi-colons are used to show the link between two connected clauses, when a comma would be too weak and a full stop too strong:

Seven people applied for the post; six were shortlisted and then interviewed.

Nobody questioned the results; they were quite conclusive.

Semi-colons are also used to divide up items in a list when they have a complex structure, as in a multiple citation:

(Maitland, 2006; Rosenor, 1997; The Economist, 2017b; University of Michigan, 2000).

6. Colons (:)

Colons have three main uses:

a) to introduce explanations   *The meeting was postponed: the Dean was ill.*

b) to start a list   *Three aspects were identified: financial, social and ethical.*

c) to introduce a quotation   *As Keynes said: 'In the long run we are all dead'.*

7. Quotations marks/inverted commas (" "/' ')

a) Single quotation marks are used to show quotations from other writers:

Goodwin's (1977) analysis of habit indicates that, in general, 'It will be more difficult to reverse a trend than to accentuate it'.

NB: Make sure that the final quotation mark comes before the full stop.

Longer quotations are usually indented (i.e. have a wider margin) and/or are set in smaller type:

More recently, she has stated the point even more directly:

> *Government, I hold, should not give people an option to be treated with respect and nonhumiliation. . . . Government should treat all people respectfully and should refuse to humiliate them (Nussbaum, 2011b, p.26).*

b) Double quotation marks are used to show quotations inside quotations (nested quotations):

As Kauffman remarked: 'his concept of "internal space" requires close analysis'.

NB: American English uses double quotation marks to show standard quotations.

c) They are also used to emphasise a word or phrase:

The word 'factory' was first used in the seventeenth century.

The Swedish 'third way' or welfare state is a possible model.

d) To show direct speech:

'Can anyone find the answer?' asked the lecturer.

▶ **See Written British and American English – a short guide**

e) In references, quotation marks are used for the names of articles and chapters, but book or journal titles normally use italics:

Russell, T. (1995) 'A future for coffee?' *Journal of Applied Marketing* 6, 14–17.

▶ **See Unit 1.8 References and Quotations**

8. Others

a) Hyphens (-) are used with certain words which fit together, such as 'long-lived' or 'high-profile', and in some structures:

A well-researched, thought-provoking book.

Her three-year-old daughter is learning to read.

But note that the use of hyphens is generally declining e.g. 'proofreading' rather than 'proof-reading'. Many words with prefixes re-, pre- and co- no longer require hyphens:

Cooperation is vital for successful group projects.

b) Exclamation marks (!) and question marks (?):

'Well!' he shouted, 'who would believe it?'

c) Brackets or parentheses ( ) can be used to give additional detail, without interfering with the flow of the main idea:

Employee attitudes do not affect other dimensions of customer satisfaction (price and quality).

9. Practice A

■ Punctuate the following sentences.

a) the study was carried out by christine zhen-wei qiang of the national university of singapore

b) professor rowans new book the end of privacy 2019 is published in new york

c) as keynes said its better to be roughly right than precisely wrong

d) banks such as hsbc and barclays were in penny pinching mode in the 1990s

e) as Matheson 1954 wrote it was the germ that was the villain

f) thousands of new words such as app enter the english language each year

g) the bbcs world service is broadcast in 33 languages including somali and vietnamese

h) she scored 56% on the main course the previous semester she had achieved 67%

i) their article a reassessment of the spanish housing market 2005 2015 was well received

j) before submitting her essay on irish smes she checked for spelling grammar and punctuation

10. Practice B

■ Punctuate the following text.

studying will play a vital part in your life as an oxford student but you will also find an enormous amount to do in oxford in your spare time oxford is the youngest city in england and wales and has two universities oxford university and oxford brookes 35% of people who live here are aged 15 29 and 27% 40,000 of a total population of 150,000 are university students if you ever feel like a change of scene the bus to london takes around 90 minutes and runs 24 hours a day there are now two railway stations the central oxford station and the recently opened oxford parkway oxford is a youthful and cosmopolitan city with plenty to see and do there are dozens of historic and iconic buildings including the bodleian libraries ashmolean museum sheldonian theatre the cathedral and the colleges in the city centre you will find lots of shops cafés restaurants theatres cinemas pubs and clubs there are plenty of green spaces too riverside walks englands oldest botanic garden the university parks and college gardens

3.6 Singular or Plural?

The choice of singular or plural can be confusing in several situations, such as in the use of countable and uncountable nouns. This unit illustrates the main areas of difficulty and clarifies the correct structures.

1. Five difficult areas

■ Working with a partner, find the mistakes in the following sentences.

    i.   The proposal has both advantages and disadvantage.

    ii. A majority of workers in Bangladesh is under 30.

    iii. There are few young people in rural area.

    iv. Many places are experiencing an increase in crimes.

    v.   Each companies have their own policies.

These five sentences show the main problem areas with singular/plural for international students:

a)   Nouns should agree with verbs, and pronouns with nouns:

    *There **are many arguments** in favour.*

    ***Those problems** are unique.*

b)   Uncountable nouns and irregular plurals usually have no final 's':

    *Most students receive free **tuition**.*

    *The main export is tropical **fruit**.*

c) General statements normally use the plural:

*State **universities** have lower **fees**.*

d) 'Each/every' are followed by singular noun and verb forms:

*Every **student gets** financial support.*

e) Two linked nouns should agree:

*Both the **similarities** and **differences** are important.*

■ Link each problem area (a–e) with one of the first five sentences (i–v).

2. Group phrases

■ Study the following 'group' phrases.

singular + plural	plural + singular *	plural + uncountable
half the universities	two types of institution	three areas of enquiry
a range of businesses	various kinds of brick	several fields of research
one of the elements	many varieties of response	different rates of progress

* In these structures the use of the singular is with the second noun:

*Several sorts of **revolution** occurred in the Balkans.*

emphasises that 'revolution' here is a general concept, not a specific event.

Note that if a verb has more than one subject it must be plural, even if the preceding noun is singular:

*Scores of students, some teachers and the president **are** at the meeting.*

*Their valuable suggestions and hard work **were** vital.*

Certain 'group' nouns e.g. team/army/government can be followed by either a singular or plural verb, depending on the situation:

*The team **was** defeated three times last month.* (collectively)

*The team **were** travelling by train, bus and taxi.* (separately)

It is not always clear, in sentences with two nouns, which one the verb agrees with. Compare these:

*The quality of candidates **was** improving.*

*The majority of candidates **were** French.*

In the first case the verb should agree with 'quality', in the second with 'candidates'.

3. Uncountable nouns

a) Most nouns in English are countable, but the following are generally uncountable i.e. they are not usually used with numbers or the plural 's'.

accommodation	information	scenery
advice	knowledge	staff
chaos	money	traffic
commerce	news	travel
data	permission	trouble
education	progress	vocabulary
equipment	research	weather
furniture	rubbish	work

Many of these can be 'counted' by using an extra noun:

A piece of advice

An item of equipment

Six members of staff

b) Another group of uncountable nouns consists of materials:

wood/rubber/iron/coffee/paper/water/oil/stone

Little **wood** is used in the construction of motor vehicles.

How much **paper** is needed to produce these magazines?

But many of these nouns can be used as countable nouns with a rather different meaning:

How many daily **papers** are published in Delhi?

Most **woods** are home to a wide variety of birds.

c) The most difficult group can be used either as countable or uncountable nouns, often with quite different meanings:

She developed **an interest** in genetics.   (countable)

The bank is paying 4% **interest**.   (uncountable)

(further examples: business/capital/experience)

Other nouns with a similar pattern are used for general concepts e.g. love/fear/hope:

Most people feel that **life** is too short.   (uncountable – in general)

Nearly 20 **lives** were lost in the mining accident.   (countable – in particular)

▶ **See Unit 4.3 Academic Vocabulary: Nouns and Adjectives**

4. Practice A

■ Choose the correct alternative in these sentences.

a) Little/few news about the takeover was released.

b) He established three successful businesses/business before he was 25.

c) Substantial experiences/experience of report writing are/is required.

d) It is often claimed that travel broadens/travels broaden the mind.

e) The college was built of grey stones/stone.

f) How much advice/many advices were they given before coming to Australia?

g) She had little interest/few interests outside her work.

h) The insurance policy excludes the effects of civil war/wars.

i) Irons were/iron was first powered by electricity in the twentieth century.

j) They studied the work/works of three groups of employees over two years.

5. Practice B

■ Read the text and choose the correct alternatives.

TRAVEL TROUBLE

As the volume of traffic/traffics has grown, travel/travels to work/works has/have become slower for many college staffs/staff. Research/researches on commuting time in five capitals/capital shows that on average drivers spend 125 minutes in their vehicles/vehicle each day/days. This means that they are spending more than 10% of their waking life/lives driving, and also consuming a large quantity/quantities of petrol/petrols in traffic jams/jam. Another negative factor/factors is the stress/stresses caused by commuting, so the best advices/advice to drivers are/is to relax by listening to classical music/musics. An alternative strategy is for employees to work at home/homes several days a week, although permission/permissions to do this is/are not always granted.

3.7   **Style**

There is no one correct style of academic writing, but in general it should attempt to be accurate, impersonal and objective. For example, personal pronouns like 'I' and idioms (i.e. informal language) are used less often than in other kinds of writing. Students should study examples of writing in their own subject area, and then aim to develop their own 'voice'. This unit gives guidelines for an appropriate style, and provides practice.

---

1. Style in the Business school

Students of Business may be required to write essays in academic English, but also to write reports for company use. How will the style of writing vary between these two?

■ **Discuss any likely differences with a partner.**

Although company reports are likely to be less formal than academic essays and will not contain references, they share many features of good style: both, for example, aiming to be clear, impersonal and precise.

■ **Working with a partner again, underline examples of bad style in the sentences below. Then rewrite the sentences in a more suitable style.**

a)   Regrettably these days lots of people don't have jobs.

b)   Another thing to think about is the chance of inflation getting worse.

c)   Years ago the Brazilian money, the peso, was worth a lot less.

d)   Luckily the firemen soon got the fire under control.

e) You can't always trust the numbers in that report.

f) Lots of people think the economy is getting better.

g) He was over the moon when he won the prize.

h) I think we should pay students to study.

i) They sacked the boss for cooking the books.

j) A few years ago the price of property in Spain went down a lot.

2. Guidelines

There are no rules for academic style which apply to all situations and all academic disciplines, but the following guidelines should help you develop a style of your own.

a) Do not use idiomatic or colloquial vocabulary: e.g. *kids, boss.* Instead use standard English: *children, manager.*

b) Use vocabulary accurately. There is a difference between *rule* and *law,* or *weather* and *climate,* which you are expected to know if you study these subjects.

c) Be as precise as possible when dealing with facts or figures. Avoid phrases such as *about a hundred* or *hundreds of years ago.* If it is necessary to estimate numbers use *approximately* rather than *about.*

d) Conclusions should use tentative language. Avoid absolute statements such as *unemployment causes crime.* Instead use cautious phrases: *unemployment may cause crime* or *tends to cause crime.*

e) Avoid adverbs that show your personal attitude: *luckily, remarkably, surprisingly.*

f) Do not contract auxiliary verb forms: *don't, can't.* Use the full form: *do not, cannot.*

g) Avoid complicated expressions of gender. Instead of writing:

each candidate had his or her presentation prepared

write: *all candidates had their presentations prepared*

Try not to use sexist language such as *chairman, fireman* or *policeman.* Use *chairperson, firefighter* or *police officer.*

h) Avoid the following:

– *like* for introducing examples. Use *such as* or *for instance.*
– *thing* and combinations *nothing* or *something.* Use *factor, issue* or *topic.*
– *lots of.* Use *a significant/considerable number.*
– *little/big.* Use *small/large.*

-    'get' phrases such as *get better/worse*. Use *improve* and *deteriorate*.
-    *good/bad* are simplistic. Use *positive/negative* e.g. *the changes had several positive aspects*

i)   Do not use rhetorical question forms such as *What were the reasons for the decline in exports?* Instead use statements: *There were three reasons for the decline . . .*

j)   Avoid numbering sections of your text, except in reports and long essays. Use conjunctions and signposting expressions to introduce new sections (*Turning to the question of taxation . . .*).

▶ **See Unit 1.10 Organising Paragraphs**

k)   When writing lists, avoid using *etc.* or *and so on*. Insert *and* before the last item:

     The main products were pharmaceuticals, electronic goods and confectionery.

l)   Avoid using two-word verbs such as *go on* or *bring up* if there is a suitable synonym e.g. *continue* or *raise*.

▶ **See Unit 4.4 Academic Vocabulary: Verbs and Adverbs**

3. Developing a suitable style

■   **Study this paragraph and underline any examples of poor style.**

Trains are often run by the state. The state pays for new lines and new equipment. This is because they do an important job moving people around. What's more, developing the railways costs lots of money, which only governments can find. But in some countries like England the railways have been privatised, so as to offer more choice to passengers. The problem is that the private trains still need money from the government to keep running. That's the only way to get everyone to work in big cities. So either way I think that there's no easy answer to the problem.

     The paragraph could be rewritten in a more suitable style:

> In many countries railways are operated by the state, partly because the provision of mass transit is seen as a public service, but also because railway systems demand large-scale capital investment which is often beyond the reach of the private sector. However, there has been a trend towards railway privatisation, for example in Britain, since there it was thought useful to introduce some competition into the industry. Yet even these systems still often require public money to subsidise passenger services, which are essential to allow millions of people to travel safely to work each day. Neither the public nor the private model seems to provide a fully satisfactory answer to the issue.

4. Avoiding repetition and redundancy

Instead of repeating the same word in a short text:

*Most family businesses employ fewer than ten people. These **businesses** . . .*

Try to make the text more interesting by using synonyms:

*Most family businesses employ fewer than ten people. These **firms** . . .*

▶   **See Unit 4.8 Synonyms**

Redundancy, i.e. repeating an idea or including an irrelevant point, suggests that the writer is not fully in control of the material. It gives the impression that either he does not properly understand the language or is trying to 'pad' the essay by repeating the same point. Avoid statements such as:

Homelessness is a global problem in the whole world.

Good writing aims for economy and precision:

Homelessness is a global problem.

■   **In the following text, remove all repetition and redundancy, rewriting where necessary.**

FAST FOOD

Currently these days, fast food is growing in popularity. Fast food is the kind of food that people can buy ready to eat or cook quickly. It's called fast food because it doesn't take long to make. This essay examines the advantages of fast food and the drawbacks of fast food. First above all, fast food is very convenient. Most of the people who work in offices are very busy, so that they do not have time to go to their homes for lunch. But the people who work in offices can eat in restaurants such as McDonald's, which are franchised in hundreds of countries, because they are very popular. In addition, the second benefit of fast food is its cheapness. It is produced in large quantities, and this high volume means that the companies can keep costs down. As a result fast food is usually less expensive than a meal in a conventional restaurant.

5. Varying sentence length

Short sentences are clear and easy to read:

Many companies are trying to develop driverless cars.

But too many short sentences are monotonous:

Many companies are trying to develop driverless cars. These vehicles may be functioning by 2023. Their use will radically alter road transport. Individual car ownership may become outdated. Driverless cars could be used more intensively. This would reduce congestion on the roads.

Long sentences are more interesting but can be difficult to construct. Effective writing normally uses a mixture of long and short sentences, often using a short sentence to introduce the topic:

Many companies are trying to develop driverless cars. These may be functioning by 2023, and their use will radically alter road transport. Individual car ownership may become outdated, since driverless cars could be used more intensively, and this would reduce congestion on the roads.

■ **Rewrite the following paragraph so that instead of seven short sentences there is one short sentence and three longer ones.**

Even large companies can find recruitment problematic. They often employ specialist recruitment firms to find new senior staff. These firms may use a range of assessment methods and tests. But there is some doubt about how effective their methods are. The managers recruited in this way often perform badly. An alternative is to promote from inside the company. These people are familiar with the company culture.

Until you feel confident in your writing, it is better to use shorter rather than longer sentences. This should make your meaning as clear as possible.

6. The use of caution

A cautious style is necessary in many areas of academic writing to avoid making statements that can be contradicted in some way:

*Demand for housing in cities **usually** exceeds supply.*

***Most** students find writing exam essays difficult.*

*Fertility rates **tend to** fall as societies get richer.*

Areas where caution is particularly important include:

a)   outlining a hypothesis which needs to be tested, (e.g. in an introduction)

b)   discussing the results of a study, which may not be conclusive

c) commenting on the work of other writers

d) making predictions (normally with **may** or **might**)

Caution is also needed to avoid making statements which are too simplistic:

Crime is linked to poor education.

Such statements are rarely completely true. There is usually an exception which needs to be considered. Caution can be shown in several ways:

*Crime **may** be linked to poor education.*   (modal verb)

*Crime is **frequently** linked to poor education.*   (adverb)

*Crime **tends to** be linked to poor education.*   (verb)

■ **Complete the table below with more examples of each.**

Modals	Adverbs	Verb/phrase
may	*frequently*	*tends to*

▶ **See Unit 2.6 Generalisations**

7. Using modifiers

Another way to express caution is to use **quite**, **rather** or **fairly** before an adjective:

*She wrote a **fairly** accurate summary of the problem.*

*That is a **rather** inconvenient location for our warehouse.*

*The research team made **quite** a significant discovery last week.*

NB: **quite** is often used before the article. It is mainly used positively, while **rather** tends to be used negatively.

■ **Insert quite/rather/fairly in the following to emphasise caution.**

a) The company's efforts to save energy were successful.

b) The survey was a comprehensive study of student opinion.

c) His second book had a hostile reception.

d)   The first year students were fascinated by her lectures.

e)   The latest type of arthritis drug is expensive.

f)   This mountain tiger has become rare.

g)   The class found the essay topic challenging.

8. Practice

■   Rewrite the following sentences in a more cautious way.

a)   Private companies are more efficient than state-owned businesses.

b)   Exploring space is a waste of valuable resources.

c)   Older students perform better at university than younger ones.

d)   Word-of-mouth is the best kind of advertising.

e)   English pronunciation is confusing.

f)   Some cancers are caused by psychological factors.

g)   Global warming will cause the sea level to rise.

h)   Most shopping will be done on the internet in ten years' time.

i)   Online education is inferior to taught classes.

j)   By 2025 driverless cars will be in common use.

3.8 Time Markers

When describing a sequence of events it is important to make clear what happened when. Time markers such as 'ago' and 'since' are often used to explain the timing of events. But the application of some of these words is restricted to particular tenses. This unit explains these limitations and practises their application.

1. How time markers are used

■ Study the following:

*She went on a training course **for** six weeks.*	(with numbers, without start date)
*The report must be finished **by** 12 June.*	(on or before)
*He has been president **since** 2007.*	(with present perfect, must specify start date)
*They are studying in Bristol **until** March.*	(end of a period)
*The library was opened two years **ago.***	(usually with past)
*The hotel is closed **during** the winter.*	(with noun)
***Before** writing he studied over 100 sources.*	(often followed by the -ing form; also **after**)
*He applied in May and was accepted two months **later**.*	(often used with numbers; also **earlier**)
*She bought the car **while** working at Harvard.*	(two things happening at the same time)

2. Practice A

■ Choose the best alternative in each case.

a) Currently/Recently she has been researching French internet start-ups.

b) He worked there until/during he retired.

c) Dr Hoffman has lived in Melbourne since/for 16 years.

d) Last month/In the last month a new book was published on upcycling.

e) Applications must be received by/on 25 November.

f) Since/During her arrival last May she has reorganised the department.

g) During/For the winter most farmers in the region find work in the towns.

h) After/While giving the lecture she answered all their questions.

3. Tenses

■ Compare the tenses used with the following time markers:

Last year there **was** an election in Spain.	(past – finished event)
In the last year there **has been** a decline in inflation.	(present perfect – unfinished)
While he **was doing** the experiment, he **saw** his mistake.	(past continuous + past)
Recently, there **has been** a sharp rise in internet use.	(present perfect – unfinished)
Currently, there **is** widespread concern about plagiarism.	(present – focus on now)

4. Practice B

■ Study the details of Henry Ford's life, and complete the biography below with suitable time markers (one word per gap).

1863	Born on a farm near Detroit, USA.
1879	Left home to work as a machinist.
1888	Married Clara Bryant and worked the family farm.
1893	Became Chief Engineer with the Edison company. Began to experiment with petrol engines.

1903	The Ford Motor Company was formed to build the car that he had designed.
1908	The Model T was introduced at a price of $825. It was successful because it was easily maintained and simple to drive.
1909	The price of the Model T was regularly reduced and sales climbed sharply.
1914	Ford shocked the industry by increasing wages to $5 a day. This successfully reduced labour turnover and attracted the best engineers to the company.
1916	The price of the Model T was cut to $360 and sales reached 472,000 annually.
1927	Production of the Model T was finally stopped, after selling over 15 million, because sales had been declining for years. It was replaced by the Model A.
1941	After years of conflict with the labour unions Ford finally recognised the Union of Automobile Workers.
1945	Having kept effective control of the company into his 80s, he allowed his grandson, Henry Ford II, to become president.
1947	Henry Ford died at the age of 83.

Henry Ford

Henry Ford was born on a farm near Detroit and lived there a) _____ he was 16.

He returned to the farm nine years b) _____ to marry Clara Bryant. However,

he was more interested in machinery than farming and c) _____ a few years he

became an engineer with the Edison company, working there until 1899.

d) _____ this period he experimented with petrol engines and eventually built a

car. e) _____ 1903 he was confident enough to form a manufacturing company to

produce cheap vehicles, called the Ford Motor Company. The Model T, introduced

in 1908, dominated the American market f) _____ the next 20 years. Although

Ford had been one of the leading American car makers g) _____ the 1920s, unions

were only recognised in 1941, h) _____ a long struggle. Henry Ford retained con-

trol of his company i) _____ old age, though j) _____ his death he allowed his

grandson to take over.

5. Practice C

■ Complete each gap in the following text with a suitable time marker.

Because it's there?

Nearly 200 years a) _____, in 1841 a Himalayan survey team, led by George Everest, recognised that what was b) _____ called Mount Everest was the world's highest peak, at over 8,840 metres above sea level. But there were no attempts to climb the mountain c) _____ 80 years, d) _____ 1921 when a British team made the first attempt.

e) _____ the 1920s and 30s there were a few more unsuccessful expeditions, but it was not f) _____ 1953 that a New Zealand/Nepalese pair, Hillary and Tenzing, were successful. g) _____ then there have been over 4,000 ascents, although these are only possible h) _____ a short period in May. Reaching the summit has become a profitable business, with companies charging up to $75,000 to organise an ascent. But i) _____ 2010 there has been growing concern that the routes are becoming dangerously overcrowded, with climbers dying every year. Just a few years j) _____, in 2015, 22 died when an avalanche struck base camp.

Progress Check 3

These exercises will help you assess your understanding of Part 3 – Language Issues

1. ■ *Study the following text and link the reference words to the words they refer to:*

The Rolls Royce Company was founded in 1906. It was the creation of two men, Henry Royce and Charles Rolls. The former was an engineer, the latter a salesman. When demand for their cars grew, they built a new factory at Derby. This was opened in 1908, and was expanded as sales increased. Today there is still a Rolls Royce factory there, but it now builds aircraft engines, not cars.

The Rolls Royce Company _____
Henry Royce _____
Charles Rolls _____
Henry Royce and Charles Rolls _____
a new factory _____
Derby _____

2. ■ *List eight situations where the definite article is always used (e.g. the dollar – currencies).*

3. ■ *Complete the following text by inserting a/an/the (or nothing) in each gap. (Note that in some cases more than one answer is possible).*

The origins of @

Giorio Stabile, a professor of a) _____ history at La Sapienza University in Rome, has demonstrated that b) _____ @ sign, now used in email addresses, was actually invented 500 years ago. Professor Stabile has shown that c) _____ @, now d) _____ symbol of e) _____ inter-net, was first used by f) _____ Italian merchants during g) _____ sixteenth century.

He claims that it originally represented h) _____ unit of volume, based

on i) _____ large jars used to carry liquids in j) _____ ancient

Mediterranean world. He has found k) _____ first example of its use in

l) _____ letter written in 1546 by m) _____ merchant from

Florence. n) _____ letter, which was sent to Rome, announces

o) _____ arrival in Spain of p) _____. ships carrying gold from

q) _____ South America.

4. ■ *Rewrite the paragraph, simplifying the numerical expressions.*

250 international students were interviewed about their experience of study abroad. Of this total 51 were from China, 48 from India, 24 from Nigeria and the rest were from a variety of European countries. 196 students were satisfied with their courses, but the other 54 had concerns about the quantity of work required. Just 25 complained about the quality of teaching. 124 students said they found it easy to adapt to a different culture and way of life, but of the others 39 disliked the food, 26 found the cost of living too expensive, and nine mentioned bad weather.

5. ■ *The following text is in the active voice. Change to the passive where appropriate.*

Our research aimed to find the best taxi business for campus use, so we compared the performance of six local taxi companies. We selected companies that had their offices within a kilometre of the campus. We timed the response of each company to requests made at the same time of day (7 p.m.). Response times varied from ten to 24 minutes. The passengers then asked each driver to take them to the railway station. They recorded the friendliness of the drivers and the length of time taken, as well as the fare the driver asked for. Overall we found that AZ Taxis had the fastest response and the cheapest fare, but not the most friendly driver.

6. ■ *Write two sentences, one active and one passive, using the information below.*

Google	1996	began	as a research project	by Page and Brin

7. ■ *Punctuate the text.*

the twentyfirst century has seen the rise of the so called bric economies brazil russia india and china the acronym was first used in a paper written by jim oneill in 2001 today it is clear that china and india are both powerful manufacturers while russia and brazil are mainly sources of raw materials

8. ■ *Choose the correct verb form in each sentence.*

a) Several types of response was/were recorded.

b) Three avenues of research were/was suggested.

c) One of the groups was/were eliminated from the competition.

d) Half the graduates were/was from Indonesia.

e) The government was/were defeated at the election.

f) The performance of the athletes were/was improved by his training method.

9. ■ *What are the three main aims of good academic style?*

10. ■ *Study Dr Gonzalez's schedule. Then complete the sentences with time markers. Today is 13 June.*

8 June   Fly to Berlin for conference

9 June   Give lecture at conference

10 June   Train to Prague

11 June   Meet colleagues at Charles University, Prague

12 June   Fly home

a) Dr Gonzalez went to Berlin five days ———————.

b) He was in Berlin ——————— two days.

c) ——————— his stay in Berlin he gave a lecture.

d) ——————— leaving Berlin he went to Prague.

e) ——————— staying in Prague he met colleagues at Charles University.

f) ——————— 10 June he had travelled 2,300 kilometres.

Vocabulary for Writing

International students may be understandably concerned by the quantity and complexity of vocabulary required for reading academic texts. But developing an effective vocabulary in English involves more than learning lists of words. These units, arranged alphabetically, provide a variety of approaches to improving students' understanding in this area, from learning abbreviations to recognising synonyms.

4.1 Approaches to Vocabulary

This unit examines some of the key issues students face when reading academic texts, such as processing new vocabulary, avoiding confusion with similar words and recognising phrases from other languages. Some of the vocabulary needed to discuss language features is also practised.

1. Vocabulary issues

■ The text below (part of a journal abstract) illustrates some of the vocabulary difficulties students experience when reading and writing academic texts. Read it carefully and underline any words or phrases you do not understand.

Drawing on insights from creativity theory, hypotheses on the relationship between a firm's HR practices and its ability to produce innovations are developed. We are not so much trying to push the frontier on creativity research, but use it as a framework to theorise on the relationship between innovation and strategic HRM and empirically relate HR practices to innovation.

Likely problems include:

hypotheses

HR/HRM

innovations

to push the frontier

empirically

■ Discuss the meaning of these with a partner.

These vocabulary issues are explained below:

Item	Issue	Meaning
hypotheses (plural noun)	semi-formal academic vocabulary	– theories that need to be tested
empirically (adverb)		– by observation or experience
innovations (plural noun)		– new methods or practices
HR/ HRM	abbreviations	– Human Resources/Management
to push the frontier	idiomatic phrase	– to expand the limits of knowledge

Building vocabulary is more than learning lists of 'words'. It is useful to adopt a critical approach, and focus on the most important items, such as those semi-formal academic items listed above.

▶ **See Unit 4.2 Abbreviations, 4.3 Academic Vocabulary: Nouns and Adjectives and 4.4 Academic Vocabulary: Verbs and Adverbs**

2. Dealing with new vocabulary

Instead of trying to learn all the new vocabulary you encounter, you should screen it to select which words are worth learning. It can be a mistake to attempt to learn too many new words: for most students subject-specific language will have priority. This can be seen as a process:

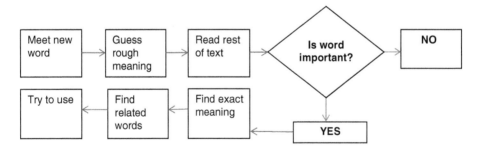

When you have selected a word or phrase to learn, make a note of its part of speech and any useful related words, along with its meaning:

    innovate (verb)   *– to introduce a new method*

    innovation (noun)   *– a new method*

You should also check the register of the word or phrase. Most vocabulary you read in academic work will be standard English, but 'empirically' is rather formal, while 'to push the frontier' is idiomatic. It is generally better to use standard English in your own written work.

3. Language features

The following words (all nouns) are used to describe common features of language.

■ **Discuss the words in the list with a partner. Try to think of another example for each.**

Ambiguity	Where more than one interpretation is possible; lack of clarity
	His feelings towards his old school were a mixture of love and hate.
Anecdote	A story told to illustrate a situation or idea
	At the beginning of the lecture Professor Chang told them about an accident she had seen that morning.
Cliché	An over-used idea or phrase; lacking in freshness
	Paris is the capital of romance; the city for lovers.
Euphemism	Word or phrase used to avoid naming something unpleasant directly
	The author of the report passed away on 21 November.
Idiom	Phrase used in colloquial speech, the meaning of which is not obvious
	He was over the moon when he won the scholarship.
Metaphor	A word used to describe something different from the original meaning
	He told the class that their new course was a voyage over an uncharted ocean.
Paradox	An idea that seems wrong but yet may be true
	She said that the older she got, the less she seemed to know.
Proverb	A traditional statement or rhyme containing advice or a moral
	It is said that the early bird catches the worm.
Saying	An often-repeated comment that seems to contain some truth
	There's no such thing as a free lunch, he warned them.
Simile	A comparison of two things, using 'like' or 'as'
	After the price rise, sales fell like a stone.
Slogan	A frequently-repeated phrase used in advertising or politics
	'Finger lickin' good' has sold millions of chicken meals.
Statement	A rather formal comment on a situation
	The President said she regretted the loss of life in the typhoon and sympathised with the survivors.
Synopsis	A summary of something
	Their teacher explained that the report consisted of two parts; the first an overview of the industry, the second a case study.

4. Confusing pairs

Certain common words can cause confusion because they have similar but distinct spellings and meanings:

*The drought **affected** the wheat harvest in Australia.*

*An immediate **effect** of the price rise was a fall in demand.*

'Affect' and 'effect' are two different words. 'Affect' is a verb, while 'effect' is commonly used as a noun.

■ **Study the differences between other similar confusing pairs (most common form of use in brackets).**

accept (verb)/except (prep)

*It is difficult to **accept** their findings.*
*The report is finished **except** for the conclusion.*

compliment (noun/ verb)/complement (verb)

*Her colleagues **complimented** her on her presentation.*
*His latest book **complements** his previous research on South African firms.*

economic (adj)/ economical (adj)

*Sharing a car to go to work was an **economical** move.*
*Inflation was one **economic** result of the war.*

its (possessive pronoun)/it's (subject pronoun + verb)

***It's** widely agreed that carbon emissions are rising.*
*The car's advanced design was **its** most distinct feature.*

led (verb – past tense of lead)/ lead (noun)

*His research **led** him to question the orthodox opinion.*
***Lead** (Pb) is a valuable mineral.*

lose (verb)/loose (adj)

*No general ever plans to **lose** a battle.*
*He stressed the **loose** connection between religion and psychology.*

principal (adj/noun)/ principle (noun)

*All economists recognise the **principle** of supply and demand.*
*Zurich is the **principal** city of Switzerland.*

rise (verb – past tense rose)/ raise (verb – past tense raised)

*The population of Sydney **rose** by 35% in the last century.*
*The university **raised** its fees by 10% last year.*

site (noun)/sight (noun)

> The **site** of the battle is now covered by an airport.
>
> His **sight** began to weaken when he was in his 80s.

tend to (verb)/trend (noun)

> Young children **tend to** enjoy making a noise.
>
> In many countries there is a **trend** towards smaller families.

■ Choose the correct word in each sentence.

a) The company was founded on the <u>principals/principles</u> of quality and value.

b) Millions of people are attempting to <u>lose/loose</u> weight.

c) Sunspots have been known to <u>affect/effect</u> radio communication.

d) Professor Poledna received their <u>compliments/complements</u> politely.

e) The ancient symbol depicted a snake eating <u>it's/its</u> tail.

f) Both social and <u>economical/economic</u> criteria need to be examined.

g) It took many years for some of Einstein's theories to be <u>accepted/excepted</u>.

h) The Eiffel tower is one of the most famous <u>sites/sights</u> in Paris.

5. Words and phrases from other languages

When reading academic texts you may meet words and phrases from other languages, usually Latin, German or French. They are generally used because there is no exact English equivalent, and they are often printed in italics:

> During her father's illness she was the *de facto* CEO.

You are not expected to use these phrases in your own writing, but it is useful to understand them when you read. They can be found in a dictionary, but some of the more common ones are listed below:

<u>Latin</u>

ad hoc	unplanned
de facto	as it really is
de jure	according to law
inter alia	among others
pro rata	proportional

<u>French</u>

à *propos de*	on the subject of
ancien régime	old ruling system
coup d' état	military take-over
déjà vu	sensation of having seen something before
fait accompli	accomplished fact
raison d'être	reason for living

<u>German</u>

Bildungsroman	a story of growing-up
Mitteleuropa	central Europe
Realpolitik	political reality
Schadenfreude	pleasure from another's misfortune
Weltanschauung	world view
Zeitgeist	spirit of the times

6. Practice

■ Look back over this unit. List the new vocabulary that you think is worth learning. Add any related words, note the meaning and an example. Try to use the words in conversation or writing where possible.

Word	Meaning	Example
Empirical – adj. *Empirically –adv.*	*Based on observation or experience.*	*In Europe, empirical research began in the sixteenth century.*

4.2 Abbreviations

> Abbreviations are an important and expanding feature of contemporary English, widely used for convenience and space-saving. Students need to be familiar with business, general and academic abbreviations.

1. Types of abbreviation

Abbreviations take the form of shortened words, acronyms or a set of letters, as shown below.

a) **Shortened words** are often used without the writer being aware of the original form. 'Bus' comes from 'omnibus', which is hardly used in modern English, and 'disco' is more common than 'discothèque', but 'refrigerator' is still better in written English than the informal 'fridge'. Yet 'lab' for 'laboratory', 'memo' for 'memorandum' and 'vet' for 'veterinary surgeon' are quite acceptable.

b) **Acronyms** are made up of the initial letters of a name or phrase (e.g. SWOT = Strengths, Weaknesses, Opportunities, Threats). They are pronounced as words. In some cases users have forgotten that these are acronyms and they are treated as ordinary words e.g. 'radar' comes from 'radio detection and ranging'.

c) **Other abbreviations** are read as sets of individual letters. They include names of countries, organisations and companies (USA/ BBC/ IBM), and also abbreviations which are only found in written English (e.g. PTO means 'please turn over'). Note that in many cases abbreviations are widely used without many users knowing what the individual letters stand for (e.g. DNA).

2. Business abbreviations

As with all academic subjects, Business and Economics employ abbreviations to save time and space. Common examples include:

AGM	annual general meeting
ATM	automated teller machine (cash machine)
B2B	business to business
CEO	chief executive officer
CV	curriculum vitae
DIY	do-it-yourself (retail sector)
EPS	earnings per share
GDP	gross domestic product
GNP	gross national product
HRM	human resource management
ICT	information and communications technology
IMF	International Monetary Fund
IPO	initial public offering
IOU	I owe you
M & A	mergers and acquisitions
OECD	Organisation for Economic Cooperation and Development
PLC	public limited company
PPP	purchasing power parity
PR	public relations
R & D	research and development
SOE	state-owned enterprise
SME	small or medium enterprise
RPI	retail prices index
TQM	total quality management
USP	unique selling point
VAT	value-added tax
VC	venture capital
WHO	World Health Organisation
WTO	World Trade Organisation

Depending on the area of study, it is also useful to be familiar with abbreviations for major companies and organisations, for example (in the UK):

BT	British Telecom
NHS	National Health Service
RBS	Royal Bank of Scotland
UCL	University College London

3. Common abbreviations

There are thousands of abbreviations in ordinary use, but these are frequently employed in an academic context.

ASAP	as soon as possible
BA	Bachelor of Arts
BCE	before the common era (previously BC)
BSc	Bachelor of Sciences
CAD	computer aided design
CE	common era (previously AD)
EU	European Union
FE	further education (non-university study above 18)
GM	genetically modified
HE	higher education (university study above 18)
LLB	Bachelor of Laws
MA	Master of Arts
MBA	Master of Business Administration
MSc	Master of Science
PG	postgraduate
PGCE	Postgraduate Certificate of Education
PhD	Doctor of Philosophy
UCAS	Universities and Colleges Admissions Service (UK)
UG	undergraduate
UN	United Nations
URL	uniform resource locator (website address)
VC	Vice-Chancellor

However, writers often employ more specialised, subject-specific abbreviations:

> *Starting from the **resource-based view** (RBV) of the firm, it is argued that ...*

> *The **Technology Readiness Index** (TRI) was introduced by Parasuraman (2000).*

Note that the first time a phrase is used it must be written in full, but on subsequent occasions the abbreviation can be used alone.

4. Punctuation

Many standard abbreviations have a full stop after them to show that they are a shortened form of a word (e.g. Wed. = Wednesday). Other examples are govt. (government), co. (company) and Oct. (October). With acronyms and other abbreviations it is now normal to write the letters without full stops e.g. BBC, ABS.

5. Duplicate abbreviations

Abbreviations can be confusing. PC, for example, may stand for 'personal computer' but also 'politically correct' or 'Police Constable'. It is useful to be aware of these potential confusions. A good dictionary should be used to understand more unusual abbreviations.

6. Abbreviations in writing

While all academic subjects have their own abbreviations, there are certain abbreviations common to most types of academic writing. They include:

anon.	anonymous (no author)
c.	*circa* (in dates – about)
cf.	compare
ed.	editor/ edition
e.g.	for example
et al.	and others (used for giving names of multiple authors)
etc.	*et cetera* (and so on – do not use this in formal academic work)
Fig.	figure (for labelling charts and graphs)
ibid.	in the same place (to refer to source mentioned immediately before)
i.e.	that is
K	thousand
NB:	take careful note
nd.	no date (i.e. an undated source)
No.	number
op. cit.	in the source mentioned previously
p.a.	yearly (per annum)
pp.	pages
PS	postscript
re:	with reference to
sic	in quotations, used to show a mistake in the original
vs	versus

NB: 'i.e.' and 'e.g.' are commonly confused. Study these examples:

*The world's largest company **i.e.** Walmart has reported increased profits.*

*Many of the world's largest companies **e.g.** BP are in the oil business.*

▶ **See Unit 1.8 References and Quotations, Unit 2.5 Examples and Unit 3.5 Punctuation**

7. Practice

■ Explain the abbreviations in the following sentences.

a) The failure rate among ICT projects in SOEs reaches 40% (Smith *et al.*, 2015).

b) The radio's USP was its retro style.

c) The world's most populous country (i.e. China) joined the WTO in 2001.

d) NB: CVs must be submitted to HR by 30 Sep.

e) See the OECD's recent report on the UAE.

f) The EU hopes to achieve a standard rate of VAT.

g) The CEO plans to raise spending on R & D next year.

h) Fig. 4 – Spanish GNP 2010–2019.

i) The MP claimed that the FE sector was underfunded.

j) Director of PR required – salary approx. $75K p.a.

k) Re: next month's AGM: the report is needed asap.

l) Dr Wang argued that the quality of MBA research was falling.

4.3 Academic Vocabulary

Nouns and Adjectives

> To read and write academic papers effectively students need to be familiar with the rather formal vocabulary widely used in this area. This unit focuses on nouns and adjectives; Unit 4.4 looks at verbs and adverbs.

1. Introduction

The quantity and complexity of vocabulary needed to read academic texts often concerns international students. But it is worth remembering that much of that vocabulary is specific to your subject area, for example in the sentence:

> *At the **employee level**, there has been a general **consensus** that **employee attitudes** and **performance** are positively **correlated**.*

'employee level' and 'employee attitudes' will be understood by Business students, while 'consensus' 'performance' and 'correlated' are general academic vocabulary which all students, including students of Business, need to understand.

2. Nouns

■ Study the following table of common academic nouns, with examples of use. With a partner, discuss the meaning of each noun.

accuracy	*Repeating the experiment will improve the **accuracy** of the results.*
analysis	*His **analysis** of the survey showed a low level of employee satisfaction.*
approach	*Professor Han has brought a new **approach** to the study of insurance.*

assessment	She failed the first module **assessment** but passed the final one.
assumption	He made the **assumption** that all the students spoke French.
authority	Dr James is our leading **authority** on labour law.
category	Her work established two **categories** of corporate governance.
claim	Their **claim** that the business was founded in the 1750s is false.
controversy	Climate change is an issue that has caused much **controversy**.
correlation	They found a **correlation** between height and wealth.
deterrent	Weak consumer demand acted as a **deterrent** to expansion.
emphasis	Their teacher put the **emphasis** on practical research.
evidence	The fall in profits provided **evidence** of his poor management.
exception	The Tesla is an **exception** to the idea of slow, small electric cars.
extract	He read a short **extract** from his paper on Adam Smith to the class.
ideology	Military power was at the heart of Roman **ideology**.
implication	The **implication** of the report is that we need to do more research.
innovation	Steam power was a significant **innovation** in the eighteenth century.
intuition	**Intuition** has been described as 'a gut feeling'.
motivation	Money is often claimed to be the primary **motivation** for most workers.
perspective	Sigmund Freud's work opened a new **perspective** on human behaviour.
phenomenon	Earthquakes are an unusual **phenomenon** in Britain.
	(NB: Irregular plural – phenomena)
policy	The university has a zero-tolerance **policy** on plagiarism.
preference	Her **preference** was criminal law, but other fields were more profitable.
process	The product evaluation **process** took two years.
proposal	The professor's **proposal** for more lectures was rejected.
provision	The library has increased its **provision** of computer terminals by 100%.
sequence	Writing is a **sequence** of reading, note-taking, planning and drafting.
strategy	His **strategy** for greater profitability involved several redundancies.
substitute	To what extent can natural gas be a **substitute** for oil?
technique	She developed a new **technique** for measuring innovation.
validity	Events confirmed the **validity** of his prediction.

■ Complete each sentence with a suitable noun.

a) The enquiry found no _____ of corruption in the tendering process.

b) The tutor asked the class for their _____ for next semester's topics.

c) Many great discoveries were based on _____ rather than logic.

d) Due to the rising birth rate _____ was made for more school places.

e) Few believed Galileo's _____ that the earth went round the sun.

f) Hurricanes and typhoons are both weather _____

g) The new _____ for making steel boosted production by 60%.

h) They looked for a _____ between birth month and longevity.

3. Nouns and adjectives

A simple way of expanding vocabulary is to learn related parts of speech. Many of the nouns in the list above have a corresponding adjective e.g. accuracy/accurate.

■ Write example sentences to show the meaning of the related adjectives given below.

accurate   *The arrival of railways created a demand for accurate timekeeping*

analytical

approachable

authoritative

controversial

emphatic

exceptional

ideological

innovative

intuitive

motivational

phenomenal

preferential

provisional

sequential

strategic

technical

valid

4. Confusing nouns and adjectives

It is easy to confuse the noun and adjective form of words such as 'possible' and 'possibility'.

■ **Compare these sentences:**

> The **efficiency** of the machine depends on the **precision** of its construction.

> **Precise** construction results in an **efficient** machine.

The first sentence uses the nouns 'efficiency' and 'precision'. The second uses the adjectives 'precise' and 'efficient'. Although the meaning is similar, the first sentence is more formal. Effective academic writing requires accurate use of both nouns and adjectives.

■ **Complete the gaps in the table below.**

Noun	Adjective	Noun	Adjective
approximation	approximate		particular
superiority		reason	
	strategic		synthetic
politics		economics/economy*	
	industrial		cultural
exterior		average	
	high		reliable
heat		strength	
	confident		true
width		probability	
	necessary		long
danger		relevance	

* Compare the three nouns:

Economics is a demanding undergraduate degree course.   (academic subject)

The Italian **economy** is heavily in debt.   (national economy, countable)

Economy is needed to reduce the deficit.   (saving money, uncountable)

5. Practice A

■ Insert a suitable noun or adjective from the table into each sentence.

a) The students were _____ their project would be successful.

b) One of Tokyo's _____ is its excellent transport system.

c) There is a strong _____ that fees will rise next year.

d) The students complained that the lecture was not _____ to their course.

e) The results are so surprising it will be _____ to repeat the experiment.

f) The _____ household size in Turkey is 4.1 people.

g) Regularly backing up computer files reduces the _____ of losing vital work.

h) Revising for exams is a tedious _____

i) These data appear to be _____ and should not be trusted.

j) The _____ sales figure for the last quarter is ten million.

k) The _____ consequences of the war were inflation and unemployment.

l) They attempted to make a _____ of all the different proposals.

6. Similar adjectives

Certain common adjectives have two forms, with slightly different meanings:

*High inflation is an **economic** problem.* (related to the economy)

*It is more **economical** to travel by bus than train.* (saving money)

*Martin Luther King made his **historic** speech in Washington.* (memorable or significant)

*Cleopatra was a **historical** character, born in 69 BCE.* (real person in past)

*The **electric** guitar was developed in the 1930s.* (worked by electricity)

***Electrical** engineering was a popular course.* (relating to electricity)

*The Aston Martin is a **classic** British sports car.* (fine example of a type)

***Classical** music is becoming more popular with the young.* (having traditional form)

7. Academic adjectives

The following adjectives are best understood and learnt as pairs of opposites:

absolute	*relative*
abstract	*concrete*
accurate	*inaccurate*
ambiguous	*unambiguous*
analytic	*synthetic*
effective	*ineffective*
exclusive	*inclusive*
logical	*illogical*
metaphorical	*literal*
precise	*vague* or *approximate* or *rough*
rational	*irrational*
reliable	*unreliable*
relevant	*irrelevant*
specific	*non-specific*
subjective	*objective*
theoretical	*practical* or *empiric* or *pragmatic*

*Inflation is an **abstract** concept.*

*The **metaphorical** use of the word 'key' is probably more common than its **literal** one.*

*The study of mathematics is highly **relevant** to economics.*

*Her paper on women in management was criticised for being too **subjective**.*

8. Practice B

■ Complete each sentence with a suitable adjective from the table above.

a) The teacher complained that the quotes were _____ to the title.

b) His _____ approach led him to ignore some inconvenient facts.

c) _____ examples are needed to make the argument clear.

d) It is sufficient to give _____ figures for national populations.

e) Poverty is usually regarded as a _____ concept.

f) They approached the task in a _____ way by first analysing the title.

g) The students preferred examining case studies to _____ discussion.

h) The results were _____: the fire had been started deliberately.

9. Practice C

■ Underline the adjective in each sentence and write the related noun in brackets.

Example:
Several steel producers are <u>likely</u> to shut down next year. (likelihood)

a) The HR team have just completed a strategic review of pay. (_____)

b) Dr Lee adopted an analytical approach to the inquiry. (_____)

c) Nylon was one of the earliest synthetic fibres. (_____)

d) Her major contribution to the research was in developing a model. (_____)

e) All advertising must respect cultural differences. (_____)

f) Some progress was made in the theoretical area. (_____)

g) A frequent complaint is that too much reading is expected. (_____)

h) We took a more critical approach to marketing theory. (_____)

i) The Department of Social Policy is offering three courses this year. (_____)

j) Finally, the practical implications of my findings will be examined. (_____)

Students wishing to develop their academic vocabulary should study the Academic Word List (AWL). This is a list of 570 items commonly found in academic texts across various disciplines, created by Averil Coxhead.

See: https://canvas.bham.ac.uk/courses/12947/pages/vocabulary-and-the-academic-word-list for links to various websites on this subject.

Academic Vocabulary

Verbs and Adverbs

When reading a text it is useful to identify and understand the main verb: this is often the key to understanding the whole sentence. This unit looks at the more formal verbs used in academic writing, the verbs of reference used to introduce summaries, and outlines the use of adverbs.

1. Understanding main verbs

■ Study the following sentence and underline the main verbs:

The government has consistently encouraged entrepreneurship through courses in schools and colleges, and has considerably reduced the barriers to starting a business by eliminating bureaucratic requirements.

To follow the writer's meaning, the reader needs to be clear that 'encouraged' and 'reduced' are the main verbs in the two parts of the sentence.

■ Underline the verbs in the following:

We empirically distinguish between three types of customer satisfaction and examine the impact of employee attitudes on each component of customer satisfaction. In doing so, we improve our understanding of how employee attitudes affect customer satisfaction.

Academic writing tends to use rather formal verbs to express the writer's meaning accurately:

*In the last decade the pace of change has **accelerated**.*

*Could Keynes have **envisaged** the controversy his work would cause?*

In spoken English we are more likely to use 'speed up' and 'imagined'.

2. Common academic verbs

■ Study the list below and find a synonym in each case.

(Some of these verbs e.g. 'hold' are used in academic writing with a special meaning).

Verb	Example of use	Synonym
to adapt	the tax system has been **adapted** from Norway	*modified*
to arise	a similar situation **arises** when we look at new businesses	
to conduct	the largest study was **conducted** in Finland	
to characterise	developing countries are **characterised** by ...	
to clarify	the project was designed to **clarify** these contradictions	
to concentrate on	that study **concentrated on** female managers	
to be concerned with	the programme is **concerned** primarily **with** ...	
to demonstrate	further research has **demonstrated** that few factors ...	
to determine	the water content was experimentally **determined**	
to discriminate	a failure to **discriminate** between the two systems	
to establish	the firm was **established** in 1879	
to exhibit	half of the businesses **exhibited** signs of improvement	
to focus on	her work **focused on** short-term loans	
to generate	a question which has **generated** a range of responses	
to hold	Newton's second Law, F=ma, **holds** everywhere	
to identify	three main areas have been **identified**	
to imply	his absence **implies** a lack of interest	
to interact	understand how the two systems **interact**	
to interpret	the result can be **interpreted** as a limited success	
to manifest	as **manifested** in more business failures	
to overcome	both difficulties were **overcome** in the first week	
to propose	they **propose** that social class is the main factor	
to prove	the use of solar power is **proving** successful	
to recognise	he is now **recognised** as a leading expert	
to relate to	the pattern was **related to** both social and physical factors	
to supplement	the research was **supplemented** with a survey	
to undergo	the system **underwent** major changes in the 1980s	
to yield	both programmes **yielded** mixed results	

▶ See Unit 4.7.7 Verbs and prepositions

3. Using verbs of reference

Referring verbs are used to summarise another writer's ideas:

> *Previn **argued** that interest rates were too low.*

> *Bakewell (1992) **found** that most managers tended to use traditional terms.*

They may also be used to introduce a quotation.

> *As Scott **observed**: 'Comment is free but facts are sacred'.*

Most of these verbs are followed by a noun clause beginning with 'that'.

a) The following mean that the writer is presenting a case:

argue   claim   consider   hypothesise   suggest   believe   think   state

> *Melville (2007) **suggested** that tax rates should be harmonised.*

b) A second group describe a reaction to a previously stated position:

accept   admit   agree with   deny   doubt

> *Handlesmith **doubts** Melville's suggestion that tax rates should be harmonised.*

c) Others include:

assume   conclude   discover   explain   imply
indicate   maintain   presume   reveal   show

> *Patel (2013) **assumes** that inflation will remain low.*

4. Practice A

■ Write a sentence referring to what the following writers said (more than one verb may be suitable). Make sure you use the past tense.

Example:

> Z: 'My research shows that biofuels are environmentally neutral'.
> Z **claimed/argued** that biofuels were environmentally neutral.

a) A: 'I may have made a mistake in my calculations of the cost of living'.

b) B: 'I did not say that women make better economists than men'.

c) C: 'Small firms are more dynamic than large ones'.

d) D: 'I support C's views on small firms'.

e) E: 'I'm not sure, but most people probably work to earn money'.

f) F: 'After much research, I've found that family firms are more efficient'.

g) G: 'I think it unlikely that electric cars will replace conventional ones'.

h) H: 'There may be a link between age and entrepreneurial ability'.

5. Further verbs of reference

A small group of verbs is followed by the pattern (**somebody/thing + for + noun/gerund**):

blame   censure   commend   condemn   criticise

*Lee (1998) **blamed** the media for creating uncertainty.*

NB: all except 'commend' have a negative meaning.

Another group is followed by (**somebody/thing + as + noun/gerund**):

assess   characterise   classify   define   describe

evaluate   identify   interpret   portray   present

*Terry **interpreted** rising oil prices as a result of the Asian recovery.*

▶ **See Unit 1.8.3 Reference verbs**

6. Practice B

■ Rewrite the following statements using verbs from the lists in Section 5.

Example:

> K: 'Guttman's work is responsible for many of the current social problems'.
> K **blamed** Guttman's work for many of the current social problems.

a) L: 'She was very careless about her research methods'.

b) M: 'There are four main types of long-term investments'.

c) N: 'That company has an excellent record for workplace safety'.

d) O: 'Falling unemployment must be a sign of economic recovery'.

e) P: 'Wind power and biomass will be the leading green energy sources of the future'.

f) Q: 'Adam Smith was the most influential economist of the eighteenth century'.

7. Using adverbs

In the sentence in Section 1, adverbs are used to give information about time (consistently) and degree (considerably).

> *The government has **consistently** encouraged entrepreneurship through courses in schools and colleges, and has **considerably** reduced the barriers to starting a business by eliminating bureaucratic requirements.*

1. Adverbs are used in academic writing in a variety of ways. Among the most important are:

    a) to provide more detail, with verbs and adjectives:

    > ***Reasonably*** *good data are available for only the first two years.*

    > *Economists **traditionally** argue for import controls.*

    b) individually, often at the beginning of sentences, to introduce new points or link sentences together:

    > ***Currently***, *the Earth's atmosphere appears to be warming up.*

    > ***Alternatively***, *the use of non-conventional renewable energies is worth exploring.*

    NB: adverbs used individually need to be employed with care. It is dangerous to over-use them, since they can be like the author's 'voice'; commenting on the topic. As an academic writer aims to be objective, adverbs such as 'fortunately' or 'remarkably' may be unsuitable.

2. Adverbs linked to verbs and adjectives usually fall into three groups.

    a) Time (when?)

    > ***previously*** *published*

    > ***retrospectively*** *examined*

    b) Degree (how much?)

    > *declined **considerably***

    > *contribute **substantially***

    c) Manner (in what way?)

    > ***financially*** *complicated*

    > ***remotely*** *located*

Further common examples include:

Time	Degree	Manner
recently	*clearly*	*(un)surprisingly*
increasingly	*particularly*	*factually*
originally	*broadly*	*politically*
presently	*highly*	*locally*
currently	*wholly*	*alternatively*
traditionally	*crucially*	*similarly*
continuously	*emphatically*	*psychologically*

▶ **See Unit 3.4.4 Adverbs with passives**

8. Practice C

▣ Insert suitable adverbs from the table above into the gaps in the sentences.

a) Most houses do not have electricity. _____, then, there is little chance of improving living standards.

b) _____, the internet was mainly used for academic purposes.

c) Some courses are assessed purely by exams. _____, coursework may be employed.

d) _____, there has been growing concern about financing the health service.

e) There was strong opposition _____ to building the dam.

f) _____, the development should be acceptable environmentally.

g) Despite some disagreement, the team were _____ united on the next step.

h) Although _____ correct, many details were missing from the report.

9. Practice D

▣ Complete the text by inserting a suitable adverb from the box into each gap.

virtually   conventionally   basically   originally   recently   illicitly   significantly

substantially

Locking up

_____, the earliest keys were made by the Egyptians from wood, and

_____ improved by the Romans, who used metal. Today's keys are

_____ the same: a piece of metal with teeth, _____ produced by

cutting and stamping. But _____ a new technology, 3D printing, has made

it possible to manufacture much more intricate designs which are _____

impossible to copy _____. Although _____ more expensive,

these hi-tech keys offer remarkable security.

Conjunctions

4.5

Conjunctions are words or phrases which join sections of text together. Effective reading and writing requires clarity about the specific meaning of conjunctions. This unit describes the different functions of conjunctions and practises their use. Other ways of linking sections of text are explained in Unit 3.1 Cohesion.

1. How conjunctions work

When reading a text, conjunctions are like signposts, helping the reader to follow the ideas.

■ **Read the paragraph below and study the functions of the conjunctions (in bold).**

BIOFUELS

Newly published research examines some important questions about the growing use of biofuels, **such as** ethanol made from maize. The production of these has increased sharply recently, **but** the replacement of food crops with fuel crops has been heavily criticised. **Although** initially seen as a more environmentally-friendly type of fuel, the research shows that producing some biofuels, **for instance** biodiesel palm oil, is more polluting than using conventional oil. The ethanol produced from sugar cane, **however**, can have negative emissions, **in other words** taking carbon dioxide from the atmosphere, which is a beneficial process. **Consequently**, it can be seen that the situation is rather confused, **and** that biofuels are **neither** a magical solution to the energy problem, **nor** are they the environmental disaster sometimes suggested.

Note that some conjunctions link parts of sentences together:

> *The production of these has increased sharply recently,* **but** *the replacement of food crops with fuel crops has been heavily criticised.*

While others join a new sentence to the previous one:

> *… carbon dioxide from the atmosphere, which is a beneficial process.* **Consequently,** *it can be seen that the situation is rather confused …*

2. Types of conjunctions

Note the way conjunctions work in the following sentences:

> *Demand for food is increasing* **because** *the population is growing.*

> *Mechanisation has increased crop yields,* **yet** *production is still inadequate.*

In the first sentence 'because' introduces a reason, in the second 'yet' indicates opposition between the two parts of the sentence.

■ Underline the conjunctions in the following sentences.

a) A few inventions, for instance the internet, have had a major impact on everyday life.

b) Furthermore, many used cars are sold through dealerships.

c) The definition of 'motivation' is important since it is the cause of some disagreement.

d) The technology allows consumers a choice, thus increasing their sense of satisfaction.

e) Four hundred people were interviewed for the survey; then the results were analysed.

f) However, another body of opinion associates globalisation with unfavourable outcomes.

■ There are six main types of conjunction. Match each of the types below to one of the sentences above.

i) Addition (*b*)

ii) Result (_____)

iii) Reason (_____)

iv) Opposition (_____)

v) Example (_____)

vi) Time (_____)

■ Read the paragraph on biofuels above and decide what the function of each conjunction is (i.e. types i–vi above).

Conjunction	Type	Conjunction	Type
a) *such as*	*example*	f)	
b)		g)	
c)		h)	
d)		i)	
e)			

▶ See Unit 2.2 Cause and Effect

3. Common conjunctions

■ Working with a partner, complete the table with as many examples of conjunctions as possible.

Addition	Result	Reason	Opposition	Example	Time
and	*consequently*	*since*	*yet*	*such as*	*then*

4. Practice A

■ Insert a suitable conjunction into each gap.

a) _____ checking the equipment the experiment was repeated.

b) _____ most people use the train, a minority walk or cycle.

c) Brick is a thermally efficient building material. It is, _____, cheap.

d) Demand has increased for summer courses, _____ extra ones are offered this year.

e) Many writers, _____ Chekhov, have also been doctors.

f) _____ the increase in residence fees more students are moving out.

g) _____ teaching at the Sorbonne she was writing a novel.

h) _____ he was studying Italian he spent a semester in Bologna.

5. Practice B

■ Insert a suitable conjunction into each gap.

Geoengineering

Geoengineers believe that it may be possible to counteract the effects of global warming by large-scale engineering projects, a) _____ the 'solar umbrella' designed to reflect sunlight back into space. b) _____ no major schemes have yet been attempted, there is already controversy about the risks involved.

Two quite different approaches are suggested: to block incoming sunlight, c) _____ alternatively to take carbon dioxide out of the atmosphere. One proposal, d) _____, consists of putting iron into the sea e) _____ to encourage the growth of the tiny sea creatures which absorb carbon dioxide. f) _____ this second approach is unlikely to create major problems, blocking sunlight is potentially dangerous, g) _____ the risk of affecting rainfall patterns h) _____ even ocean currents. i) _____ bioengineers are anxious to establish clear guidelines before any large-scale experiments are carried out.

6. Confusing conjunctions

In a few cases conjunctions have two meanings:

While there were risks with the drug, he thought they were minor. (opposition)

While listening to the lecture she was planning the essay. (time)

He has been in Washington since Tuesday. (time)

Since she couldn't read Russian she had the paper translated. (reason)

7. Conjunctions of opposition

In some ways these are the most important type of conjunction, and can be the most difficult to use accurately. Note the position of the conjunctions in the following sentences:

Although/While there are frequent strikes the economy is strong.

In spite of/Despite the frequent strikes the economy is strong.

There are frequent strikes. *However/Nevertheless,* the economy is strong.

The economy is strong, *but/yet* there are frequent strikes.

■ Make sentences using conjunctions of opposition.

Example: expensive/unreliable

The equipment was expensive but unreliable.

Although the equipment was expensive it was unreliable.

relevant/limited   interesting/ambiguous amusing/subjective old-fashioned/effective

a) _____

b) _____

c) _____

d) _____

8. Practice C

■ Finish the sentences in a suitable way.

a)   In contrast to America, where gun ownership is common,

b)   Despite leaving school at the age of 14

c)   The majority displayed a positive attitude to the proposal, but

d)   While the tutor insisted that the essay was easy,

e)   Although the spring was cold and dry

f)   He finished the project before the deadline, yet

g)   She usually speaks French, nevertheless

h)   He preferred to travel by train. Flying, however

4.6 Prefixes and Suffixes

Prefixes and suffixes are the first and last parts of certain words. Understanding the meaning of prefixes and suffixes can help you work out the meaning of a word, and is particularly useful when you meet specialist new vocabulary.

1. How prefixes and suffixes work

'Unsustainable' is an example of a word containing a prefix and suffix. Words like this are much easier to understand if you know how prefixes and suffixes affect word meaning.

Prefixes change or give the meaning.

Suffixes show the meaning or the word class (e.g. noun, verb).

Prefix	Meaning	STEM	Meaning	Suffix	Word class/Meaning
un-	negative	**sustain**	support	**-able**	adjective/ability

*The rate of growth was **unsustainable** (i.e. could not be continued).*

■ Study the meaning of the words in bold:

Prefabrication of the flats speeded up the building process.

He was revitalised by the holiday in the mountains.

Prefix	Meaning	STEM	Meaning	Suffix	Word class
pre-	before	**fabric**	manufacture	**-ation**	noun
re-	again	**vital**	full of life	**-ise**	verb

2. Prefixes

a) Negative prefixes: non-, un-, in-, im-, mis-, de- and dis- often give adjectives and verbs a negative meaning:

nonsense, unclear, incapable, impossible, mishear, decrease, disagree

NB: There are a few exceptions e.g. 'invaluable' means very useful.

b) A wide variety of prefixes define meaning e.g. pre- usually means 'before', hence

prefer, prehistory and, of course, *prefix*!

Common prefixes of meaning

■ Find the meaning(s) of each prefix (NB: some prefixes have more than one meaning).

Prefix	Example	Example	Meaning
anti	antidepressant	**Antidepressant** drugs are often over-prescribed.	*against*
auto	automatically	Over-18s **automatically** have the right to vote.	
co	co-ordinator	The **co-ordinator** invited them to a meeting.	
ex	ex-president	The **ex-president** gave a speech on climate change.	
ex	exclusive	It is difficult to join such an **exclusive** club.	
fore	forecast	The long-term **forecast** is for higher inflation.	
inter	intervention	Government **intervention** in the market is needed.	
macro	macroeconomics	Keynes focused on **macroeconomics**.	
micro	microscope	She examined the tiny animals with a **microscope**.	
multi	multinational	Ford is a **multinational** motor company.	
non	nonfiction	They specialise in publishing **nonfiction**.	
over	oversleep	He missed the lecture because he **overslept**.	
poly	polyglot	She was a true **polyglot**, speaking five languages.	
post	promote	The meeting is **postponed** until next Monday.	
re	retrain	The firm **retrained** staff to use the new software.	
sub	subtitle	Chinese films often have **subtitles** in the West.	
tele	televise	Parliament was first **televised** in 1989.	
trans	transmitter	Early radio **transmitters** were short-range.	
under	undergraduate	Most **undergraduate** courses last three years.	
under	undervalue	Buying **undervalued** assets can be profitable.	

3. Practice A

Prefixes allow new words to be created e.g. 'unfriend' (to delete a 'friend' from social media).

■ **Suggest possible meanings for the recently developed words in bold.**

   a)   Criminal activity seems to be very common among the **underclass**.

   b)   Some passengers found the plane was **overbooked** and had to wait for the next flight.

   c)   The **microclimate** in this district allows early vegetables to be grown.

   d)   It is claimed that computers have created a **post-industrial** economy.

   e)   Most film stars have **ex-directory** phone numbers.

   f)   The class was **underwhelmed** by the quality of the lecture.

   g)   The couple decided to draw up a **prenuptial** agreement.

   h)   The company is looking for a **proactive** manager.

   NB: It can be difficult to decide whether to use a hyphen with a prefix e.g. 'co-operate' or 'cooperate'?

▶   **See Unit 3.5.8 Punctuation**

4. Suffixes

a)   Some suffixes like -ion, -ive or -ly help the reader find the word class e.g. noun, adjective or adverb.

b)   Other suffixes add to meaning e.g. -ful or -less after an adjective have a positive or negative effect (thought**ful**/care**less**).

Word class suffixes

Nouns	-er often indicates a role: *teacher, gardener* -ee can show a person who is the subject: *employee, trainee* -ism and -ist are often used with belief systems and their supporters: *socialism/socialist* -ness converts an adjective into a noun: *sad/sadness* -ion changes a verb to a noun: *convert/conversion*
Adjectives	-ive *effective, constructive* -al *commercial, agricultural* -ious *precious, serious*

Verbs	-ise/-ize to form verbs from adjectives: *private/privatise* NB: in the USA only -ize spelling is used, but both forms are accepted in the UK
Adverbs	-ly most (but not all) adverbs have this suffix: *happily*

Meaning suffixes

A few suffixes contribute to the meaning of the word:

–   ABLE has the meaning of 'ability': *a **watchable** film, **changeable** weather*
–   WARDS means 'in the direction of': *the ship sailed **northwards**, he walked **homewards***
–   ful and -less: ***hopeful** news, a **leaderless** team*

5. Practice B

■   **Give the word class for the following:**

a)   cancellation   f)   unpredictable
b)   coincidental   g)   saleable
c)   uncooperatively   h)   interviewee
d)   evolutionary   i)   consumerism
e)   protesters   j)   symbolically

■   **Complete each sentence with one of the words above.**

i)   The police arrested dozens of _____ in the main square.

ii)   Her new book proved very _____ and was reprinted twice.

iii) The hurricane's arrival and the climate change conference were

      _____

iv)   All the _____ were asked to watch a video on the company's plans.

v)   He claimed that the firm's growth was an _____ process.

vi)   The country's flag _____ links the different races.

6. Practice C

▓ Study each sentence and find synonyms for the words underlined.

Example: The film is an Anglo-Italian <u>coproduction</u> made by a <u>subsidiary</u> company.

joint production/subordinate

a)   When the car crashed she screamed <u>involuntarily</u> but was <u>unharmed</u>.

b)   Using <u>rechargeable</u> batteries has <u>undoubted</u> benefits for the environment.

c)   They <u>rearranged</u> the <u>preschool</u> tests.

d)   The <u>unavailability</u> of the product is due to the <u>exceptional</u> weather.

e)   The <u>miscommunication</u> led to a <u>re-organisation</u> of their software system.

f)   Her <u>incorrect</u> pronunciation was <u>laughable</u>.

g)   He was told to <u>rewrite</u> his <u>unreadable</u> essay.

▶   **See Unit 4.3 Academic Vocabulary: Nouns and Adjectives**

Prepositions

Prepositions are generally short words such as 'by' or 'at', which have a variety of uses. This unit explains how they can be understood and learnt, by linking them to nouns, adjectives and verbs. Students should consult a standard English grammar book for a full list of prepositional combinations.

1. Using prepositions

a) Many international students find the use of prepositions confusing. This is partly because, although they are mainly short words, a different preposition can change the meaning of a sentence.

■ **Compare:**

*Essays must be handed in **on** 15 January.*

*Essays must be handed in **by** 15 January.*

In the first sentence essays have to be submitted on the exact date, but in the second the date is the final deadline and essays can be submitted earlier.

b) ■ **Study the use of prepositions in the following text:**

Satisfying customers is **critical to** a firm's success. **In the last decade** a substantial **body of** research **in management** has **focused on** the **relationship between** employee attitudes and customer satisfaction, with most studies suggesting that positive employee attitudes **lead to** customer satisfaction. But **in general** the causal mechanisms have rarely been made explicit. **In this section**, we review the **findings of** empirical research **in this area**.

c) ■ The table lists the main ways of using prepositions. Find examples of each in the text.

Noun + preposition	*body of*
Verb + preposition	_____
Adjective + preposition	_____
Preposition of place	_____
Preposition of time	_____
Phrase	_____

Note that prepositions linked to nouns, verbs and adjectives often follow the word they are connected with, while prepositions of time and place generally come before the word.

2. Practice A

■ Study these further examples of prepositional use and decide on their type.

a)   There are a number **of** limitations to be considered.   (*noun +* _____)

b)   The results would be applicable **to** all employees.   (_____)

c)   The data were gathered **from** a questionnaire.   (_____)

d)   All the items were placed **within** their categories.   (_____)

e)   The results **of** the investigation are still pertinent. (_____)

f)   The respondents had spent **on** average 4.9 years ...   (_____)

g)   Most countries **in** sub-Saharan Africa ...   (_____)

h)   **Within** a short spell of four years he had ...   (_____)

3. Prepositions and nouns

■ Insert a suitable preposition into the sentences below.

a)   Evidence is presented in support _____ the value of women's work.

b)   A small change _____ demand can lead to large price fluctuations.

c)   Many examples _____ tax evasion were found.

d)   The answer _____ the problem was 0.585.

e)   The head _____ the council has just resigned.

f)   The second point is their impact _____ developing countries.

4. Prepositions in phrases

◼ Complete the following phrases with the correct preposition.

a) _____ the whole

e) in support _____

b) point _____ view

f) _____ the other hand

c) in respect _____

g) _____ order to

d) _____ spite of

h) standard _____ living

5. Prepositions of place and time

Note the difference between 'among' and 'between':

Among 14 students in the class, only two were from Africa. (large group)

He divided his time between the offices in Barcelona and Madrid. (limited number)

◼ Complete the following sentences with suitable prepositions of place or time.

a) _____ the respondents, few had any experience of working abroad.

b) The illiteracy rate declined gradually _____ 1995 _____ 2015.

c) Most workers _____ the European Union retire before the age _____ 60.

d) Adam Smith was born _____ Scotland _____ 1723.

e) Chocolate sales fall _____ summer and peak _____ Christmas.

f) _____ the surface, there is no difference _____ male and female responses.

g) The countries _____ the Mediterranean held a meeting _____ 20 May.

h) _____ 15 and 20 students study marine insurance every year.

▶ See Unit 3.8 Time Markers

6. Practice B

◼ Complete the following text with suitable prepositions.

This study attempts to answer the controversial question a) _____ whether increased food supply b) _____ a country makes a significant contribution

c) _____ reducing malnutrition d) _____ children. It uses data col-

lected e) _____ 75 countries f) _____ 2005 and 2015. The findings

are that there was a considerable improvement g) _____ the majority

h) _____ countries, despite increases in population i) _____ the

period. However, a clear distinction was found j) _____ the poorest coun-

tries (e.g. k) _____ South Asia), where the improvement was greatest, and

the wealthier states such as those l) _____ North Africa. Other factors, nota-

bly the educational level m) _____ women, were also found to be critical

n) _____ improving childhood nutrition.

7. Verbs and prepositions

The following verbs are generally used with these prepositions:

Verb + prep.	Example
add to	The bad weather **added to** the team's difficulties.
agree with	Yu (2012) **agrees with** Martin and Jenks (2000).
associate with	Monetarism is an economic policy **associated with** Mrs Thatcher.
believe in	The survey showed that 65% **believed in** Keynesian theory.
blame for	He **blamed** unfair questions **for** his poor exam results.
concentrate on (*also: focus on*)	She dropped all her hobbies to **concentrate on** her work.
consist of	Parliament **consists of** two Houses: the Commons and the Lords.
depend on (*also: rely on*)	The company **depends on** ITC for a rapid flow of sales data.
derive from	Modern computers **derive from** wartime decoding machines.
divide into	Trees are **divided into** two main types: conifers and deciduous trees.
invest in	Far more money needs to be **invested in** training programmes.
learn from	All successful students **learn from** their mistakes.
pay for	Goods delivered in April must be **paid for** by 30 June.
point out	Goodson (2001) **points out** the dangers of over-generalisation.
specialise in	This department **specialises in** entrepreneurial research.

8. Practice C

■ Complete the following with suitable verbs and prepositions.

a) The enquiry _____ the cause of the accident, not the consequences.

b) Dr Cracknell _____ that there were only two weeks before the deadline.

c) After graduating he _____ designing security software.

d) Albert Einstein is commonly _____ the theory of relativity.

e) A football pitch is _____ two halves.

f) A series of strikes were _____ the decline in production during May.

g) Millions of men died for the cause they _____

h) She _____ French _____ her mother, who came from Rouen.

Synonyms

4.8

Synonyms are different words with a similar meaning, such as 'figures' and 'numbers'. A good writer uses synonyms to avoid repetition and thus provide more interest for the reader. Synonyms should also be used when paraphrasing or note-making to avoid plagiarism.

1. How synonyms work

■ Underline the synonyms in the following text and complete the table.

Royal Dutch Shell is the <u>largest</u> oil company in the world by revenue, with a significant share of the global hydrocarbon market. The <u>giant</u> firm employs over 100,000 people internationally, including over 8,000 employees in Britain. Shell produces about 13% of the UK's oil and gas.

Word/phrase	Synonym
largest	*giant*
oil	
company	
in the world	
people	
Britain	

a) Synonyms are not always exactly the same in meaning, so that in the example above 'employees' is more specific than 'people'. It is important not to change the register: 'firm' is a good synonym for 'company', but 'boss' is too informal to use for 'manager'. The table illustrates the validity of some synonyms for 'company':

Possible synonyms for 'company'	Validity
firm	Good
business	Used generally for small and medium companies
concern	Rather informal
enterprise	Suggests a small entrepreneurial business
corporation	Used generally for larger companies
organisation	Can be also used for non-commercial bodies

b) Many common words e.g. culture, economy, or industry have no effective synonyms.

2. Common synonyms in academic writing

■ Match the academic synonyms in each list.

Nouns		Verbs	
area	advantage	accelerate	**take apart**
authority	part	alter	help
behaviour	argument	**analyse**	question
benefit	disadvantage	assist	change
category	tendency	attach	explain
component	**field**	challenge	evolve
controversy	source	clarify	examine
difficulty	emotion	concentrate on	establish
drawback	target	conduct	insist
expansion	explanation	confine	speed up
feeling	conduct	develop	join
framework	topic	evaluate	decrease
goal	possibility	found	demonstrate
interpretation	production	maintain	increase
issue	research	predict	reinforce
method	increase	prohibit	focus on
option	figures	raise	forecast

Nouns		Verbs	
results	type	reduce	ban
statistics	structure	respond	carry out
study	system	retain	limit
trend	findings	show	keep
output	problem	strengthen	reply

NB: these pairs are commonly synonymous, but not in every situation.

3. Practice A

■ Find synonyms for the words and phrases underlined, rewriting the sentences where necessary.

    a)   Professor Hicks questioned the findings of the research.

    b)   The statistics show a steady increase in applications.

    c)   The institute's prediction has caused a major controversy.

    d)   Cost seems to be the leading drawback to that system.

    e)   They will concentrate on the first option.

    f)   After the lecture she tried to clarify her concept.

    g)   Three issues need to be examined.

    h)   The framework can be retained but the goal needs to be altered.

    i)   OPEC, the oil producers' cartel, is to cut production to raise global prices.

    j)   The trend to smaller families has speeded up in the last decade.

4. Practice B

■ Identify the synonyms in this text by underlining them and linking them to the word they are substituting for.

Example: pets – domestic animals

Keeping pets has become increasingly popular in wealthier countries. In America 95% of owners of domestic animals say that they regard them as part of their family. Since most people in Asian cities live in flats, felines are more popular there, as they require less care from urban apartment dwellers. Alongside this trend is the growth of businesses that cater for dogs and cats. Specialist companies offer a huge variety of pet foods, including canine ice cream and vegan fare, while luxurious pet hotels pamper their guests in South Korea. But there is debate about the benefits of keeping animals in the home: there seems little evidence that domestic owners gain any tangible advantages from owning pets, though it is clear that the animals themselves do.

5. Practice C

■ In the following text, replace all the words or phrases in bold type with suitable synonyms.

Many motor manufacturers are currently introducing electric cars. Their aim is to **manufacture cars** which are cheaper to run and less polluting. But these **motor manufacturers** face several key difficulties. One **key difficulty** is the limited range of the battery, while another **difficulty** is its cost and weight. But the **motor manufacturers** predict that these **difficulties** will soon be overcome and **predict** that 20% of cars will be powered by electricity in five years' time. However, electrical **power** must be generated by something, and unless it is **generated** by renewables (e.g. wind or solar power) such **cars** may not be as 'green' as their makers claim.

▶ See Unit 1.7 Summarising and Paraphrasing

Progress
Check 4

These exercises will help you assess your understanding of Part 4 – Vocabulary for Writing.

1. ■ *Which of the following should be avoided in academic writing?*

   a) a cliché   b) a synopsis   c) a proverb   d) an idiom

2. ■ *Choose the correct form in each sentence.*

   a) The Democratic Liberal Party may lose/loose the election.

   b) I finished the essay accept/except for the conclusion.

   c) The site/sight of the accident was guarded by police.

   d) Mint can be a good complement/compliment to lamb.

3. ■ *Explain the following:*

   a) The IMF has revised its GDP forecast for next year.

   b) Their IPO was valued at £350 million after trading opened on the LSE.

   c) His 200 pp. MSc dissertation was on cryptocurrencies.

4. ■ *Give the opposite adjectives:*

   a) relative

   b) literal

   c) objective

   d) vague

   e) concrete

5. ■ *Find the nouns related to these adjectives:*

   a) high

   b) synthetic

   c) long

   d) probable

   e) relevant

6. ■ *Rewrite the sentences using verbs of reference.*

   a) X: I have found that eating spiders keeps you healthy.

   b) Y: I don't agree with X's theory; it is based on poor research.

   c) Z: I support Y's opinion of X's work.

7. ■ *Add a suitable adverb from the box to each sentence.*

   rarely   particularly   traditionally   locally   increasingly   continuously   obviously

   a) The site of London has been occupied _____ since Roman times.

   b) As central government was weak, decisions were taken _____

   c) In the past, there was a high mortality rate among children, _____ the youngest.

   d) Young adults are _____ delaying marriage until their late 20s.

   e) _____, becoming a carpenter required a seven-year apprenticeship.

8. ■ *Complete the paragraph with suitable conjunctions.*

   a) _____ she was tired, she had to finish the essay that night, b) _____ the deadline was 9 a.m. next morning. c) _____ she made a cup of coffee d) _____ sat down to write. e) _____ she could not write a word, f) _____ she was feeling so hungry. g) _____ she remembered she had not eaten all day, h) _____ she had been on the train. i) _____ she cooked an omelette, ate it with some salad, j) _____ felt much better.

9. ■ *Find the word class of the following:*

a) saleable

b) salvation

c) privatise

d) attendee

e) agnosticism

10. ■ *Link the words on the left to the meanings on the right, using the prefixes.*

antidote	under the skin
correspondent	preliminary section of a book
foreword	relation of one thing to another
polytechnic	institute where many scientific subjects are taught
proportion	assess worth of something too cheaply
subcutaneous	medicine to counter effects of poison
undervalue	person you write to regularly

11. ■ *Find the correct prepositions to complete the text.*

a) _____ the eighteenth century, news travelled as fast as a horseman or sailing ship. It could take weeks b) _____ news c) _____ a battle d) _____ Europe to reach America. e) _____ the mid-nineteenth century railways had accelerated the distribution f) _____ newspapers, so that they reached distant provinces g) _____ hours, and then the telegraph allowed news to be sent h) _____ seconds. Today we can be overwhelmed i) _____ the volume j) _____ news k) _____ all over the world which we can continuously receive l) _____ our phones and laptops.

12. ■ *Find synonyms for the underlined words, rewriting the sentence where necessary.*

a) Their research <u>methods</u> caused serious <u>argument</u>.

b) The <u>statistics</u> <u>demonstrate</u> the <u>benefits</u> of increased investment.

c) There is a <u>possibility</u> of <u>studying</u> the family records.

d) Her <u>findings</u> <u>reinforce</u> Keynes' theory.

e) Her <u>area</u> of <u>research</u> was the economy of war-time India.

f) They <u>conducted</u> a survey into the <u>behaviour</u> of international students.

Writing Models

The types of writing that students need to produce vary enormously, according to both level (undergraduate, postgraduate) and subject. However, most students will have to write case studies and literature reviews, often as part of longer papers, and many will write reports of some kind, while almost all need to write letters and emails during their course. This section provides examples of these formats, and also introduces the practice of writing in a group.

Case Studies

Both essays and reports may include case studies, which are detailed examples illustrating the topic under discussion. One case study may be the main subject of an essay, or several may be included to illustrate different situations.

1. Using case studies

A case study attempts to show exactly what happened in a particular situation. For example, if you are studying microfinance, you might look at the performance of one particular scheme in a district of Dhaka, in Bangladesh.

What are the advantages of including case studies?

Are there any disadvantages?

■ Match the topics on the left with the example case studies on the right.

Topics	Case studies
Improving crop yields in semi-deserts	A study of a French supermarket training programme
Encouraging entrepreneurship in Africa	
Approaches to motivation in the service sector	The Berlin experiment: increasing public participation in collecting and sorting waste
The impact of the housing market on the wider economy	Using solar power to operate irrigation pumps in Ethiopia
Improving recycling rates in large cities	A Moroccan scheme for supporting new business start-ups
	The effect of the Spanish property price crash of 2008

2. Model case study

■ Read the following example of a case study, taken from a longer essay, and answer the questions below.

Topic: Adapting international brands to local markets

Case Study: The experience of IKEA in China

Introduction

The Chinese economy has expanded at an annual average rate of about 7% for the past 20 years. Parallel to this, the Chinese furniture industry has grown vigorously, with annual sales recently rising by over 20% a year. Legislation to privatise home ownership and rapidly rising income levels have created unprecedented growth in the home improvement sector, and China is now the world's second largest furniture market. This demand has boosted domestic production and also prompted international furniture manufacturers to enter this lucrative market.

IKEA, a Swedish furniture company, was one of the international companies which moved into China. It is a major furniture retailer operating in over 52 countries around the world and had annual sales of over €38 billion in 2018 (IKEA website). It entered the Chinese market in 1998 with its first store in Beijing, and sees great potential in the country, having already expanded to 30 stores and five distribution centres. Despite this successful growth, IKEA has found itself facing a number of challenges in terms of local differences in culture and business practices.

Marketing IKEA in China

Marketing management needs to be largely tailored to local contexts. IKEA has kept this notion in mind when designing marketing strategies and trying to appeal to local customers while maintaining profitability. The company attempts to find the best possible compromise between standardisation and adaptation to local markets. Its product policy pays careful attention to Chinese style and integrates the set of product attributes effectively (Armstrong and Kotler, 2006).

The store layouts reflect the floor plan of many Chinese apartments, and since many of these have balconies, the stores include a balcony section. In contrast with traditional Chinese furniture, which is dark with much carving, IKEA introduces a lighter and simpler style. However, efforts have been made to adapt its products to Chinese taste. For instance, it has released a series of products just before each Chinese New Year. In 2008, the year of the rat, the series 'Fabler' was designed, using the colour red which is associated with good luck.

Changes were also made to some product ranges. In Sweden, people are used to sleeping in single beds, or to putting two single beds together to form a double bed. However, this idea was not very well received by Chinese couples, due to the fact that sleeping in separate beds symbolises a poor relationship and is believed to bring bad luck. In addition, Chinese brand names should have positive connotations. The Chinese name of IKEA (Yi Jia) means 'comfortable home', which gives the company a useful advantage in the market.

An important feature of a retailer is the services it offers. The Shanghai store, for instance, has a children's playground and a large restaurant, which make it distinctive. However, Chinese consumers expect free delivery and installation, and although IKEA has reduced its charges for these, it still compares unfavourably with its competitors.

Price

When the company first entered China its target market was couples with an income of 5,000–8,000 Rmb per month. Following steady price reductions this has now been lowered to families with just over 3,000 Rmb. Various strategies have been adopted to achieve these reductions; the most effective being to source locally. 70% of its products sold in China are now made in the country (Song, 2005). Furthermore, IKEA replaced its thick annual catalogue with thinner brochures which now appear five times a year. These not only cut printing costs but also give greater flexibility to adjust prices.

Accessibility is also an important issue for the Chinese market. In most countries IKEA stores are sited near main roads, but as only a minority of likely customers own cars in China, easy access to public transport is vital (Miller, 2004).

Advertising plays an important role in the total promotional mix. IKEA uses advertising effectively, with adverts in the local newspapers to keep customers informed of special offers. All TV commercials are produced locally with Chinese characters. Public relations is also vital to building a good corporate image. In China, IKEA co-operates with the World Wide Fund for Nature (WWF) on forest projects. The company insists on using environmentally friendly and recyclable materials for the packaging of its products, as part of its efforts to build a good corporate image.

238 Part 5: Writing Models

Discussion and conclusion

IKEA's product policy in China has been to successfully standardise products as much as possible, but also customise as much as needed. But quality and price are not the only factors in its success. It has learned that service is also vital: free delivery and installation are the perceived rules in the local market which it needs to follow. It has further found that it is better to locate in a downtown area, easily accessible with public transport, when free delivery is not provided. Currently there is a programme to open smaller stores, which offer a limited range of products, in the centres of large cities, as an alternative to the large stores on the outskirts of the cities.

International companies which operate in China, such as IKEA, face more complicated marketing decisions than local companies. They must become culture-conscious and thoroughly research local requirements rather than simply introduce a standard model of business. However, if these considerations are effectively managed the Chinese market offers great potential for innovative retailers.

(*890 words*)

a)   Give examples of problems the company has faced in this market.

b)   What has IKEA done to adapt to the Chinese market?

c)   What could be done to improve the case study?

5.2 Literature Reviews and Book Reviews

Literature reviews are sections of a paper in which the writer summarises published work on the topic. They are standard in dissertations, but in most essays a summary of relevant and recent authorities is included in the introduction.

Book reviews may be written by graduate students for academic journals in order to broaden their knowledge and achieve publication.

1. Literature reviews

In some cases the whole focus of an essay may be a lengthy literature review, but in most student writing it will only form a relatively short section of the paper. Only a minority of essays have a separate section headed 'The literature' or 'Literature review'. But in all cases it is necessary to show that you are familiar with the main sources, to provide your work with credibility and so that your writing can build on these sources.

A literature review is not simply a list of sources that you have studied. It can be used to show that there is a gap in the research that your work attempts to fill:

This article has a different standpoint from other studies, because it believes that the influence of the state on the market has structurally increased since the neo-liberal era.

This article focuses on information production, not information accessibility. That is the difference between this research and previous studies.

It is also common to use the literature section to clarify the varying positions held by other researchers:

The political competition literature comprises two main strands – voter monitoring and political survival.

▶ **See Unit 1.9 Contrasting Sources**

2. Example literature review

■ Study the following example from a student essay on motivation theory. Answer the questions which follow.

CONTENT AND PROCESS THEORIES

The various theories of motivation are usually divided into content theories and process theories. The former attempt to 'develop an understanding of fundamental human needs' (Cooper *et al.*, 1992:20). Among the most significant are Maslow's hierarchy of needs theory, McClellan's achievement theory and Herzberg's two-factor theory. The process theories deal with the actual methods of motivating workers, and include the work of Vroom, Locke and Adams.

Content theories

Maslow's hierarchy of needs theory was first published in 1943 and envisages a pyramid of needs on five levels, each of which has to be satisfied before moving up to the next level. The first level is physiological needs such as food and drink, followed by security, love, esteem and self-fulfillment (Rollinson, 2005:195–196). This theory was later revised by Alderfer, who reduced the needs to three: existence, relatedness and growth, and re-named it the ERG theory. In addition, he suggested that all three needs should be addressed simultaneously (Steers *et al.*, 2004:381). McClelland had a slightly different emphasis when he argued that individuals were primarily motivated by three principal needs: for achievement, affiliation and power (Mullins, 2006:199).

In contrast, Herzberg suggested, on the basis of multiple interviews with engineers and accountants during the 1950s, a two-factor theory: that job satisfaction and dissatisfaction had differing roots. He claimed that so-called hygiene factors such as conditions and pay were likely to cause negative attitudes if inadequate, while positive attitudes came from the nature of the job itself. In other words, workers were satisfied if they found their work intrinsically interesting, but would not be motivated to work harder merely by good salaries or holiday allowances. Instead workers needed to be given more responsibility, more authority or more challenging tasks to perform (Vroom and Deci, 1992:252). Herzberg's work has probably been the most influential of all the theories in this field, and is still widely used today, despite being the subject of some criticism, which will be considered later.

Process theories

Vroom's expectancy theory hypothesises a link between effort, performance and motivation. It is based on the idea that an employee believes that increased effort will result in improved performance. This requires a belief that the individual will be supported by the organisation in terms of training and resources (Mullins, 2006). In contrast, Locke emphasised the importance of setting clear targets to improve worker performance in his goal theory. Setting challenging but realistic goals is necessary for increasing employee motivation: 'goal specificity, goal difficulty and goal commitment each served to enhance task performance' (Steers *et al.*, 2004:382). This theory has implications for the design and conduct of staff appraisal systems and for management by objective methods focusing on the achievement of agreed performance targets.

Another approach was developed by Adams in his theory of equity, based on the concept that people value fairness. He argued that employees appreciate being treated in a transparently equitable manner in comparison with other workers doing similar functions, and respond positively if this is made apparent (Mullins, 2006). This approach takes a wider view of the workplace situation than some other theories, and stresses the balance each worker calculates between 'inputs' i.e. the effort made, and 'outputs', which are the rewards obtained.

As many of these theorists did their research over 60 years ago there has clearly been a huge change in the nature of employment since then. Therefore it is worth asking whether they still have relevance to the situation of many workers in the modern, post-industrial economy, and this study attempts to answer that question.

a)   How many types of motivation theory are described?

b)   How many different theorists are mentioned?

c)   How many sources are cited?

d)   Why has the writer not referred to the work of the theorists directly but used secondary sources instead?

3. Book reviews

Writing a book review gives a student the opportunity to critically examine a topic in detail. Journals normally specify the length they require (often about 400 words). In general a review should contain two parts:

a) A description of the scope and organisation of the book. Who is the author, and what has he/she written before? What kind of reader is the book aimed at? In the case of an edited volume, who are the editors and principal contributors?

b) The second part should evaluate how successful the book is in its aims. It is better to avoid excessive praise or criticism, and to mention both positive and negative features. Is the book breaking new ground and adding significantly to current debates? It is also worth commenting on the author's style, and how easy it is to read for specialist or non-specialist readers.

Writers are recommended to first read a selection of reviews in their subject area before attempting their own.

4. Model book review

■ **Study the following review and discuss with a partner whether there is anything else that you think the reviewer should have included.**

Atlantic Crossing: a comparison of European and American society by Marcus Montero (ed.) York: York University Press, 2018. 378 pp., £35.00, ISBN 987 0 15 980456 3.

This useful and important edited volume partly fills a gap in the comparative political science literature. The book compares the society and politics of the European Union (treated here as a single state) with the United States. The book examines 'convergences and divergences' between these two global powers, similar in size and economic weight 'but asymmetric in terms of political influence and military might' (p. 1).

The book has eight chapters. The introductory and concluding chapters, which hold the volume together, are written by the editor. The first briefly outlines the adopted comparative approach and methodological challenges faced in producing this study. Montero then goes on to argue that the EU and the US offer two contrasting models of Western modernity. The final chapter argues that the process of constructing the EU has led to convergence, not divergence, between the EU and the US. In between are six sectoral chapters; of particular interest is the third, by Kuhl, which argues that the *quality* of the democratic experience is in decline on both sides of the Atlantic.

The style of the book is generally clear and accessible, and could be useful background reading for both undergraduate and graduate students. It breaks new ground in treating the EU as a single state, but the book tends to focus on the western half of the EU and has little to say regarding the more recent members such as Romania. This neglect of the newest member states is repeated throughout the volume and brings into question the validity of the book's wider conclusions.

5.3 Writing Longer Papers

Long essays of 3,000–5,000 words may be required as part of a module assessment. These require more time, research and organisation than short essays, and this unit provides a guide to how such an assignment can be approached.

1. Planning your work

Longer assignments are normally set many weeks before their deadline, which means that students should have plenty of time to organise their writing. However, it is worth remembering that at the end of a semester you may have to submit several writing tasks, so it may be a good idea to finish one well before the deadline.

You should also check the submission requirements of your department. These include style of referencing, method of submission (i.e. electronic, hard copy or both) and place and time of submission. Being clear about these will avoid last-minute panic.

▶ **See Unit 1.5 From Understanding Titles to Planning**

a) The first thing is to prepare a schedule for your work. An eight-week schedule might look like this:

Week	Stages of work	Relevant units in this book
1	Study title and make first outline. Look for and evaluate suitable sources.	1.2, 1.5
2	Reading and note-making. Keep record of all sources used.	1.2, 1.3, 1.6, 1.8
3	Reading, note-making, paraphrasing and summarising. Modify outline.	1.2, 1.3, 1.5, 1.7

4	Write draft of main body.	1.10
5	Write draft introduction and conclusion.	1.11
6	Rewrite introduction, main body and conclusion, checking for logical development of ideas and relevance to title.	1.12
7	Organise list of references, contents, list of figures and appendices if required. Check all in-text citations.	1.8
8	Proofread the whole essay before handing it in. Make sure that the overall presentation is clear and accurate (e.g. is page numbering correct?).	1.12

b) How you actually plan your schedule is up to you, but the important thing is to organise your time effectively. At some point you have to stop researching and start writing (Week 4 in the example above). Leaving the writing stage until the last minute will not lead to a good mark, however much research you have done. There is little value in collecting a large quantity of data or ideas if you cannot use it to answer the question effectively. Although you may be tempted to postpone writing, the sooner you start the sooner you will be able to begin refining your ideas. Remember that late submission of coursework is usually penalised.

2. Formatting the paper

Longer papers may include the following features, in this order:

Title page	Apart from the title, this usually shows the student's name and module title and number.
Contents page	This should show the reader the basic organisation of the essay, with page numbers.
List of tables or figures	If the essay includes visual features such as graphs, these need to be listed by title and page number.
Introduction	
Main body	The main body may be divided into sections with sub-headings in bold for each. Your department may require a numbering system, so the sections of the main body are normally numbered 1, 2, 3 and then subdivided 1.1, 1.2 etc.
Conclusion	

Acknowledgements	A space to thank any teachers or others who have assisted the writer.
Notes	These are used to give extra details without interfering with the main narrative. Arabic numbers should be used for these.
List of references	This is a complete list of all the sources cited in the text. Writers occasionally also include a bibliography, which is a list of sources read but not cited.
Appendices (Singular – appendix)	These sections are for data related to the topic which the reader may want to refer to. Each appendix should have a title and be mentioned in the main body.

You must check with your department for details regarding typeface, line spacing, margins and other items. You may have the choice of using endnotes, which are collected in a section before the list of references, or footnotes at the bottom of each page.

Page numbers: use Roman numbers (i, ii, iii) for the preliminary section from the title page to the end of the contents page, and then use Arabic numbers (1, 2, 3) to number the rest of the text.

Overall, success with longer papers depends on:

- Having a schedule and keeping to it

- Starting to write the main body early enough

- Being ready to modify your outline if necessary

- Allowing adequate time for editing and proofreading

- Being consistent in formatting e.g. with references

5.4 Reports and Executive Summaries

Students of Business and Economics may often have to write reports as well as essays. Reports and essays are similar in many ways, but this unit explains and illustrates the differences. Executive summaries are commonly used in business to provide senior managers with a short synopsis of lengthy reports.

1. Writing reports

While essays are often concerned with abstract or theoretical subjects, a report is a description of a situation or something that has happened. In academic terms it might describe:

a)   a problem that you have studied and developed several solutions for

b)   a survey you have carried out

c)   a proposal for a new product or service.

Most reports should include the following features:

Introduction
  – background to the subject
  – reasons for carrying out the work
  – review of other research in the area

Methods
  – how you did your research
  – description of the tools/materials/equipment used

Results
  – what you discovered
  – comments on likely accuracy of results

Discussion
- of your main findings
- comments on the effectiveness of your research

Conclusion
- summary of your work
- practical implications of the research
- suggestions for further research

2. Essays and reports

In comparison with essays, reports are likely to

a) be based on primary as well as secondary research

b) be more specific and detailed

c) use numbering (1.1, 1.2) and sub-headings for different sections.

In most other respects reports are similar to essays since both:

a) have a clear and logical format

b) use an objective and accurate academic style

c) include citations and references

d) make use of visual information in the form of graphs, diagrams and tables

e) include appendices where necessary.

■ **Decide whether the following titles are more likely to be written as reports or essays.**

Topic	Report	Essay
1. The development of trade unions in South Africa (1900–2015)		
2. Two alternative plans for improving college open days for prospective students		
3. A survey you conducted to compare male and female attitudes to writing essays		
4. A study of a struggling retail business and proposals to improve its performance		
5. The macroeconomic consequences of negative interest rates		

3. Practice

■ Read the following report and answer the questions which follow.

A report on student accommodation at Bullbridge College

Introduction

The quality of accommodation is a crucial concern for most students, since having comfortable and affordable housing can be seen as essential for focussing on academic work. Rising student numbers are putting pressure on existing student residences on the campus, so that the College is currently considering building three new blocks in the College grounds which would accommodate approximately 350 students. However, as the estimated cost of these is about £2.75 million ($3.4 million) there is a counter-proposal to spend the money on better teaching facilities and instead rely on private landlords to provide accommodation off-campus.

This report sets out to establish what kind of accommodation students prefer, and secondly to discuss how this can be best provided, given the current financial climate. In order to research this question we conducted a survey of 194 current students living in a range of accommodation. On the basis of these results, we then attempted to evaluate the two main options available to the College.

Accommodation survey

We tried to find out why a cross-section of students had chosen their current rooms and how satisfied they were with their choices by conducting a short survey. About 250 students were sent an online questionnaire and 194 of these were completed. Of these, 55% (106) were from female students and 45% (88) were from males. This broadly reflects the gender balance of the College.

Question 1: What kind of accommodation do you have now?

Type	College residence on-campus	Student residence off-campus	Shared house or flat – private landlord	At home with parents
Male	36	14	33	5
Female	57	11	29	9
Total	93	25	62	14

It can be seen that the most common type of accommodation is in the College residences, and that only a small minority live with their parents. The results also demonstrate that substantially more females than males live in College residences and with their families.

Question 2: How satisfied are you with your current accommodation?

(Rated 1–5, average results)

Type	College residence on-campus	Student residence off-campus	Shared house or flat – private landlord	At home with parents
Male	3.7	4.6	3.4	2.9
Female	4.2	4.1	3.6	4.0
Average	3.95	4.35	3.5	3.45

These results show that the highest levels of satisfaction are found with the off-campus purpose-built residences, provided by private companies. The on-campus College residences are also quite well-liked, but shared houses and flats seem less satisfactory.

Question 3: What do you like and dislike about your current accommodation?

Type	College residence on-campus	Student residence off-campus	Shared house or flat – private landlord	At home with parents
Likes	convenient make friends	well-equipped near town centre	cheap can choose friends to share with	economical comfortable
Dislikes	expensive noisy	small rooms expensive	arguments with flatmates poor quality fittings	less freedom can't have friends to stay

Analysis

The survey might have been improved by asking a greater number of students, but 194 responses does provide a significant sample. Perhaps a more serious drawback is that it did not distinguish between different years: first year students may well have different priorities (e.g. making friends) to final year students (who may value the independence of a shared house). However, the results obtained do support anecdotal reports of student preferences.

Conclusion

Clearly living with parents is an option only open to a limited number of students with families living locally, so there are basically three types of student accommodation. Some students will prefer to save money by sharing flats and houses with their friends, and in fact there is a good supply of this type of accommodation provided by private landlords.

The off-campus student residences appear to be rather more popular than the College residences, and from the College's point of view they require no investment. Provided that more of these can be built to accommodate rising student numbers it would seem better for the college to spend its limited capital on new teaching facilities.

a) *How could the report be improved?*

b) *Is anything missing from the report?*

4. Executive summaries

As the name suggests, with business reports and proposals it is common to preface the texts with a short summary of the main points and conclusions. This allows senior managers to keep abreast of the situation, without needing to study unnecessary detail.

The summary should be written after the report is finalised, and in general will be no more than 10% of the original length.

An effective summary will, depending on the situation:

- explain the issue being discussed
- describe the various options
- identify the best course of action
- give reasons to support this.

There is no need to include statistical data and other details since the reader always has the option of studying the full report.

▣ **Write an executive summary of the report above in 60–70 words.**

5.5 Reflective Writing

> As part of studying a course in Business, it is increasingly common for students to be asked to reflect on their performance in various activities, as part of the learning process. This unit explains the purpose of this reflection and illustrates some ways it can be approached.

1. The purpose of reflective writing

Reflective writing aims to improve the benefit that students gain from various activities on their academic course, especially from more practical ones such as taking part in a group project or conducting a survey. It recognises the value to students of assessing their experience, thinking about the positive and negative aspects, and drawing conclusions from this which will inform future performance.

Gibbs (1988) portrayed reflective writing as a cycle, moving from a description of what happened to an analysis of a student's reactions to the event, followed by an explanation of the situation and then an evaluation of how well they dealt with the issue. Finally the student could consider how this might impact on their behaviour in future.

2. Example

■ Study the following extract from a piece of reflective writing on a survey you have recently conducted as part of a group project on public transport. Answer the questions below.

Our research into demand for local bus services used a questionnaire which consisted of ten questions, all with a yes/no format. The survey was carried out in the local shopping precinct on 19 May, with the group working in pairs. We completed 112 questionnaires during the morning, with 74 women and 38 men taking part. The results showed that a majority of respondents (67% overall) would pay more to use the bus service if it was more reliable. However, among the car owners (44% of respondents) only 26% would ever consider using buses (see full report below).

I was quite nervous about interviewing people in the street but almost everyone we asked agreed to take part. However, I feel that the format of our questions was too rigid and some 'open' questions would have been productive. Due to the timing, most of the interviewees were women shoppers, and we should have tried to get a better male/female balance. Looking back, I think we could have trialled the questionnaire with a small group and been prepared to modify some of the questions. I had thought about this earlier, but was worried about suggesting it to the group. In future I must be prepared to give my opinions even if it creates extra work for the team. Overall it seems difficult to design a set of questions in a large group of ten people and perhaps it would be better to form a sub-committee to deal with this.

a)   What has the writer learned from the experience about her behaviour?

b)   What does the writer suggest might improve group work in future?

3. Style

Reflective writing is different in style from the bulk of academic writing. As it is more personal, using 'I' or 'we', it will be more subjective than normal. However, like other academic genres, it aims to be clear and precise as well as logical. The emphasis will be on critical analysis rather than description. In the example above (Section 2) the first paragraph gives an outline of the situation, but the second paragraph contains the crucial evaluation.

4. Practice A

■   **Work with a partner. Think about a seminar or lecture you both have recently attended, or a project you have been involved in. Ask each other questions such as:**

•   What did you expect from this?

•   What benefit did you get from it?

•   How could it have been improved?

•   Would you change your behaviour with a similar event in future?

■   **Write a short account of the event with a brief description of what happened, and then an account of your reactions to it and an analysis of any changes you might make to your participation in future.**

5. Practice B

Consider keeping a learning journal. This is a kind of diary which records some of the academic tasks you are required to do and your analysis of how useful they were, as well as how well you dealt with them. This is just for your own interest and nobody else need read it. Example:

> *5 October – We were given two weeks to write a 1,000 word report on local taxi services, working with two other students. I felt rather nervous at first, but after meeting them I thought we got on well and we made a plan for our research.*

> *6 October – We talked to a taxi driver from A–Z Taxis. He gave us some ideas, but we should have prepared our questions better before meeting him. However, on the basis of this we modified our plans for researching the project, which I was pleased with.*

Writing in Groups

5.6

Courses in Business may expect students to complete written tasks as part of a group of four to eight students. This unit explains the reasons for this, and suggests the best way to approach group work in order to achieve the maximum benefit from the process.

1. Why write in groups?

■ Read the text and complete the following exercise.

THE IMPORTANCE OF GROUP WORK

Some students, especially those from other academic cultures, may be surprised to find that they are expected to work in groups to complete some academic assignments. These groups may meet face-to-face or they may be virtual groups with members in various locations.

For those who have always worked on their own this may cause a kind of culture shock, especially as all the students in the group will normally be given the same mark for the group's work. In addition, students are normally told who they will have to work with, although with some kinds of project students may be able to choose their colleagues. Yet there are several good reasons for this emphasis on group work in many English-speaking institutions.

First of all, employers are generally looking for people who can work in a team. Most managers are not looking for brilliant individuals; instead they want employees who are comfortable working with a mixed group, with different skills and backgrounds. So familiarity with teamwork has become an essential qualification for many jobs, and this task provides students with an opportunity to strengthen their experience of working in this way.

Furthermore, working in groups allows individuals to achieve more than they could by working on their own. A team can tackle much larger projects than individual students can, and this applies to most research projects at university, as well as business development in companies. Therefore, by taking part in these activities students are able to provide evidence in their portfolio and CV that they have succeeded in this critical area.

Finally, in the academic world, many journal articles and other publications are the product of a group of researchers. By collaborating, academics are able to pool their knowledge and bring their varied expertise and backgrounds to focus on an issue, thereby often achieving more credibility than they could when working alone.

■ Working in pairs, decide if the following statements are true or false.

a) Most students react positively to the idea of group work.

b) All the group members receive the same mark.

c) Students in groups can normally choose who they work with.

d) There are two main reasons for setting group work.

e) Most employers look for successful team members.

f) Group work on university courses has no connection to teamwork in companies.

2. Making group work successful

■ Below is a list of suggestions for organising the process of completing group work successfully. The correct order (1–7) has been mixed up. Working with a partner, put them into the most logical sequence, using the table below.

A. Analyse the task.
Get everyone to discuss the assignment and agree on the best methods to complete it. At this stage it is important to have complete agreement on the objectives.

B. Divide up the work fairly, according to the abilities of the members.
Your group may include a computer expert or a design genius, so make sure that their talents are used appropriately. It is most important to make sure that everyone feels they have been given a fair share of the work.

C. Make everyone feel included.

Nobody should feel an outsider, so make special efforts if there is only one male student, or one non-native speaker, for instance. Make a list of all members' phone numbers and email addresses and give everyone a copy.

D. Finish the assignment on time.

This is the most important test of your group's performance. When you have finished and handed in your work, it may be helpful to have a final meeting to discuss what you have all learned from the task.

E. Get to know the other members.

Normally you cannot choose who you work with, so it is crucial to introduce yourselves before starting work. Meet informally in a café or somewhere similar (but be careful not to choose a meeting place which may make some members uncomfortable, such as a bar).

F. Select a co-ordinator/editor.

Someone needs to take notes about what was agreed at meetings and send these to all members as a reminder. The same person could also act as editor, to make sure that all the individual sections conform to the same layout and format. However, you should all be responsible for proofreading your own work.

G. Plan the job and the responsibilities.

Break down the task week by week and allocate specific roles to each member. Agree on times for regular meetings – although you may be able to avoid some meetings by using group emails. You may want to book a suitable room, for example in the library, to hold your meetings.

	Schedule for successful group work
1	E. Get to know the other members
2	
3	
4	
5	
6	
7	

NB: this process applies to both face-to-face and virtual groups, though clearly in the latter case it will have to be modified.

■ **Discuss with a partner how it could be adapted to a virtual group.**

3. Dealing with problems

■ **Working in groups of three, discuss the best response to the following situations. You may choose an alternative strategy to the ones provided.**

a) In a group of six, you find that two students are not doing any work. Not only do they not come to meetings, they have not done the tasks they were given at the beginning. Should you ...
   i)   decide that it's simplest to do the work of the missing students yourself?
   ii) find the students and explain that their behaviour is going to damage the chances of all six members?
   iii) tell your teacher about the problem?

b) You are the only non-native speaker in the group. Although you can understand normal speech, the other students speak so fast and idiomatically that you have difficulty taking part in the discussions. Should you ...
   i)   tell your teacher about the problem?
   ii) keep quiet and ask another student in the group to explain decisions later?
   iii) explain your problem to the group and ask them to speak more slowly?

c) One member of the group is very dominant. He/she attempts to control the group and is intolerant of the opinions of others. Should you ...
   i)   explain to them, in a group meeting, that their behaviour is having a negative effect on the group's task?
   ii) tell your teacher about the problem?
   iii) let them do all the work, because that's what they seem to want?

4. Points to remember

Finally, remember that:

- You may learn a lot by listening to other people's ideas.
- Negotiation is important in a group – nobody is right all the time.
- Working in groups is an ideal opportunity to make new friends – make the most of it.
- Respect the values and attitudes of others, especially people from different cultures – you may be surprised what you learn.

Glossary

Abbreviation
    The short form of a word or phrase (see 4.2)

Abstract
    A short summary of the aims and scope of a journal article (see 1.3)

Acknowledgements
    A list of people the author wishes to thank for their assistance, found in books and articles

Appendix (plural – appendices)
    A section at the end of a book or article containing supplementary information

Assignment
    A task given to students, normally for assessment

Authority
    A well-known expert or reference work on a subject

Back issue
    A previous issue of a journal or magazine

Bias
    A subjective preference for one point of view

Bibliography
    A list of sources an author has read but not specifically cited

Brainstorm
    A process of collecting ideas on a topic at random (see 1.5)

Case study
    A section of an essay which examines one example in detail (see 5.1)

Citation
    An in-text reference providing a link to the source (see 1.4 and 1.8)

Cohesion
Linking ideas in a text together by use of reference words (see 3.1)

Coursework
Assessed assignments given to students to complete during a course

Conclusion
The final section of an essay or report (see 1.11)

Contraction
A shortened form of pronoun and verb e.g. she's, I'd (see 3.5)

Criteria (singular – criterion)
The principles on which something is judged or based

Deadline
The final date for completing a piece of work

Draft
An unfinished version of a piece of writing

Edited book
A book with contributions from a number of writers, controlled by an editor

Extract
A piece of text taken from a longer work

Flowchart
A diagram that illustrates the stages of a process

Formality
In written work, the use of a non-idiomatic style and vocabulary

Format
The standard organisation of a text

Heading
The title of a section of text

Higher degree
A Master's degree or Doctorate

Hypothesis
A theory which a researcher is attempting to explore or test

Introduction
The first part of an essay or article (see 1.11)

Journal
An academic publication in a specialised area, usually published quarterly (see 1.2)

Literature review
A section of an article describing other research on the topic in question (see 5.2)

Main body
> The principal part of an essay after the introduction and before the conclusion

Margin
> The strip of white space on a page around the text

Module
> Most academic courses are divided into modules, each of which focuses on a specified topic

Outline
> A preparatory plan for a piece of writing (see 1.5)

Paraphrase
> A rewriting of a text with substantially different wording and organisation but similar ideas

Peer review
> The process of collecting comment from academic authorities on an article before publication in a journal. This system gives increased validity to the publication.

Phrase
> A few words which are commonly combined (see 1.1)

Plagiarism
> Using another writer's work without acknowledgement in an acceptable manner (see 1.4)

Primary research
> Original research e.g. a laboratory experiment or a sociological enquiry

Quotation
> Use of the exact words of another writer to illustrate an argument or idea (see 1.8)

Redundancy
> The unnecessary repetition of ideas or information (see 3.7)

References
> A list of all the sources cited in a paper (see 1.8)

Register
> The level of formality in language

Restatement
> Repeating a point in order to explain it more clearly

Scan
> A method of reading in which the eyes move quickly over the page to find a specific item

Skim
> A related reading technique to quickly find out the main ideas of a text

Source
> The original text used to obtain an idea or piece of information

Summary
> A shorter version of something (see 1.7)

Synonym

    A word or phrase with a similar meaning to another (see 4.8)

Synopsis

    A summary of an article or book

Term

    A word or phrase used to express a special concept

Word class

    A grammatical category e.g. noun, adjective

Answers

Providing answers for a writing course is less clear cut than for other language areas. In some exercises there is only one possible answer, but in other cases several possibilities exist. Teachers need to use common sense, and accept any reasonable answer. In the case of exercises where students can choose their own topic and it is therefore impossible to provide a definite answer, students may still appreciate having a model answer, and so some have been given.

Academic writing quiz

1	b (see Unit 1.1)	2	c (see Unit 1.1)	3	a (see Unit 1.5)	4	c (see Unit 1.11)
5	a (see Unit 1.11)	6	c (see Unit 1.6)	7	a (see Unit 1.8)	8	b (see Unit 1.7)
9	c (see Unit 1.10)	10	b (see Unit 1.12)	11	c (see Unit 1.3)	12	c (see Unit 3.5)
13	a (see Unit 4.8)	14	b (see Unit 4.4)	15	b (see Unit 1.3)	16	c (see Unit 4.6)
17	b (see Unit 1.6)	18	b (see Unit 2.8)	19	c (see Unit 1.1)	20	a (see Unit 1.11)

PART 1 THE WRITING PROCESS

1.1 Basics of Writing

1. **The purpose of academic writing**

   Other reasons might include:
   - To present a hypothesis for consideration by others
   - To make notes on something read or heard or seen

2. **Features of academic writing**

   Possibilities include:
   - Semi-formal vocabulary, lack of idioms
   - Use of citation/references
   - Use of both passive and active voices
   - Precision
   - Caution

3. **Common types of academic writing**

   Report – A description of something a student has done e.g. conducting a survey or experiment.
   Essay – The answer to a question set by the teacher, often on a theoretical subject.
   Dissertation/Thesis – The longest piece of writing normally done by a student, often for a higher degree (20,000+ words).
   Paper – A general term for any academic essay, report, presentation or article.
   Case study – A detailed report on a particular situation or organisation.
   Survey report – The presentation of the results of a piece of research you have conducted, using interviews or questionnaires.
   Reflection – A piece of writing in which you critically examine how you dealt with a situation or task and what you learned from it.
   Proposal – A persuasive text written to convince a potential customer of the value of a new product or strategy.

4. **The format of written assignments**
   a) abstract
   b) references
   c) appendix
   d) acknowledgements
   e) literature review
   f) case study
   g) foreword

5. **The components of academic writing**
   a) title
   b) sub-title
   c) heading
   d) phrase
   e) sentence
   f) paragraph

7. **Simple and complex sentences**
   (*Example sentences*)
   a) In 2019 the Human Resources programme had predominantly female students.
   b) There was a small majority of female students on the Marketing programme.
   c) The Finance programme had the greatest gender imbalance: over 70% of the students were male.
   d) There was a small majority of male students studying Economics, but in the Accounting programme there was a substantial majority of men.

8. **Writing in paragraphs**
   See Unit 1.10.1 Organising paragraphs for initial questions

para 2 begins:	However, some economists …
para 3 begins:	But this effect …
para 4 begins:	The macroeconomic model …

9. **Practice**
   (*Example sentences*)
   a) Energy efficiency was thought to benefit both consumers and the environment.
   b) More efficient engines should reduce demand for fossil fuel.
   c) Recent research has questioned this idea, using the example of the USA from 1960 to 2011.
   d) Researchers claim that cheaper energy costs lead to more energy being used, with no overall benefit for the environment.

1.2 Reading: Finding Suitable Sources

1. **Academic texts**

   A. Worldwide pressures – Possibly – it mentions two sources, and contains a lot of information, but some of the language is subjective e.g. 'reckless lack of control', 'shrinking alarmingly'.

   B. A drying world? – No – no sources are mentioned, and the style is very informal e.g. 'the stuff we drink'.

   C. Measuring scarcity – Yes – a more critical, formal and objective style, and a citation provided.

   (Possible answers)

Feature	Examples
Formal or semi-formal vocabulary	The more complex indicators are not widely applied because data are lacking to apply them and the definitions are not intuitive.
Sources are given	Rijsberman (2006)
Objective, impersonal style	It is surprisingly difficult to determine whether water is truly scarce in the physical sense at a global scale (a supply problem) or whether it is available but should be used better (a demand problem).

2. **Types of text**

   (Possible answers)

Text type	Advantages	Disadvantages
Website	Easily accessed, probably up-to-date	Possibly unreliable and/or unedited
Journal article	Often focuses on a very particular area	May be too specialised or complex
Official report (e.g.from government body)	Contains a lot of detail	May have a narrow focus
Newspaper or magazine article	Easy to read and up-to-date	May not be objective and not give sources
E-book	Easily accessible	Must be read on screen
Edited book	A variety of contributors provide a range of views	May lack focus

4. **Using library catalogues**

   Title 1 appears to be an edited general study, recently published.
   Title 2 is also quite up-to-date and general.
   Title 4 is a third edition, so might be worth consulting although rather dated.
   The others seem to be too specific or outdated.

7. **Reading methods**

Choosing suitable texts

Read title and sub-title carefully

Survey text features (e.g. abstract, contents, index)

Ask yourself how this relates to your own knowledge of the subject and reasons for reading

Skim text for gist – is it relevant?	Scan text for information you need (e.g. names)

Read extensively when useful sections are found

Read intensively to make notes on key points

Other reading skills – possible answers:
- Text genre recognition
- Dealing with new vocabulary

8. **Practice**
   a) Text is relevant
   b) Three sources are mentioned which could be useful

9. **Reading abstracts**
   a) Purpose/aim   to analyse the contribution ... 1978 to 2013.
   b) Method   We use a massive ... the United States
   c) Findings/results   We find that ... between firms.
   d) Explanation of results   However, this rising ... (i.e., segregation rose).

1.3 Reading: Developing Critical Approaches

1. **Fact and opinion**

A
   a) opinion
   b) fact (not true)
   c) opinion
   d) fact (true) + fact (true)
   e) fact (true) + opinion

B

(Objective version with facts corrected)

New Zealand is an island nation in the southern Pacific Ocean, consisting of two main islands. Nearly 1,000 miles east of Australia, it was one of the last places on Earth to be settled by man: Polynesians who arrived in about 1250 CE, and who developed the Maori culture. In the eighteenth century European settlers started to land, and in 1841 New Zealand became part of the British Empire. Due to its long period of isolation many distinctive plants and animals evolved, such as the kiwi, now the nation's symbol. The country suffers from frequent earthquakes, such as the one that hit Christchurch in 2011, causing serious damage and loss of life.

3. Critical thinking

The responses to these questions will vary from student to student, which is the nature of the critical approach.

(Model Answer)

Statements	*Comments*
A	
It is claimed that in one year nearly half of Harvard's history professors were on sabbatical leave. As a consequence, students work less …	The link between these two situations is not made clear.
B	
… it has been calculated that the average UK university graduate will earn £400,000 ($600,000) more over their lifetime compared to a non-graduate.	Who has made this calculation? What basis is there for this claim?

4. Practice

(Example answers)

	A. Volkswagen plugs in	*B. How electric cars will change the world*
Negative points	Subjective language – 'tough talking', 'exciting new technology' Inaccurate – '11 billion vehicles' is clearly a mistake Narrow focus on one company	Rather an uncritical acceptance of the scenario with no counter-arguments presented
Positive points	Some useful information about the economics of building vehicles Contains up-to-date news of the company	Presents a global view of the situation Reference to other studies and reports

1.4 Avoiding Plagiarism

3. Degrees of plagiarism

1. Y
2. Y
3. Y
4. N
5. Y

6. N
7. Y
8. N
9. Y/N
10. Y

4. **Avoiding plagiarism by summarising and paraphrasing**
   a) Plagiarised – No citation given
   b) Plagiarised – original wording with minor changes
   c) Acceptable – a correctly referenced summary of the original
   d) Acceptable – a correctly referenced summary and quotation
   e) Technically plagiarism – mistake in spelling the author's name

5. **Avoiding plagiarism by developing good study habits**
   (Possible further suggestions)
   - Check that your quotations are exactly the same wording as the original.
   - When paraphrasing, alter the structure as well as the vocabulary.
   - Make sure your in-text citations are all included in the list of references.

6. **Practice**
   Kaufman (2017) argues that wealth (expressed as GDP per head) rather than size of population is the key to national success in the Olympics.

   Large populations alone do not guarantee good national results at the Olympics. Countries must also be wealthy enough to have healthy citizens and be able to provide resources for training. As Kaufman points out: 'When many people are affected by poverty and illness it is not easy to be ordinarily healthy, let alone be an Olympic athlete' (Kaufman, 2017:3).

7. **Further practice**
   Source – The origin of ideas or information
   Citation – Short in-text note giving the author's name and publication date
   To summarise – To reduce the length of a text while keeping the main points
   Quotation – Using the exact words of the original text in your work
   Reference – Full publication details of a text or other source
   To cheat – To gain advantage dishonestly
   Paraphrase – Using different words or word order to restate a text

1.5 From Understanding Essay Titles to Planning

2. **Analysing essay titles**
   a) <u>Summarise/discuss</u>
      Give the factors behind the development, and explore the possible consequences.

   b) <u>Critically evaluate</u>
      Decide if these theories are valid.

   c) <u>Describe/critically examine</u>
      Discuss some of the difficulties in this area with reference to methods companies use.

   d) <u>Discuss/consider</u>
      Explain how knowledge and power inter-relate and what this means for management.

3. **Practice: key words**
   Analyse – Break down into the various parts and their relationships
   Assess/Evaluate – Decide the value or worth of a subject
   Describe – Give a detailed account of something

Discuss – Look at various aspects of a topic, compare benefits and drawbacks
Examine/Explore – Divide into sections and discuss each critically
Illustrate – Give examples
Outline/Trace – Deal with a complex subject by reducing it to the main elements
Suggest/Indicate – Make a proposal and support it
Summarise – Explain a topic briefly and clearly
(NB: 'summarise' and 'outline' are very similar)

5. **Brainstorming**

(Possible answers)

How and why?
- Number of travellers has increased sharply
- More people plan their own holidays, using the internet
- Greater demand for different types of holidays

What?
- Older, retired people spend more on travel
- Rising disposable incomes in many countries e.g. China allow spending on travel

6. **Essay length**

(NB: These figures are only a guide and individual students may have a different approach)

a) Explain/discuss
   Approximately 50/50

b) What/discuss
   Approximately 60/40

c) Examine/political/economic/cultural
   Approximately 10 describing the company, then 30/30/30

7. **Outlines**

c) Lists can help develop a logical structure and make it easier to allocate space, but are rather inflexible.
   Mind maps are more flexible as extra items can be added easily.

8. **Practice**

(Model outline – list)

The likely results
- Retailers must compete on logistics (delivery times)
- Increased demand for warehouse space esp. near big cities
- New businesses created (e.g. returns)
- More delivery traffic > demand for drivers
- Many stores will close
- Character of shopping streets will change > more cafes and entertainment

1.6 Finding Key Points and Note-making

1. Finding key points

(Example titles)

The cost of internet fraud

Compensating victims of internet scams

Key points:

- The cost of internet scams in the USA may be + $50bn per year
- Scammers becoming more sophisticated
- Victims often wealthier, retired, well-educated people who over-estimate financial ability
- Normally banks refuse to compensate people who have lost money
- In Britain some victims may be compensated – but who will fund the scheme?

2. Finding relevant points

Key points:

1. The practice of imposing taxes on products which are thought to have a negative social impact, such as alcohol, has been accepted for several hundred years …
2. It has recently been suggested in the USA that so-called junk food should be taxed in order to compensate for the social costs of the obesity it is believed to cause. This proposal is based on the estimate of the medical costs of obesity, which is thought to be linked to cancer, diabetes and heart disease.
3. A study of the long-term effects of changes in food prices (Goldman, Lakdawalla and Zheng, 2009) argues that significant changes in consumption, and hence obesity levels, can be achieved over time.
4. But the link between junk food and ill-health is not easily determined. A physically active person could eat hamburgers daily and still keep slim.
5. It has even been suggested that such a 'fat tax' might have the opposite effect and reduce activity levels by forcing people to spend more time preparing food for themselves, instead of buying it from fast-food outlets (Yaniv, Rosin and Tobol, 2009).
6. … other studies on the effects of alcohol and tobacco taxes indicate that the heaviest users of these products are the least influenced by price rises …

3. Why make notes?

(Other answers possible)

b) To avoid plagiarism
c) To keep a record of reading/lectures
d) To revise for exams
e) To help remember main points

4. Practice A

(Other answers possible)

The notes are paraphrased, not copied from the text
The source is included
Symbols are used (>)
Abbreviations (esp.) to save space
Notes are organised in numbered lists

6. **Practice B**

   (Example notes)

   > <u>Taxing junk food</u>
   > 1) Goods > social harm e.g. alcohol have been taxed since 18th C.
   > 2) US proposal to tax junk food > reduce obesity > cut medical costs (diabetes, heart disease)
   > 3) Goldman, Lakdawalla and Zheng, 2009 claim that raising food prices can reduce consumption in long term
   > 4) No clear link health/ junk food – active people stay thin
   > 5) Yaniv, Rosin and Tobol, 2009 argue that tax on fast food might have undesired effect of making people cook more > cut their exercise time
   > 6) Research on tax on alcohol shows that main users are unaffected by increase in prices
   >
   > (Source: Rohan, J. (2010) Can taxation reduce obesity? *Public Health Review* 8 p. 36)

7. **Practice C**

   (Source: Caballero J. and Poledna Z. (2010) *European Business Prospects.* London: Capital University Press, p. 351)

   <u>Predatory pricing</u> (PP) = using size to lower prices below cost to harm competitors
   In USA 1890 Sherman Antitrust Act – example of govt. attempt to control monopolies

   <u>But</u> low prices benefit customers + predation hard to prove legally
   – good reasons for selling below cost e.g. new product promotion
   – bundling (selling several items together) makes proof harder (i.e. calculating individual profit margins)

   <u>Example</u>: 5/09 EU fined Intel €1 bn. for PP against rival AMD – but very complex case and Intel appealed verdict

1.7 Summarising and Paraphrasing

1. **What makes a good summary?**

   A good summary requires:
   • selection of most important aspects
   • clear organisation
   • accuracy

2. **Stages of summarising**

   1   c)
   2   d)
   3   b)
   4   a)
   5   e)

3. **Practice A**

   1 = c (includes all essential details; clearly written)
   2 = b (does not specify the advantages of digital cameras)
   3 = a (lacks detail and includes information – expensive film – not in original)

4. **Practice B**

    (Model answers)

    b)
    - i)   Mobile phones have helped to establish new businesses in Africa.
    - ii)   Link between higher phone ownership and increase in GDP.
    - iii) Only half of Africans (wealthier and urban) have a mobile phone.
    - iv)   New developments should reduce costs and increase availability of telecom services.
    - v)   But growth is still held back by high levels of taxation on telecom companies.

    c) *(Model summary)*

    ### The impact of mobile phones in Africa

    Recently, mobile phones have helped to establish new businesses in Africa, and there is a link between higher phone ownership and an increase in GDP. However, only half of Africans (mainly the wealthier and urban ones) currently have a mobile phone. New technical developments should reduce costs and increase the availability of telecom services, but growth is still held back by high levels of taxation on telecom companies.

    d) *(Example summary)*

    Although mobiles help create new businesses in Africa, their use is limited to wealthier people. Advanced technology may make them more accessible, but high taxes threaten the providers.

5. **Practice C – The economics of happiness**

    (Example summary)
    Regular surveys in over 100 nations attempt to measure personal satisfaction with life. Economists expect to find rising satisfaction alongside increasing GDP per person, as is seen in China, but in other countries, such as India, this is not found. Called the 'Easterlin Paradox', reasons for this situation still cause argument among economists.

7. **Practice D – The causes of the Industrial Revolution**
    1) b. The best paraphrase, with all main points included and a significantly different structure.
    2) a. Quite good, but lack of precision (at that time) and unsuitable register (bosses).
    3) c. A poor paraphrase, with only a few words changed and extra and inaccurate information added (Britain was the only country …).

9. **Practice E – Green dreams**

    (A number of possibilities are acceptable here. These are suggestions)

    a) It is <u>frequently claimed</u> that governments can create <u>jobs</u> and <u>cut</u> carbon emissions by investing in renewable energy <u>schemes</u>. These so-called 'green jobs' have the <u>attraction</u> of helping to <u>fight</u> global warming while <u>lowering</u> a <u>nation's</u> dependence on imported fuels.
    b) But there are <u>claims</u> by critics of these schemes that the <u>benefits</u> are less than they seem. Firstly, <u>spending</u> the money on other projects such as road-building would also allow the <u>creation</u> of jobs.
    c) Secondly, the taxpayer has to finance higher government borrowing to pay for the investment, and all business borrowing may eventually be affected. In addition, the price of electricity for consumers may be raised by subsidising solar and wind power, which are relatively inefficient sources of energy.
    d) A Spanish study examined the value of providing subsidies for renewable energy over 25 years. It found that each of the 50,000 jobs created cost €570,000, with an estimated total spending

of €29bn. But had the state permitted the same sum to be spent by private businesses they would have produced over twice as many jobs: 113,000. According to these calculations the subsidies in Spain would have effectively eliminated more than 50,000 posts.

10. Practice F – The power of the BID

(Example answers)

a) Business Improvement District or BIDs were created to prevent crime in commercial urban areas of America. Cook and MacDonald from Pennsylvania University examined how well they functioned in LA. Their conclusion was that they were useful, since the guards who were employed could be more focussed than the police, and were also cheaper. The BIDs were paid for by the local companies, and these benefitted from less crime and more valuable property. Finally the police could focus on crime in the rest of the city, although there seemed to be no sign of increased crime there.

b) A study of the value of Business Improvement Districts (BIDs) in the USA has found that they are an effective method of reducing crime in commercial areas. Paid for by local businesses, they employ guards who just concentrate on securing the area of the BID, freeing the police to work elsewhere.

1.8 References and Quotations

1. Why use references?

a) N
b) Y
c) Y
d) N

e) Y
f) N
g) Y

2. Citations and references

Smith (2009) argues that the popularity of the Sports Utility Vehicle (SUV) is irrational, as despite their high cost most are never driven off-road. In his view 'they are bad for road safety, the environment and road congestion' (Smith, 2009:37).

The first is a summary, the second a quotation.

A summary allows the writer to condense ideas, while a quotation uses the words of the original author, which have authenticity and may be difficult to improve.

6. Practice

(Example answers)

a) According to Kelman (2016), McEwan (2015) points out that with an increasingly diverse body of both students and teaching staff, the need to reduce the gap in their distinct expectations is vital.

b) McEwan maintains that 'student success at university level is partly dependent on narrowing the difference between student and staff expectations' (Kelman, 2016:45).

c) According to Kelman, McEwan (2015) points out that with an increasingly diverse body of both students and teaching staff, the need to reduce the gap in their distinct expectations is vital: 'the student body includes an increasing proportion of international students, who may take longer to adapt to the university culture' (Kelman, 2016:45).

10. Organising the list of references

a) *(Any of)*

 i) Anderson, E. (1999) *Code of the Street.* New York: Norton.
 Beck, J. (2011) *Cognitive Therapy: Basics and Beyond.* New York: Guilford.
 Kahneman, D. (2011) *Thinking, Fast and Slow.* London: Macmillan.

 ii) Blattman, C., J. Jamison and M. Sheridan (forthcoming) 'Reducing crime and violence: Experimental evidence on adult noncognitive investments in Liberia'. *American Economic Review.*

 iii) *Doe v. Cook County* (2007) No. 99 C 3945 (N.D. Ill.)

 iv) Cunningham, T. (2015) 'Hierarchical aggregation of information and decision-making'. Unpublished Manuscript, New York: Columbia University.

 v) *(Any of)* Anderson, M. (2008) 'Multiple inference and gender differences in the effects of early intervention: A re-evaluation of the Abecedarian, Perry Preschool, and Early Training projects'. *Journal of the American Statistical Association* 103, 1481-1495.

 Ellis, A. (1957) 'Outcome of employing three techniques of psychotherapy'. *Journal of Clinical Psychology* 13, 344-350.

 Jensen, R. (2010) 'The (perceived) returns to education and the demand for schooling'. *Quarterly Journal of Economics* 125, 515-548.

 Manski, C. (1993) 'Dynamic choice in social settings: Learning from the experiences of others'. *Journal of Econometrics* 58, 121-136.

 vi) *(Either of)* Ellis, A. and R. Harper (1975) *A New Guide to Rational Living.* Upper Saddle River, NJ: Prentice Hall.

 Nisbett, R. and R. Lee (1991) *The Person and the Situation.* New York: McGraw-Hill.

 vii) Anon. (1990) *Coping Better, Anytime, Anywhere: The Handbook of Rational Self-Counselling.* Alexandria, VA: RBT Center.

 viii) Blattman, C., J. Jamison and M. Sheridan (forthcoming) 'Reducing crime and violence: Experimental evidence on adult noncognitive investments in Liberia'. *American Economic Review.*

b) Books: Author/Date/Title/Edition/Place of publication/Publisher

 Journal articles: Author/Date/Article title/Journal title/Issue/Page numbers

c) Book and journal titles

d) Book and journal titles are capitalised, journal article titles are not

e) Name of publication e.g. *The Times*

f) i) Aizer and Doyle (2015)
 ii) Allensworth and Easton (2005)
 iii) Anderson (1999)

1.9 Contrasting Sources

1. Referring to sources

a) 8

b) 4

c) *(Any two of)* Bound and Johnson 1992; Katz and Murphy 1992; Juhn, Murphy, and Pierce 1993; Acemoglu and Autor 2011

d) Discussion of lack of growth in well-paid skilled jobs since 2000.

e) To support the writer's thesis that this lack of growth has occurred.

2. **Contrasting sources**

(Example answers)

2.2 Ziadah	*Summary*
However, it appears that most of the change has been seen in office work, and in other areas there has been little recent progress. In fact, across the economy men still work mainly with other men, and women with women.	Ziadah (2018), however, points out that as there has been little progress in employment patterns since the 1970s and 80s, the process may have stalled.
… women … are less likely than men to get work in that field, and are more likely to leave it, possibly due to discrimination. Motherhood poses a further barrier to integration.	Discrimination and the demands of their families, she maintains, are both significant contributory factors.

a) emphasises, considers, points out, argues, maintains
b) however
c) though

3. **Practice**

(Example answer)

There is good evidence that globalisation has resulted in a considerable increase in world trade over the past 20–30 years (Costa, 2016). However, it has been pointed out (Lin, 2012) that the benefits of this are not evenly shared. While multi-nationals are able to use the cheapest labour for manufacturing, people in the poorest countries are no better off than they were 40 years ago. In addition, Brokaw (2014) maintains that these large companies benefit from reduced import duties and so can compete more successfully with local businesses, further strengthening their market dominance. Moreover, they are often able to cut their tax payments by basing themselves where taxes are lowest.

1.10 Organising Paragraphs

1. **Paragraph structure**
   a) Decentralising government
   b) By using conjunctions

2. **Practice A**

Topic sentence	Today's civil servants no longer need to all work in the same district and be able to meet face-to-face.
Reason	Recent developments such as emails and video-conferencing make this pattern of dispersal, which has many apparent benefits, more feasible.
Result 1	Moreover, away from the pressures of the capital with its lobbyists and politicians, workers may have a more objective and detached viewpoint.

| Result 2 | Another benefit of dispersal is to improve the quality of life of the civil servants, detached from over-crowded and expensive capitals. |
| Result 3 | Finally there should be economic benefits for remote and possibly run-down regions in receiving an injection of well-paid employment. |

3. Practice B

a)

Topic sentence	Despite these advantages there are serious drawbacks to relocating government departments.
Supporting point 1	One of the gravest is that many employees, especially younger ones, are reluctant to leave lively capital cities to live in remote provincial towns.
Example 1	In some cases more than half the staff has resigned rather than move, fearing the loss of social life.
Supporting point 2	In addition, new locations may be chosen for political rather than economic reasons.
Example 2	Politicians may attempt to bring jobs to their own constituencies, as when Pinochet moved Chile's congress to his home town, Valparaiso.
Summary	So although there are many apparent gains from relocation, putting such a move into practice can be full of problems.

b) One of the/In some cases/In addition/as when/So although
c) Despite these

4. Practice C

(Example answers)

Title: Decentralising government
Subtitle 1: Spreading the work
Subtitle 2: Benefits of dispersal
Subtitle 3: Some disadvantages

6. Practice D

(Example answer)

Trams

Trams were first introduced in the late nineteenth century, when they provided cheap and convenient mass transport in many cities in America and Europe. But their drawbacks were that the rail-based systems were expensive to maintain, and the fixed tracks made them inflexible as cities developed. Consequently, by the 1950s many European and Asian cities had closed their tramway systems.

Today, however, trams are regaining their popularity. They are seen as less polluting than cars and relatively cheap to operate. As a result, cities such as Paris and Manchester have built new systems. Despite this, the high cost of constructing tramways and difficulties with traffic congestion blocking the tracks mean that trams remain a controversial transport option.

1.11 Introductions and Conclusions

1. Introduction components

a)

Components	Y/N
i) A definition of any unfamiliar terms in the title	Y
ii) Your personal opinion on the subject of the essay	N
iii) Mention of some sources you have read on the topic	Y
iv) A provocative idea or question to interest the reader	N
v) A suitable quotation from a famous authority	N
vi) Your aim or purpose in writing	Y
vii) The method you adopt to answer the question	Y
viii) Some background or context of the topic	Y
ix) Any limitations you set yourself	Y
x) An outline of the main body	Y

b)
   i)   Aim/purpose (vi)
   ii)   Method (vii)
   iii)   Definition (i)
   iv)   Limitation (ix)
   v)   Outline (x)
   vi)   Background (viii)
   vii)   Sources (iii)

2. Introduction structure

a) Definition: *... in this paper 'e-learning' refers to any type of learning situation where content is delivered via the internet.*

b) Context: *Learning is one of the most vital components of the contemporary knowledge-based economy. With the development of computing power and technology the internet has become an essential medium for knowledge transfer.*

c) Reference to other researchers: *Various researchers (Webb and Kirstin, 2003; Honig et al., 2006) have evaluated e-learning in a healthcare and business context ...*

d) Aim: *The purpose of this study was to examine students' experience of e-learning in an HE context.*

e) Method: *A range of studies was first reviewed, and then a survey of 200 students was conducted to assess their experience of e-learning.*

f) Limitations: *Clearly a study of this type is inevitably restricted by various constraints, notably the size of the student sample ... students of Pharmacy and Agriculture.*

g) Outline: *The paper is structured as follows ... the delivery of e-learning programmes.*

3. Opening sentences

(Example answers)

a) In recent years there has been steady criticism of the lack of women in senior management positions.

b) The spectacular growth in international tourism in the last forty years has been caused by several significant 'pull' factors.

c) In the last 20 years most Western economies have seen a steady decrease in inflation rates.

d) Monopoly industries were a feature of the command economies of the communist bloc countries such as Czechoslovakia before 1990.

4. **Practice A**

Example introduction:

State control can be defined as meaning that industries are publicly financed, usually with ultimate control exercised by government ministers. Over the last two decades there has been a global tendency to privatise many key industries which had formerly been in public ownership such as electricity and gas supply, railways and iron and steel production. There is continuing debate as to how far this process can continue; for example some countries have privatised railways while in others they remain under state control.

This paper aims to evaluate the benefits and drawbacks of state control of industry. Using examples from Germany and France between 2000 and 2010, a comparison will be made of two key industries: electricity and railways. The first section will examine the benefits obtained from public ownership, then the disadvantages will be analysed. The final section will attempt to assess the limits of the privatisation process.

5. **Conclusions**
   a) Yes
   b) Yes
   c) No
   d) Yes
   e) Yes
   f) Yes
   g) Yes
   h) No
   i) f
   ii) b
   iii) e
   iv) a
   v) g
   vi) d

7. **Practice B**
   1. e
   2. c
   3. a
   4. b
   5. d

1.12 Editing and Proofreading

2. **Practice A**

   (Comments on the first draft might include some of the following)

   a) No sources are mentioned

   b) Too much space given to basic points

   c) Sentences are too short

   d) Style: e.g. *I personally think* not suitable

   e) Question in title not properly addressed

3. **Practice B**

(Example rewrite)

Organisations inevitably face risks by permitting researchers to interview employees, so these must be understood and minimised by the design of the research project. If employees criticise other workers in the organisation they may be punished, or alternatively they may feel unable to express their true feelings and so invalidate the interviews. Consequently, researchers must protect the reputation of the organisation and the value of their own work by carefully explaining the purpose of the study and insisting on strict anonymity through the use of false names. By doing this both parties should benefit from the research.

5. **Practice C**

i) Africa is not a country: *such as Nigeria*
ii) Prosperousness is not a word. Use *prosperity*
iii) Question mark needed
iv) Present perfect needed with 'since': *Since 2017 there have been …*
v) Money is incorrect. Use *currency*
vi) 'pervious' is incorrect: *previous*
vii) 'one of the … ' needs plural noun: *one of the largest companies …*
viii) Repetition: a multinational business by definition operates in many countries
ix) Time periods need the definite article: *the nineteenth century*
x) *Three skills are needed for success …*

6. **Practice D**

a) Style – use 'managers'
b) Singular/plural – their lines
c) Vocabulary – torment is too strong, use 'frustration'
d) Word ending – different effects
e) Factual – 1973
f) Word order – overcome
g) Punctuation – its
h) Spelling – Hungary
i) Missing word – the world
j) Tense: were

7. **Practice E**

(Corrections underlined)

The Panama Canal

Ship canals are <u>an</u> important element in the development of world trade, as most manufactured <u>goods</u> travel by ship. Unlike the Suez Canal in <u>Egypt</u>, crossing the Panamanian isthmus involves lifting <u>ships</u> 26 metres and then lowering them on the other side. Construction was so difficult and <u>dangerous</u> that the original French engineers were defeated by disease, after over 20,000 men had died working on the project. <u>In</u> the early twentieth century the American government became involved and after ten years' work the canal opened to shipping <u>in</u> 1914, thereby avoiding the difficult route around South America. But since the 1970s container ships have steadily grown <u>too</u> large to fit the <u>canal's</u> locks, and so in 2007 the canal authority began a major development to expand <u>the</u> canal's capacity with locks 60% wider. When this was completed in 2016, at a cost of over $5 billion, the canal was able to handle almost all ships, including the giant cruise vessels now being operated.

PROGRESS CHECK 1

1. *(Other answers may be possible)*
    a) title
    b) schedule, timetable
    c) outline, plan
    d) sources
    e) making, taking
    f) techniques, skills
    g) draft
    h) plagiarism
    i) conclusion
    j) carefully/thoroughly
    k) references
    l) proofread

2.

a) T see p. 4	f) T see p. 20	k) T see p. 54	p) T see p. 86
b) F see p. 4	g) T see p. 28	l) F see p. 60	q) F see p. 88
c) T see p. 6	h) T see p. 80	m) F see p. 76	r) T see p. 84
d) F see p. 14	i) F see p. 39	n) F see p. 50	s) T see p. 23
e) F see p. 14	j) T see p. 47	o) T see p. 84	t) F see p. 40

3.
(Model summary)

Wild bison nearly became extinct in Europe 100 years ago, but today herds have been re-established in several eastern European countries. This has been made possible by the expansion of forests which happened during the communist period, and was followed by an exodus of population from rural areas after 1989. This has created a richly diverse habitat in which large animals can thrive alongside birds and insects. Today new businesses are being established to cater for the eco-tourists attracted by these developments.

Nitoiu, C. (2019) *Rewilding Europe*. Frankfurt: Freihaus.

PART 2 ELEMENTS OF WRITING

2.1 Argument and Discussion

1. Discussion vocabulary

(Model paragraph, other answers possible)

Every year millions of students choose to study in a foreign country. This can have considerable <u>benefits</u>, such as the chance to experience another culture, and improve another language, but also involves certain <u>disadvantages</u>, which may include feelings of isolation or homesickness. Another <u>negative</u> aspect may be the high cost, involving both fees and living expenses. However, most students appear to find that the <u>positives</u> outweigh the <u>negatives</u>, and that the chance to join an international group of students is a major <u>advantage</u> in developing a career.

2. **Organisation**
   Vertical: a simpler pattern suitable for short essays
   Horizontal: this allows a more complex approach in longer essays

3. **Practice A**
   Possible ideas include:

+	−
No time wasted commuting to work	Homeworkers may feel isolated
Gives employees more flexibility	May not suit all employees
Saves expensive office space	Home may contain distractions
	Requires different management style

   Example outline with vertical structure:
   a) Introduction: Reasons for growth of home-working: development in communication technology, demand for more flexible work patterns.
   b) Drawbacks: Employees may feel isolated and be distracted by activities at home. May not suit all employees, some prefer more direct management.
   c) Benefits: Companies need to provide less office space, less time spent on commuting = more work time, employees have more flexibility.
   d) Discussion: Of benefit to certain employees in some roles, but necessary to have regular contact with colleagues and managers.

5. **Counterarguments**
   The writer's position is that companies should pursue long-term environmental goals rather than seeking to increase profits in the short-term.
   (Example answers)

Counterargument	Your position
It has been claimed that employees may waste time at home,	but in practice there seems little evidence for this.
Although home-working may save companies money by reducing the need for expensive office space,	employees need to have a well-equipped workspace in their home.
There is some evidence that working from home only suits self-disciplined people,	although much depends on the quality of their management.

6. **Providing evidence**
   a) 2
   b) The education system
   c) Many young people do not use 'digital tools'
   d) Sceptical of the 'digital native' theory

7. **Practice B**
   (Example answer)
   It is widely believed that moderate inflation, in the range of 2–3%, can be a positive force in the economy. It creates an incentive to spend, since there is an expectation that prices will rise in the future (Costa *et al*, 2012). At the same time there is a slow reduction in the value of debt, which may

encourage long-term investment. Compared with a deflationary situation, where prices fall, limited inflation signals a healthy economy.

However, when allowed to accelerate above 5% or so, inflation can have a negative effect. Workers will demand regular pay rises to keep up with the cost of living, and ultimately people will lose faith in their currency and try to hold their savings in a more stable currency, leading to capital outflow. Runaway inflation has other costs, such as the need to constantly update prices, and may make it difficult to plan future projects (Patterson, 1998).

2.2 Cause and Effect

2. Practice A

(Example answers)

a) More people shopping on the internet results in stores closing on the high street.
   Stores are closing on the high street owing to more people shopping on the internet.
b) Her aggressive management style resulted in more disputes with the union.
   More disputes with the union were due to her aggressive management style.
c) A reduction in sales tax led to higher levels of spending.
   Levels of spending rose because of a reduction in sales tax.
d) Raising the retirement age to 70 led to fewer jobs for young people.
   There were fewer jobs for young people due to raising the retirement age to 70.
e) Owing to the opening of the Panama Canal shipping costs to Europe were lowered.
   Lower shipping costs to Europe were caused by the opening of the Panama Canal.
f) Because of a 15% rise in the price of oil fewer journeys were driven.
   There were fewer journeys driven due to a 15% rise in the price of oil.

3. Practice B

(Example answers)

a) Increasing use of email for messages has caused a decline in letter writing.
b) Rising demand for MBA courses led to stricter selection criteria.
c) Storms in the Brazilian coffee-growing areas caused coffee prices to rise.
d) Building a high-speed railway line caused journey times to fall by 25%.
e) The invention of the jet engine made cheap mass travel possible.
f) The company's bankruptcy was due to reckless over-spending.
g) The high price of bread is owing to the poor harvest last summer.
h) The fall in share prices resulted from political instability.
i) A significant rise in profits was caused by the collapse of their rival.
j) The success of their café was mainly due to her cooking.

4. Practice C – Unhappy workers

(Other answers possible)

a) due to/owing to/produced by/because of/as a result of
b) caused by/produced by/created by
c) due to/because of/resulting from/caused by
d) owing to/due to/because of
e) lead to/cause/produce/result in/create
f) results in/produces/causes/leads to
g) results in/produces/causes/leads to

5. **Practice D**

a) *(Example chart and paragraph)*

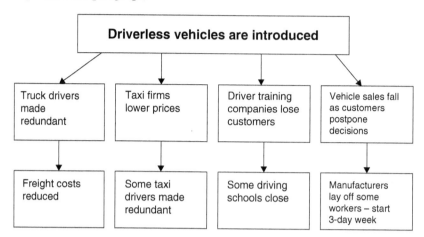

The introduction of driverless cars and trucks would have various significant results. First it would lead to many redundancies among truck drivers, but would also result in reduced freight costs, since driverless trucks could work 24 hours a day. Taxi firms would also be able to lower their prices, since many taxi drivers would be made redundant. In addition, demand for driver training would fall, leading to some driving schools having to close, with the loss of jobs for instructors. Moreover, potential customers would postpone purchases while they assessed the new technology, causing a fall in sales of new vehicles and then lay-offs and short-time working at vehicle manufacturers.

2.3 Comparisons

3. **Practice A**

In the decade between 2007 and 2017, the **largest** rise in house prices among these countries was in Canada, where prices rose by 47%. This increase was **significantly** greater **than** in New Zealand (36%) or Australia (35%). Rises in Germany were nearly the **same** as in China (31% and 30%). The **largest** falls were in Spain and Ireland (–36% and –35%), **substantially** greater than declines in the USA (–15%) or the UK (–4%).

5. **Practice B**

a) Manchester United had the highest income **in European football.**
b) Bayern Munich's income was almost twice **as** much as Tottenham's.
c) FC Barcelona earned **considerably** more than Juventus.
d) Juventus had less revenue **than** Liverpool.
e) Arsenal's income was **slightly** less than Manchester City's.
f) Arsenal earned approximately **the** same as Chelsea.

6. **Practice C**

(Other answers possible)
a) There are wide **variations** in the percentage of GDP spent on health globally.
b) The USA spends **four** times as much as Bangladesh.
c) South Africa spends **slightly** more than Denmark.

d) Madagascan spending on health is **approximately** the same as Indonesian.
e) Canada spends three times as much on health as Oman.
f) Swiss health spending is significantly higher than Bangladeshi.

7. **Practice D**

(Model paragraph)

In terms of producing energy from renewable sources, there are substantial differences between EU countries. The Scandinavian nations, Sweden, Denmark and Finland produce between a third and a half of their energy from these. For Austria, Portugal and Romania the proportion is around a third. But with Italy, Germany and the UK less than 20% of the total comes from renewable sources.

2.4 Definitions

2. **Category words**
   a) loan
   b) organization
   c) period
   d) agreement
   e) costs
   f) financial instrument

Model answers:

g) A trades union is an organisation of workers formed to protect its members' interests.
h) A monopoly is a market in which one company has total or near-total control.
i) Marketing is a process that focuses on identifying and satisfying consumer demand profitably.
j) A dividend is a payment made by a company to its shareholders.
k) A hostile takeover is the acquisition of a firm despite the opposition of its management board.

3. **Complex definitions**
   a) a failed project
   b) Development
   c) Electronic commerce
   d) Corporate governance
   e) Globalisation
   f) Empathy
   i) a, e
   ii) c
   iii) f
   iv) b (process) d (set of mechanisms)
   v) b

4. **Practice**

(Example definitions)

a) **Managing diversity** policies are a systematic and comprehensive managerial process for developing an environment in which all employees, with their similarities and differences, can contribute to the organization, and where no-one is excluded due to unrelated factors.

b) An **entrepreneurial business** is set up by somebody who demonstrates effective application of a number of enterprising attributes, such as creativity, initiative, risk taking, problem solving ability, and autonomy, and will often risk their own capital.

c) **Organisational culture** is a pattern of shared assumptions that the group learned as it solved its problems, which has proved itself and so is considered valid, and is passed on to new members.

d) **Perfect competition** is characterized by a market so open that no participant can influence prices, without barriers to entry and with large numbers of buyers and sellers.

2.5 Examples

1. Using examples

Droning on

For some years there have been predictions that drones could be used to deliver goods to customers. Amazon was one company that expressed an interest. Yet issues with regulators have delayed the arrival of airborne parcels in most countries, owing to concerns with privacy and safety. However, in remote rural regions drone deliveries are already in operation. In Rwanda, for instance, an American startup called Zipline is flying medical supplies, especially blood, to isolated clinics and hospitals. There are various reasons for beginning to operate in these places: medicines are valuable yet lightweight, while most deliveries are between a small number of fixed points. By comparison, travel by road is likely to be slower and more expensive. The pioneer companies such as Zipline and Matternet claim to be operating profitably already, and there plans to begin the service in less remote places: Zipline will bring its expertise from Africa to North Carolina.

2. Phrases to introduce examples

(Example answers)

a) Some twentieth-century inventions, such as TV and the internet, affected the lives of most people.

b) A number of sports, for example motor racing, have become very profitable due to the sale of television rights.

c) Various companies have built their reputation on the strength of one product, a case in point is Microsoft Windows.

d) Some brands, for instance confectionery such as Mars bars, have remained successful for more than fifty years.

e) In recent years the product life cycle has tended to get shorter, particularly with electronic goods.

f) A variety of products, e.g. shampoos, are promoted by celebrity endorsement.

g) Speculation in some commodities, such as oil, has created price bubbles.

h) Investors are often advised to spread their risk by putting their money into a range of investments, for instance equities, bonds and commodities.

3. Practice A – The changing face of shopping

(Model paragraph)

Widespread use of the internet has led to a major change in shopping habits, so that it is no longer necessary to visit shops to make routine purchases, **for example groceries**. With more specialised items internet retailers **such as Amazon** can offer a wider range of products than brick-and-mortar shops. They also provide extra incentives to customers, **for instance cheaper prices**, in addition to the convenience of not having to visit a real shop. As a result certain types of store

e.g. bookshops and record shops are disappearing from the high street. Other products however, **for instance clothing and footwear**, appear to require personal inspection and approval, and in addition many people enjoy the activity of shopping, so it seems unlikely that the internet will completely replace the shopping centre.

4. Practice B

(Model paragraph)

A new perspective?

Students who go abroad to study often experience a type of culture shock when they arrive in the new country. Customs which they took for granted in their own society, such as holidays or ways of greeting people, may not be followed in the host country. Even everyday patterns of life may be different, for instance types of shop and shop opening times. When these are added to the inevitable differences which occur in every country, such as language and currency, students may at first feel confused. They may experience rapid changes of mood, for example depression or elation, or even want to return home. However, most soon make new friends and, in a relatively short period are able to adjust to their new environment. They may even find that they prefer some aspects of their new surroundings, such as freedom and independence and forget that they are not at home for a while!

5. Restatement

a) The company's overheads, in other words the fixed costs, doubled last year.
b) During a bear market, that is a period of falling share prices, few investors make money.
c) The Indian capital, namely New Delhi, has a thriving commercial centre.
d) The best-selling car of all time i.e. the Toyota Corolla, has ceased production.
e) The world's lightest metal, namely lithium, is used in car batteries.

2.6 Generalisations

1. Using generalisations

a) A valid generalisation, widely agreed to be true.
b) A widely accepted fact, supported by medical evidence.
c) This may be true in some cases but is a very sweeping generalisation.
d) Clearly true in many cases, but not valid for every situation e.g. short journeys.

3. Practice A

(Example answers)

a) Job satisfaction is not always related to the rate of pay.
b) A weak currency tends to raise a country's level of exports.
c) Spending on R&D is often linked to the introduction of new products.
d) High rates of unemployment normally reduce the level of consumer spending.
e) Cold weather is likely to increase demand for gas.
f) Industrial growth is often linked to increased pollution.

4. Building on generalisations

a) To introduce the topic.
b) The study, which compared the preferences of women in a range of countries.
c) To summarise the findings of the research.

5. **Practice B**

   (Example)

   d) In many countries people tend to favour domestic products. Reasons for this preference include familiarity, patriotism and the fact that such products are often designed with local needs in mind. But with the growth of globalisation domestic products are increasingly challenged by imported rivals.

2.7 Problems and Solutions

1. **Vocabulary**

   (Other answers possible)

   a) issue/question
   b) answer/approach
   c) approach/avenue/suggestion/proposal
   d) remedy/approach
   e) approach/avenue/suggestion/proposal
   f) solution/answer

4. **Practice A – The housing dilemma**

   (Example answer)

   In many expanding urban areas there is a serious housing shortage, caused by people moving from the country to seek urban opportunities. There are various possible answers to this problem, but each has its drawbacks. The traditional response is to build family houses with gardens, which offer privacy and space but require a lot of land. Building these is slow and the growth of suburbs creates longer journeys to work.

   A second option is to build prefabricated three-storey houses, which can be erected more quickly and cheaply than traditional houses, and can be designed to achieve a higher density of population. In some places these may be the best solution, but they also require a lot of space and are too expensive for the average citizen.

   A better solution is to construct tall blocks of flats, which will accommodate more people at high density quite cheaply, while preventing cities from sprawling too widely. Although some families may find them cramped, for the majority they are a convenient and affordable answer to the housing problem.

5. **Practice B**

   (Example paragraph)

   There is widespread concern that the common use of plastic for packaging is causing serious problems on both land and sea. Various solutions have been proposed; for instance to use biodegradable plastic, although this material is still under development. Another proposal is to use glass containers which can be recycled, but their weight is likely to increase freight costs. More effort should be made to recycle all types of plastic, yet this is rarely an economic process. Perhaps the best answer is simply to use less plastic packaging in the first place.

6. **Practice C – University expansion**

   (Example argument)

   Currently there is increasing demand for university places, which frequently leads to overcrowding of student facilities, such as lectures. It has been argued that fees should be increased to reduce demand for places, but this would discriminate against students from poorer families. Another proposal is for the government to pay for the expansion of universities, but against this is the view that this would unfairly benefit the minority who attend university, who in any case go on to earn higher salaries. A fairer solution might be for the government to subsidise the fees of the poorest students.

2.8 Visual Information

1. Types of visuals

TYPES	USES	EXAMPLE
1 Diagram	g	F
2 Table	h	B
3 Map	a	H
4 Pie chart	f	D
5 Flow chart	d	E
6 Line graph	c	A
7 Bar chart	e	C
8 Plan	b	G
9 Scatter graph/plot	i	I

3. Describing visuals

A)   1 is better. It comments on the main features of the chart but does not repeat the statistics.

B)
   a)   density
   b)   demonstrates/illustrates/shows
   c)   between
   d)   less-crowded/less densely populated
   e)   role/part
   f)   since/as/because
   g)   tend

4. Practice A

(Example paragraph)

Figure 4 illustrates diverging trends in student enrolment in the UK from India and China. It can be seen that in 2007 numbers from the two countries were quite similar, with about 17,000 from India and 24,000 from China. But since then annual enrolments from India have fallen to approximately 10,000, which Chinese student numbers have increased sharply, to over 70,000 in 2017.

5. Practice B

   a)   shows/illustrates
   b)   between
   c)   majority
   d)   substantially/significantly
   e)   Spain
   f)   rise/increase
   g)   than

6. **Practice C**

(Example paragraph)

Figure 5 illustrates enrolments in private schools in a range of countries as a percentage of total school enrolments. In both Britain and Germany only about 10% of pupils attend private schools, while in Chile the figure reaches 65%. Between these extremes, in Thailand, Australia and Spain between a quarter and a third of children are educated privately.

7. **Practice D**

(Example paragraph)

The 12 largest companies in the world, by annual revenue, are shown in Table 2. Walmart, the American retailer, is the biggest, with revenues totalling $500 bn. Half of the remaining companies are in the energy market, mainly oil producers. Also in the table are two vehicle manufacturers, Toyota and Volkswagen, while the two lowest positions are occupied by electronics companies, Apple and Samsung.

PROGRESS CHECK 2

1. benefit = advantage/positive aspect
   disadvantage = drawback/negative feature

2. A position in opposition to the writer's views
   State-owned companies are often seen as inefficient, but …

3. *(Model examples)*
   a) Unemployment rose due to the economic recession.
   b) The railway accident was caused by a faulty signal.
   c) The power cut was due to the hurricane.

4. *(Model examples)*
   Australia is approximately thirty times larger than New Zealand.
   The population density of New Zealand is substantially higher than Australia's.
   Australians are significantly wealthier than New Zealanders.

5. *(Model examples)*
   a) A semester is one of the two divisions of the academic year.
   b) A limited company is a business whose owners have limited liability.
   c) An invoice is a document requesting payment for goods or services provided.
   d) Bankruptcy is a legal process to deal with a person or business heavily in debt.

7. With the plural: 'Middle managers are under threat'
   With 'the' + singular: 'The middle manager is under threat'.

8.
   In the past century, photography has gone from being an exclusive hobby to something accessible to everyone. This is largely due to the invention of the digital camera. In the last twenty years this has made it simple to take colour photographs cheaply, and also to modify pictures easily by using editing programmes. So now that everyone has a smart phone, with its built-in camera, photography has become democratic and high quality photographs can be produced by anybody.

9. *(Other synonyms may be possible)*
   a) The main challenge/difficulty/issue facing the engineers was the extreme cold.
   b) The only answer/remedy/option was to repeat the experiment.
   c) One difficulty/issue/concern faced by the company was public mistrust of internet security.
   d) The safe disposal of nuclear waste is a(n) issue/concern without an easy answer.

10.
   a) change over time
   b) function
   c) proportion
   d) statistical display

(Model example)

The table illustrates the results of a survey of student evaluation of library facilities, contrasting undergraduate with graduate opinion. Most facilities are rated highly by both groups, especially the café and staff helpfulness. Both student groups are least satisfied with the availability of short loan stock. In most areas graduates seem slightly more critical of facilities than undergraduates.

PART 3 LANGUAGE ISSUES

3.1 Cohesion

2. **Practice A**

Reference	Reference word/phrase
La Ferrera	She
new businesses	they
average life of only 4.7 years	this
one economic	the former
the other social	the latter
the former … the latter …	these

4. **Practice B – Famous for?**

a)	he	f)	he
b)	his	g)	they/he
c)	his	h)	This
d)	it/this	i)	He
e)	his	j)	his

6. **Practice C – Velcro**

Velcro is a fabric fastener used with clothes and shoes. **It** was invented by a Swiss engineer called George de Mestral. **His** idea was derived from studying the tiny hooks found on some plant seeds. **They** cling to animals and help disperse the seeds. Velcro has two sides, one of which is covered in small hooks and the other in loops. When **they** are pressed together they form a strong bond.

Mestral spent eight years perfecting **his** invention, which **he** called 'Velcro' from the French words 'velour' and 'crochet'. **It** was patented in 1955 and today over 60 million metres of Velcro are sold annually.

7. **Practice D – Gillette's blades**

a) He
b) it/this
c) His/it
d) he
e) them
f) This
g) his
h) they
i) he

8. **Practice E**

(Example answer)

Wallace Carothers, the director of research at the American DuPont Corporation, patented nylon in 1935. He had previously studied chemistry, and specialised in polymers, which are molecules composed of long chains of atoms. Nylon was a strong but fine synthetic fibre which was first mass produced in 1939. It is used to make a wide range of products which include stockings, toothbrushes, parachutes, fishing lines, and surgical thread.

3.2 Definite Articles

3. **Practice A**

a) Engineering is the main industry in **the** northern region.
b) Insurance firms have made record profits in **the** last decade.
c) Global warming is partly caused by fossil fuels.
d) **The** CEO has been arrested on suspicion of corruption.
e) **The** moons of Jupiter were discovered in **the** eighteenth century.
f) Tourism is **the** world's biggest industry.
g) **The** forests of Scandinavia produce most of Germany's paper.
h) **The** Thai currency is **the** baht.
i) Computer crime has grown by 200% in **the** last five years.
j) **The** main causes of **the** Industrial Revolution are still debated.
k) 3% of **the** working population are employed in call centres.
l) **The** latest forecast predicts warmer winters in the next decade.
m) Research on recruitment methods is being conducted in **the** Business school.
n) **The** best definition is often **the** simplest.
o) During **the** last recession there was a sharp increase in child poverty.

4. **Practice B**

A Northern model?

Norway is **a/the** global leader in **the** use of electric cars: in 2016 nearly 30% of vehicle sales were battery-powered or hybrid models. In **the** past five years sales have increased sharply due to **the** development of better batteries, so now **the** country's five million people are **the** world's largest electric car market. **The** Transport Minister talks of ending sales of cars powered by fossil fuels by 2025. **The** government is subsidising **the** installation of charging points on main roads and shopping centres. In addition, drivers of zero-emission vehicles pay no sales tax or parking fees, and may use bus lanes in cities. But this pattern may not be **a/the** model for other countries: Norway has **a** surplus of cheap electricity thanks to hydropower, and it taxes petrol and diesel fuel heavily.

3.3 Numbers

2. **Percentages**
   a)   50%
   b)   100%
   c)   400%

3. **Simplification**
   a)   Scores of students applied for the scholarship.
   b)   In the past decade the bank has closed dozens of branches.
   c)   The students thought of a few/several good topics for their project.
   d)   Various names were suggested but rejected for the new chocolate bar.
   e)   Last year dozens of books were published on insurance.

4. **Further numerical phrases**
   (Example answers)
   a)   The price of petrol has increased tenfold since 1975.
   b)   Two thirds of the students in the group were women.
   c)   The new high-speed train halved the journey time to Madrid.
   d)   The number of students applying for the Statistics course has risen by 50% since last year.
   e)   More than twice as many British students as Italian students complete their first degree course.
   f)   Tap water is seven hundred times cheaper than bottled water.
   g)   The rate of unemployment in the EU varies greatly: it is nearly ten times higher in Greece than in the Czech Republic.
   h)   A majority of members supported the suggestion, but a large proportion of these expressed some doubts.
   i)   The number of theme park visitors doubled every year between 2015 and 2017.

5. **Practice**
   (Example answers)
   b)   Management was the most popular future course.
   c)   One fifth of the group planned to study Economics.
   d)   Only one student was over 23.
   e)   Swimming was the favourite sport of one third of the group.
   f)   The least popular sports were cycling and tennis.

3.4 Passive and Active

2. **Structure**
   a)   The data was collected and the two groups (were) compared.
   b)   120 people in three social classes were interviewed.
   c)   The results were checked and several errors (were) found.
   d)   An analysis of the findings will be made.
   e)   Four managers were asked to give their opinions.
   f)   The report was written and ten copies (were) distributed.

3. **Use of the passive**

   a) It was argued that entrepreneurial skills should be taught in school.
   b) It is believed that the government should reduce its borrowing.
   c) It is suggested that that industry can be damaged by foreign competition.
   d) Eight new destinations are being offered this year (by Ryanair).
   e) It was claimed that productivity could be raised by more automation.

4. **Adverbs with passives**

   (Other adverb combinations possible)

   a) The company was profitably run by the Connors family until 2001.
   b) The reasons for the Asian currency crisis were vigorously debated (by economists).
   c) All students in the exam were helpfully provided with pencils.
   d) A presentation was vividly given by the staff of the advertising agency.
   e) The percentages were accurately calculated to three decimal places (by researchers).
   f) Their business was optimistically called the Grand Universal Trading Company.
   g) The life cycles of over 240 companies were carefully researched.

5. **Practice**

   (Model answer)

   Making bread

   Bread is traditionally made from wheat flour, salt, water and yeast. You mix the wholemeal or white flour with a little salt and yeast, and then gradually add lukewarm water. Other ingredients such as chopped nuts or seeds may be included. Then mix the dough until a soft ball is formed, which you can knead by hand. In the kneading process the dough is vigorously pounded and reshaped so that all the ingredients are fully combined. After being thoroughly kneaded leave the dough for a few hours to rise. When this is finished work the dough by hand to shape it into loaves or rolls. After two more hours the loaves will have risen again, due to the action of the yeast. Bake them in a hot oven for about half an hour and then allow to cool.

3.5 Punctuation

9. **Practice A**

   a) The study was carried out by Christine Zhen-Wei Qiang of the National University of Singapore.
   b) Professor Rowan's new book 'The End of Privacy' (2019) is published in New York.
      or
      Professor Rowan's new book *The End of Privacy* (2019) is published in New York.
   c) As Keynes said: 'It's better to be roughly right than precisely wrong'.
   d) Banks such as HSBC and Barclays were in penny-pinching mode in the 1990s.
   e) As Matheson (1954) wrote: 'It was the germ that was the villain'.
   f) Thousands of new words such as 'app' enter the English language each year.
   g) The BBC's World Service is broadcast in 33 languages including Somali and Vietnamese.
   h) She scored 56% on the main course; the previous semester she had achieved 67%.
   i) Their article 'A reassessment of the Spanish housing market 2005–2015' was well received.
   j) Before submitting her essay on Irish SMEs she checked for spelling, grammar and punctuation.

10. **Practice B**

    Studying will play a vital part in your life as an Oxford student, but you will also find an enormous amount to do in Oxford in your spare time. Oxford is the youngest city in England and Wales and has two universities: Oxford University and Oxford Brookes. 35% of people who live here are aged 15–29 and 27% (40,000 of a total population of 150,000) are university students. If you ever feel like a change of scene, the bus to London takes around 90 minutes and runs 24 hours a day. There are now two railway stations: the central Oxford station and the recently opened Oxford Parkway. Oxford is a youthful and cosmopolitan city with plenty to see and do. There are dozens of historic and iconic buildings, including the Bodleian Libraries, Ashmolean Museum, Sheldonian Theatre, the cathedral and the colleges. In the city centre you will find lots of shops, cafés, restaurants, theatres, cinemas, pubs and clubs. There are plenty of green spaces too: riverside walks, England's oldest botanic garden, the University Parks and college gardens.

3.6 Singular or Plural?

1. Five difficult areas
i)   ... and disadvantages   (e)
ii)   are under 30   (a)
iii) rural areas   (c)
iv)   ... in crime   (b)
v)   Each company has its own policy (d)

4. Practice A

a) Little
b) businesses
c) experience/is
d) travel broadens
e) stone
f) much advice
g) few interests
h) civil war
i) Irons were
j) work

5. Practice B

traffic	capitals	jams	home
travel	vehicles	factor	permission
work	day	stress	is
has	life	advice	
staff	quantity	is	
Research	petrol	music	

3.7 Style

1. Style in the Business school

(Example sentences)

a) Currently the rate of unemployment is high.
b) Another factor to consider is the possibility of inflation increasing
c) In 2005 the Brazilian currency, the peso, was devalued.
d) The firefighters were quickly able to control the fire.
e) The numbers in that report are unreliable.
f) It is commonly thought that the economy is improving.
g) He was delighted to win the prize.
h) Students should be paid to study.
i) The manager was dismissed for embezzlement.
j) In 2008–2010 the price of Spanish property fell sharply.

4. Avoiding repetition and redundancy – Fast food

(Example answer)

Currently, fast food is growing in popularity. This is food that people can buy ready to eat or cook quickly. This essay examines its advantages and drawbacks. First, it is very convenient; most office workers are very busy, so they do not have time to go home for lunch, but can eat in restaurants such as McDonalds. The second benefit is cheapness. As it is produced in large quantities the companies can keep costs down. As a result it is usually less expensive than a meal in a conventional restaurant.

5. Varying sentence length

(Example answers)

Even large companies can find recruitment problematic. They often employ specialist recruitment firms to find new senior staff, and these firms may use a range of assessment methods and tests. But there is some doubt about how effective their methods are: the managers recruited in this way often perform badly. An alternative is to promote from inside the company, since these people are familiar with the company culture.

6. The use of caution

(Others are possible)

Modals: might/may/could/should
Adverbs: often/usually/frequently/generally/commonly/mainly/apparently
Verb/phrase: seems to/appears to/in general/by and large/it appears/it seems

7. Using modifiers

a) The company's efforts to save energy were quite/fairly successful.
b) The survey was (a fairly/quite a) comprehensive study of student opinion.
c) His second book had a rather hostile reception.
d) The first year students were quite fascinated by her lectures.
e) The latest type of arthritis drug is rather expensive.
f) This mountain tiger has become quite/rather rare.
g) The class found the essay topic fairly/rather challenging.

8. Practice

(Example answers)

a) Private companies are often more efficient than state-owned businesses.
b) Exploring space seems to be a waste of valuable resources.
c) Older students may perform better at university than younger ones.
d) Word-of-mouth is commonly the best kind of advertising.
e) English pronunciation can be confusing.
f) Some cancers may be caused by psychological factors.
g) It appears that global warming will cause the sea level to rise.
h) Most shopping may done on the internet in ten years' time.
i) Online education can be inferior to taught classes.
j) By 2025 driverless cars might be in common use.

3.8 Time Markers

2. **Practice A**
   - a) Recently
   - b) until
   - c) for
   - d) Last month
   - e) by
   - f) Since
   - g) During
   - h) After

4. **Practice B**
   - a) ago
   - b) later
   - c) for
   - d) until
   - e) During
   - f) until
   - g) Since
   - h) during
   - i) since
   - j) ago

5. **Practice C – Henry Ford**
   - a) until
   - b) later
   - c) after/in
   - d) During
   - e) By/In
   - f) for
   - g) since
   - h) after
   - i) until
   - j) before

PROGRESS CHECK 3

1.

The Rolls-Royce Company	It
Henry Royce	The former
Charles Rolls	the latter
Henry Royce and Charles Rolls	their/they
a new factory	this/it
Derby	there

2. See Unit 3.2.2

3.
   - a) –
   - b) the
   - c) the
   - d) a/the
   - e) the
   - f) –
   - g) the
   - h) a
   - i) the
   - j) the
   - k) the
   - l) a
   - m) a
   - n) The
   - o) the
   - p) –
   - q) –

4.

(Model paragraph)

250 international students were interviewed about their experience of study abroad. Of these a fifth were from China, a fifth from India, a tenth from Nigeria and the remaining half from a variety of European countries. A substantial majority were satisfied with their courses, but a fifth had concerns about the quantity of work required. Just 10% complained about the quality of teaching. Half the students said they found it easy to adapt to a different culture and way of life, but of the others a significant minority disliked the food, a fifth found living too expensive, and a small minority mentioned bad weather.

5.

(Model paragraph)

Our research aimed to find the best taxi business for campus use, so the performance of six local taxi companies was compared. Companies that had their offices within a kilometre of the campus were selected. The response of each company to requests made at the same time of day (7 p.m.) was timed. Response times varied from ten to 24 minutes. Each driver was then asked to take the passenger to the railway station. The friendliness of the drivers and the length of time taken were recorded, as well as the fare the driver asked for. Overall AZ Taxis were found to have the fastest response and the cheapest fare, but not the friendliest driver.

6.

Google was begun as a research project by Page and Brin in 1996. (passive)
Page and Brin began Google in 1996 as a research project. (active)

7.

The twenty-first century has seen the rise of the so-called BRIC economies: Brazil, Russia, India and China. The acronym was first used in a paper written by Jim O'Neill in 2001. Today it is clear that China and India are both powerful manufacturers, while Russia and Brazil are mainly sources of raw materials.

8.

a) Several types of response were recorded.
b) Three avenues of research were suggested.
c) One of the groups was eliminated from the competition.
d) Half the graduates were from Indonesia.
e) The government was defeated at the election.
f) The performance of the athletes was improved by his training method.

9.

(Any three of the following)
Good academic writing is accurate, objective, clear and impersonal.

10.

(Model answer)

a) Dr Gonzalez went to Berlin five days ago.
b) He was in Berlin for two days.
c) During his stay in Berlin he gave a lecture.
d) After leaving Berlin he went to Prague.
e) While staying in Prague he met colleagues at Charles University.
f) By June 10th he had travelled 2,300 kilometres.

PART 4 VOCABULARY FOR WRITING

4.1 Approaches to Vocabulary

4. Confusing pairs

a) principles
b) lose
c) affect
d) compliments
e) its
f) economic
g) accepted
h) sights

4.2 Abbreviations

7. Practice

a) information and communications technology/state owned enterprises/and others
b) unique selling point
c) that is/the World Trade Organisation
d) Note/curricula vitae/Human Resources/September
e) Organisation for Economic Cooperation and Development/United Arab Emirates
f) The European Union/Value Added Tax
g) Chief Executive Officer/Research and Development
h) Figure 4/gross national product
i) Member of Parliament/Further Education
j) Public relations/approximately/$75,000/per annum
k) With reference to/annual general meeting/as soon as possible
l) Doctor/Master of Business Administration

4.3 Academic Vocabulary: Nouns and Adjectives

2. Nouns

(NB: not all these words have close synonyms. This list is a guide to approximate meaning. Students should use a dictionary for a full understanding.)

accuracy – precision
analysis – examination
approach – angle of study
assessment – test
assumption – informed guess
authority – expert
category – type
claim – argument/thesis
controversy – debate
correlation – link
deterrent – disincentive
emphasis – weight put on one area
evidence – proof

exception – different thing
extract – part of a longer work
ideology – belief
implication – unstated suggestion
innovation – new introduction
intuition – understanding without thinking
motivation – incentive
perspective – angle of study
phenomenon – unusual event
policy – formal guidelines
preference – favourite choice
process – series of stages
proposal – suggestion

provision – supply
sequence – series of stages
strategy – plan

substitute – replacement
technique – method
validity – truth

a)   evidence
b)   proposals
c)   intuition
d)   provision
e)   claim
f)   phenomena
g)   process
h)   correlation

3.   Nouns and adjectives

(Model examples)

Sherlock Holmes solved crimes by <u>analytical</u> methods; examining each clue.
Although quite famous, the professor was always <u>approachable</u> for students.
Her book is the most <u>authoritative</u> work on the subject.
Even today, the ideas of Karl Marx remain <u>controversial</u>.
Their position was <u>emphatic</u>; the library would remain closed all week.
His performance was <u>exceptional</u>, winning three prizes in his final year.
My objection to the book is <u>ideological</u>, despite it being well-written.
California offers an <u>innovative</u> culture where new ideas are welcomed.
She had an <u>intuitive</u> feeling she would get the job.
In addition to money, praise and recognition are both highly <u>motivational</u>.
The Harry Potter books have been a <u>phenomenal</u> publishing success.
First class passengers are sure of <u>preferential</u> treatment.
Until it's approved by the council the agreement is only <u>provisional</u>.
The courses in this faculty are <u>sequential</u>: you must pass one to move to the next.
The general's retreat was just <u>strategic</u> – he lured the enemy into a trap.
<u>Technical</u> support for computer users is available 24/7.
Your bus pass is <u>valid</u> until October next year.

4.   Confusing nouns and adjectives

Noun	Adjective	Noun	Adjective
approximation	approximate	particularity	particular
superiority	superior	reason	reasonable/rational
strategy	strategic	synthesis	synthetic
politics	political	economy	economic/al
industry	industrial	culture	cultural
exterior	external	average	average
height	high	reliability	reliable
heat	hot	strength	strong
confidence	confident	truth	true
width	wide	probability	probable
necessity	necessary	length	long
danger	dangerous	relevance	relevant

5. **Practice A**

   a) confident
   b) particularities/strengths
   c) probability
   d) relevant
   e) necessary
   f) average

   g) danger
   h) necessity
   i) unreliable
   j) approximate
   k) economic
   l) synthesis

8. **Practice B**

   a) irrelevant
   b) subjective/irrational
   c) Concrete/Relevant
   d) approximate/rough

   e) relative
   f) logical/rational
   g) theoretical/abstract
   h) unambiguous

9. **Practice C**

   a) strategic – strategy
   b) analytical – analysis
   c) synthetic – synthesis
   d) major – majority
   e) cultural – culture

   f) theoretical – theory
   g) frequent – frequency
   h) critical – criticism/critic
   i) Social – society
   j) practical – practice

4.4 Academic Vocabulary: Verbs and Adverbs

1. **Understanding main verbs**

   distinguish
   examine
   improve
   affect

2. **Common academic verbs**

   (Approximate synonyms – infinitive form)

   adapt = modify
   arise = occur
   conduct = carry out
   characterise = have features of
   clarify = explain
   concentrate on = look at closely
   be concerned with = deal with
   demonstrate = show
   determine = find
   discriminate = distinguish
   establish = found
   exhibit = show
   focus on = look at closely
   generate = create

   hold = be true
   identify = pick out
   imply= suggest
   interact = work together
   interpret = explain
   manifest = show
   overcome = defeat
   propose = suggest
   prove = turn out
   recognise = accept
   relate to = link to
   supplement = add to
   undergo = experience
   yield = produce

4. **Practice A**

   (Some other verbs may be possible)

   a) A admitted/accepted that he might have made a mistake …
   b) B denied saying that women make/made better economists than men.

c) C stated/claimed/argued that small firms are/were more dynamic than large ones.
d) D agreed with/supported C's views on small firms.
e) E assumed/presumed that most people work/worked for money.
f) F concluded that family firms are/were more efficient.
g) G doubted that electric cars will/would replace conventional ones.
h) H hypothesised/suggested a link between age and entrepreneurial ability.

6. **Practice B**

(Other verbs may be possible)

a) L criticised/censured her research methods.
b) M identified/classified four main types of long-term investments.
c) N commended the company for its record for workplace safety.
d) O interpreted falling unemployment as a sign of economic recovery.
e) P identified/presented wind power and biomass as the leading green energy sources of the future.
f) Q described/portrayed Adam Smith as the most influential economist of the eighteenth century.

8. **Practice C**

a) Clearly
b) Originally
c) Alternatively
d) Recently
e) locally
f) Clearly/Crucially
g) broadly
h) factually

9. **Practice D – Locking up**

Originally, the earliest keys were made by the Egyptians from wood, and (significantly/substantially) improved by the Romans, who used metal. Today's keys are basically the same: a piece of metal with teeth, conventionally produced by cutting and stamping. But recently a new technology, 3D printing has made it possible to manufacture much more intricate designs which are virtually impossible to copy illicitly. Although (substantially/significantly) more expensive, these hi-tech keys offer remarkable security.

4.5 Conjunctions

2. **Types of conjunctions**

a) A few inventions, for instance the internet, have had a major impact on everyday life.
b) Furthermore, many used cars are sold through dealerships.
c) The definition of 'motivation' is important since it is the cause of some disagreement.
d) The technology allows consumers a choice, thus increasing their sense of satisfaction.
e) Four hundred people were interviewed for the survey, then the results were analysed.
f) However, another body of opinion associates globalisation with unfavourable outcomes.

ii) Result   d
iii) Reason   c

iv) Opposition   f
v)   Example   a
vi) Time   e

Biofuels

Conjunction	Type		Conjunction	Type
a)	**such as**	**example**	f) in other words	example
b)	but	opposition	g) Consequently	result
c)	Although	opposition	h) and	addition
d)	for instance	example	i) neither . . . nor	opposition
e)	however	opposition		

3. Common conjunctions

(Others are possible)

Addition: moreover/as well as/in addition/and/also/furthermore/plus
Result: therefore/consequently/so/that is why/thus (**see Unit 2.2**)
Reason: because/owing to/as a result of/as/since/due to (**see Unit 2.2**)
Opposition: but/yet/while/however/nevertheless/whereas/albeit/although/despite
Example: such as/e.g./in particular/for instance (**see Unit 2.5**)
Time: after/while/then/next/subsequently (**see Unit 3.8**)

4. Practice A

(Others are possible)

a) After
b) Although/While
c) moreover/furthermore/additionally
d) therefore/so
e) for instance/for example
f) Due to/Because of
g) While
h) As/Because/Since/When/While

5. Practice B – Geoengineering

(Others are possible)

a) such as
b) Although
c) or
d) for instance/for example
e) in order to
f) While/Although
g) due to/because of
h) or
i) Therefore/That is why

7. Conjunctions of opposition

(Example answers)

a) That article is relevant to the topic but limited in scope.
    While limited in scope, the article is relevant to the topic.
b) Her views on the proposal were interesting yet ambiguous.
    Although her views on the proposal were ambiguous, they were interesting.
c) While his book on business fraud was amusing, it was rather subjective.
    Despite being subjective, his book was quite amusing.
d) Their sales methods were old-fashioned yet very effective.
    Their sales methods were effective, in spite of being old-fashioned.

8. **Practice C**
    (Example answers)
    a)   In contrast to America, where gun ownership is common, few Japanese have guns.
    b)   Despite leaving school at the age of 14 he went on to develop a successful business.
    c)   The majority displayed a positive attitude to the proposal, but a minority strongly disagreed.
    d)   While the tutor insisted that the essay was easy, the students found it difficult.
    e)   Although the spring was cold and dry the summer was warm and wet.
    f)   He finished the project before the deadline, yet he still felt dissatisfied with it.
    g)   She usually speaks French, nevertheless her English is excellent.
    h)   He preferred to travel by train. Flying, however, was cheaper and faster.

4.6 Prefixes and Suffixes

1. **How prefixes and suffixes work**
    'Prefabrication' is the process of making something in advance of installation.
    'Revitalise' is to give extra strength or impetus to something or someone.

2. **Prefixes**

auto	by itself	over	too much
co	together	poly	many
ex	(i) previous	post	later
	(ii) outside	pro	in support of
fore	in front/in advance	re	again
inter	between	sub	below
macro	large	tele	distance
micro	small	trans	across
multi	many	under	(i) below
non	negative		(ii) not enough

3. **Practice A**
    a)   social class at bottom of society
    b)   more tickets sold than seats available
    c)   very local climate
    d)   economy based on information not production
    e)   not listed in the telephone book
    f)   disappointed
    g)   before marriage
    h)   able to create or control situations

5. **Practice B**
    a)   noun
    b)   adjective
    c)   adverb
    d)   adjective
    e)   noun
    f)   adjective
    g)   adjective

h) noun
i) noun
j) adverb
i) protesters
ii) saleable
iii) coincidental
iv) interviewees
v) evolutionary
vi) symbolically

6. **Practice C**
   a) without choosing to/not hurt
   b) able to be refilled/clear and obvious
   c) found new times/before school
   d) cannot be provided/unusual
   e) failure in communication/new order
   f) faulty/ridiculous
   g) write again/hard to understand

4.7 Prepositions

1. **Using prepositions**
   c)

Noun + preposition	body of
	in management
	relationship between
	In this section
	findings of
Verb + preposition	focused on
	lead to
Adjective + preposition	critical to
Preposition of place	in this area
Preposition of time	In the last decade
Phrase	in general

2. **Practice A**
   b) adjective + preposition
   c) verb + preposition
   d) preposition of place
   e) noun + preposition
   f) phrase
   g) preposition of place
   h) preposition of time

3. **Prepositions and nouns**
   a) of
   b) in
   c) of
   d) to
   e) of
   f) on

4. **Prepositions in phrases**

a) on
b) of
c) of
d) in

e) of
f) on
g) in
h) of

5. **Prepositions of place and time**

a) Among
b) from, to/between, and
c) in, of
d) in, in

e) in, at
f) On, between
g) around, of/on
h) Between

6. **Practice B**

a) of/about
b) in/to
c) to/in
d) among/in
e) from/in
f) between
g) in

h) of
i) in/over
j) between
k) in
l) in
m) of
n) to/in

8. **Practice C**

a) focused on/concentrated on
b) pointed out
c) specialised in
d) associated with

e) divided into
f) blamed for
g) believed in
h) learned ... from

4.8 Synonyms

1. **How synonyms work**

Word/phrase	*synonym*
oil	hydrocarbon
company	firm
in the world	global/internationally
people	employees
Britain	the UK

2. Common synonyms in academic writing

(NB: Some of these pairs are approximate synonyms)

Nouns		Verbs	
area	field	accelerate	speed up
authority	source	alter	change
behaviour	conduct	analyse	take apart
benefit	advantage	assist	help
category	type	attach	join
component	part	challenge	question
controversy	argument	clarify	explain
difficulty	problem	concentrate on	focus on
drawback	disadvantage	conduct	carry out
expansion	increase	confine	limit
feeling	emotion	develop	evolve
framework	structure	evaluate	examine
goal	target	found	establish
interpretation	explanation	maintain	insist
issue	topic	predict	forecast
method	system	prohibit	ban
option	possibility	raise	increase
results	findings	reduce	decrease
statistics	figures	respond	reply
study	research	retain	keep
trend	tendency	show	demonstrate
output	production	strengthen	reinforce

3. Practice A

(Others are possible)

a)   Professor Hicks <u>challenged</u> the <u>results</u> of the <u>study</u>.
b)   The <u>figures</u> <u>demonstrate</u> a steady <u>rise</u> in applications.
c)   The institute's <u>forecast</u> has caused a major <u>debate</u>.
d)   Cost seems to be the <u>principal disadvantage</u> to that <u>method</u>.
e)   They will <u>focus on</u> the first <u>possibility</u>.
f)   After the lecture she tried to <u>explain</u> her <u>idea</u>.
g)   Three <u>topics</u> need to be <u>evaluated</u>.
h)   The <u>structure</u> can be <u>kept</u> but the <u>aim</u> needs to be <u>modified</u>.
i)   OPEC, the oil producers' cartel, is to <u>reduce output</u> to <u>increase</u> global prices.
j)   The <u>tendency</u> to smaller families has <u>accelerated</u> in the last decade.

4. Practice B

cities/urban	dogs/canine
flats/apartment	food/fare
felines/cats	benefits/advantages
businesses/companies	home/domestic

5. **Practice C**

(Example answers – others possible)

build/make vehicles	challenges
car makers	forecast
principal problem	energy
obstacle	produced
automobile producers	vehicles/machines

PROGRESS CHECK 4

1. a, c, d

2.
   a) lose
   b) except
   c) site
   d) complement

3.
   a) International Monetary Fund/Gross Domestic Product
   b) Initial public offering/£350 million/London Stock Exchange
   c) 200 page/Master of Science

4.
   a) absolute
   b) metaphorical
   c) subjective
   d) precise/accurate
   e) abstract

5.
   a) height
   b) synthesis
   c) length
   d) probability
   e) relevance

6. *(Model answers)*
   a) X claimed/argued that eating spiders is healthy.
   b) Y disagreed with X, insisting that his theory was based on poor research.
   c) Z agreed with Y's opinion of X's work.

7.
   a) continuously
   b) locally
   c) particularly
   d) increasingly
   e) Traditionally

8. *(Others are possible)*
   a) Although
   b) since/because/as

c) So/Therefore
d) and
e) But/yet
f) because/as/since
g) Then
h) because/as/since
i) Therefore/So
j) and

9.

a) adjective
b) noun
c) verb
d) noun
e) noun

10.

antidote	medicine to counter effects of poison
correspondent	person you write to regularly
foreword	preliminary section of book
polytechnic	institute where many scientific subjects are taught
proportion	relation of one thing to another
subcutaneous	under the skin
undervalue	assess worth of something too cheaply

11.

In the eighteenth century, news travelled as fast as a horseman or sailing ship. It could take weeks **for** news **of** a battle **in** Europe to reach America. **By** the mid-nineteenth century railways had accelerated the distribution **of** newspapers, so that they reached distant provinces **in** hours, and then the telegraph allowed news to be sent **in** seconds. Today we can be overwhelmed **by** the volume of news **from** all over the world which we can continuously receive **on** our phones and laptops.

12.

(Others may be possible)

a) processes/controversy
b) figures/show/advantages
c) chance/researching
d) results/strengthen
e) field/study
f) carried out/conduct

PART 5 WRITING MODELS

5.1 Case Studies

1. **Using case studies**

A case study has the advantage of providing a concrete experience/example.

The disadvantages are that it is limited in place and time, and the example may not be applicable to other situations.

Topics	Case studies
Improving crop yields in semi-deserts	Using solar power to operate irrigation pumps in Ethiopia
Encouraging entrepreneurship in Africa	A Moroccan scheme for supporting new business start-ups
Approaches to motivation in the service sector	A study of a French supermarket training programme
The impact of the housing market on the wider economy	The effect of the Spanish property price crash of 2008
Improving recycling rates in large cities	The Berlin experiment: increasing public participation in collecting and sorting waste

2. **Model case study**

    (Additional answers are possible here)

    a)

    Competition from rivals offering free delivery
    Some products e.g. single beds not suited to Chinese tastes

    b)

    Store layouts match Chinese apartments' floor plans
    Products linked to New Year celebrations
    Reduced prices by sourcing production locally
    Produced thinner but more frequent catalogues
    Used local characters in adverts
    Attempted to provide better service
    Stores located in downtown areas for public transport

    c)

    More financial details of IKEA's sales and profits in the Chinese market
    More information about IKEA's main competitors in this market

5.2 Literature Reviews and Book Reviews

2. **Example literature review**
    a) 2 (content & process)
    b) 7 (Maslow, McClellan, Herzberg, Vroom, Locke, Adams, Alderfer)
    c) 5
    d) It is more convenient to use secondary sources in this kind of short literature review. If you were studying just one of these theorists e.g. Herzberg you might be expected to use primary sources.

4. **Model book review**

    (Other responses possible)

    The reviewer might have said more about the editor i.e. whether he was well-known in this field and had previous work published.

5.4 Reports and Executive Summaries

2. Essays and reports

1) Essay
2) Report
3) Report
4) Report
5) Essay

3. Practice

(Other comments possible)

a) There is a lack of detail in the report, and no mention is made of the cost of running and maintaining student residences on campus.

b) The report does not examine the question of whether companies are prepared to build new halls off-campus, but just assumes that this will happen. Not does it really consider the situation of the students who prefer to live on campus for convenience and socialising.

4. Executive summaries

(Model answer)

The College is faced with a shortage of student accommodation on campus, and consequently is considering building residences for 350 students, costing £2.75 m. However, this sum might be better spent on enhancing teaching facilities, so a survey was conducted about student preferences in accommodation. This found that off-campus, privately-funded residences were the most preferred, which supports the case for spending on a new teaching hub instead.

5.5 Reflective Writing

2. Example

a) She has learned that she needs to be more confident about giving her opinions as she had correctly predicted some of the difficulties they met.

b) She suggests that with a large group it may be productive to form sub-committees to deal with particular issues

4. Practice A

(Model)

I went to the first seminar in our new module on Economic History last week. Professor Lee outlined the course and then we watched a short film about the inflation in Weimar Germany. I realised that I should have read the article he had sent us last week as background reading, since I knew nothing about this period. I shall have to prepare better for these seminars in future or I won't be able to keep up.

5.6 Writing in Groups

1. Why write in groups?

a) F
b) T

c) F
d) F
e) T
f) F

2. Making group work successful

1   E. Get to know the other members.

2   C. Make everyone feel included.

3   A. Analyse the task.

4   G. Plan the job and the responsibilities.

5   B. Divide up the work fairly, according to the abilities of the members.

6   F. Select a co-ordinator/editor.

7   D. Finish the assignment on time.

3. Dealing with problems

a(i)   The lazy students will learn nothing from this approach, and the same problem will occur next time they are involved in group work.

a(ii)   Although it may seem difficult, this is the only positive solution.

a(iii)   Your teachers are unlikely to help – group work is designed to make these problems your responsibility.

b(i)   Your teachers are unlikely to help – group work is designed to make these problems your responsibility.

b(ii)   This will not help you in the long run – you must learn to take part in discussion.

b(iii)   The right approach. The other members probably don't realise that you are having difficulties with their language.

c(i)   If everyone in the group takes part the offender will be forced to accept that their behaviour is unhelpful.

c(ii)   Your teachers are unlikely to help – group work is designed to make these problems your responsibility.

c(iii)   You will run the risk that they will get a poor mark and so everyone will suffer.

Index

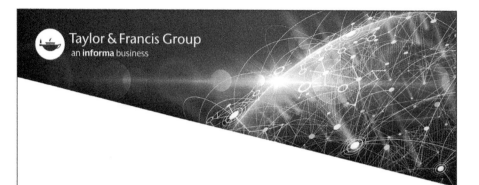